Making Money In Your PJs

Freelancing for voice-overs and other solopreneurs

Paul Strikwerda

Nethervoice Publishing
EASTON, PENNSYLVANIA

Paul Strikwerda/Nethervoice Publishing
www.MakingMoneyInYourPJs.com

Book Layout ©2013 BookDesignTemplates.com
Cover Design by Nelly Murariu, www.PixBeeDesign.com

Making Money In Your PJs/ Paul Strikwerda. —1st ed.
ISBN 978-0-9960620-7-7

Praise for Making Money In Your PJs

The sheer depth, breadth, and quality of the information on the pages of "Making Money in Your PJs" makes this book an obligatory resource in your library of VO success-building. Paul's logic builds compelling arguments for solving the chief challenges all voice actors face, no matter the level of expertise, and his deft writing style makes this book eminently readable.

Dave Courvoisier, news anchor & voice actor

Paul Strikwerda is one of the freshest and wisest voices in the entrepreneurial world today. This book is filled with humor, warmth, compassion, and, most importantly, large doses of priceless insight. Paul knows the human species and the human spirit very well, and he knows better than most how to survive in this crazy world of voiceover. For anyone looking to start his or her own business, you can't afford not to read this book. Be prepared to have your mind blown.

David Rosenthal, actor & coach

Hold on to your hats! This is a textbook on how to do it the right way. If you are a freelancer, or have ever thought about starting and running almost any kind of small business, get a copy of this book. Paul's advice is stellar. He has an uncanny knack of explaining with clear examples and situations. My business is based upon these ideas. It's a voice-over business, and it works.

TedMcaleer, voice actor

Paul Strikwerda gets triple A's - Awesome. Authentic, Accurate. A veteran voice actor with a journalist's background, Paul draws upon his experiences and wisdom to create a book that talks to us - not merely recites what to do, and what not to do, to succeed in voice overs today. And he's not afraid to admit mistakes - like the "$10,000 Mistake" we can now avoid! Thanks, Paul, for enriching us.

John Florian, Founder/PublisherVoiceOverXtra.com and Voice Actor

Paul has been an inspiration, and a mentor-of-sorts to me and a number of other voice actors. This book could be the difference between being successful and an also-ran. I intend to be among the former, not the latter!

Kent Ingram, voice actor

If you are an actor, voiceover artist, or for that matter, any type of creative freelance professional who is trying to network and market yourself, you need to read this book. While Paul's advice if fashioned from the perspective of his particular business (freelance voice acting), it really applies universally to all types of businesses where networking is vital.

Laurie Cummings, voice and on-camera actor

With that wealth of information, seasoned with his cheerful, helpful personality, *Making Money In Your PJs* is an invaluable resource for not only those beginning or maintaining their voice-over career, but for anyone wanting to take the leap and join the ranks of millions of other solopreneurs. Great reading!

Mike Harrison, voice actor

What a mine of information, and so clearly and entertainingly written – from the provocative title down to the calls for action.

Kumar Jamdagni, Dutch-English translator

Acknowledgements

Making Money In Your PJs is in part the result of the help and inspiration of numerous people. Joseph D'Agnese, author of *The Money Book for Freelancers, Part-Timers, and the Self-Employed*, ignited a flame that turned my writers' brain on fire. My British colleague Karl Littardi planted the seed that eventually grew into a book.

Mike Harrison took his fine comb and added finishing touches to the manuscript. Tracy R. Atkins of bookdesigntemplates.com was always ready to answer questions and to help me turn my manuscript into a book.

I want to thank Folkert Strikwerda and Dick Taylor for their continued encouragement, and for investing in my career. A special thank you to Jos Feitsma for believing in my dreams and for supporting me every single day of her life. I miss you, and I wish you'd still be here to hold this book in your hands.

Making Money In Your PJs would never have seen the daylight had it not been for my wife Pamela Taylor. She is the wind beneath my wings in all my endeavors, as well as an editor/proofreader extraordinaire. Pam, you keep me grounded, and sharing this journey with you is one of the greatest joys of my life!

And finally, I want to thank my beautiful daughter Skyler. Words have the power to change minds and transform lives. Use them wisely, and let your imagination take you to a world of new ideas, fascinating people and great stories!

If you want your added value to always be higher than your rate, this book is for you.

Contents

Introduction

As I am finishing the last pages of *Making Money In Your PJs*, the United States is crawling out of the worst recession in seventy-five years. People have discovered that it's easy to get fired and a lot harder to get hired.

Gone are the steady jobs with steady hours, steady paychecks and generous benefit packages. Instead, it's every man or woman for him or herself. More and more people are flying solo by becoming a freelancer.

According to the United States Government Accountability Office, there are at least 42 million consultants, independent contractors, entrepreneurs, and freelancers working multiple gigs for multiple clients. That means that at last count (in 2005), almost one-third of the U.S. workforce was made up of independent workers. By 2020, this number will have gone up to forty percent.

Perhaps you've told yourself that the current economic crisis is the ideal opportunity to finally create the career you've always wanted.

Perhaps you've been dreaming of a life of freedom and flexibility from the comfort of your home.

Perhaps you feel this is the perfect time to become a VOP, a Voice-Over Professional!

Don't let me stop you. It is an honorable profession and some voice talents are still making a six-figure income doing what they love.

I also want to caution you.

MAKING IT BIG

Here's the thing. This world needs a lot more nurses, teachers, scientists, and IT specialists, and it doesn't need too many folks who like to talk into microphones for a living. As synthesized speech is getting more and more sophisticated, robots – not people – will read to you what's on your tablet, smartphone or monitor.

A-list screen actors turned voice-overs are making millions trying to sell you anything from cars and credit cards to peanuts. Most of them are more than happy to fit a feature-length animation into their busy schedule. Lesser gods and ordinary mortals are left to pick up the crumbs.

Does that mean that you shouldn't even try to break into the voice-over business? It would be presumptuous to make that call for you. Show business is filled with daydreamers who were discouraged by family and friends. Yet, they've proven everybody wrong and made it big because they had tremendous talent and came prepared.

Thanks to the internet, the game has certainly changed. These days, one viral video can turn a homeless man with a golden voice into a national celebrity. You could be discovered by an insurance company and asked to quack like a duck for the rest of your life. A well-equipped home studio can connect you with clients on all continents.

There's definitely work out there, but here's the question: How is this book going to help you get it?

ABOUT THIS BOOK

Let me begin by telling you what this book is not.

This isn't a memoir about the good old days of voice acting, filled with juicy tales of semi-famous people the author has worked with.

If you are looking for another "get-rich-quick by doing voice-overs guide," you're out of luck, too. First off, this isn't a step-by-step course that will take you from voice-over novice to top talent in three days. Desperate people will believe anything, but you know that's just a load of hogwash.

Secondly, Fred Astaire didn't learn how to dance from a book, and Babe Ruth didn't discover how to hit a home run from a brochure. No correspondence course, website, or taped seminar has ever produced a Yehudi Menuhin, a Stephen Sondheim, or a voice-over superstar for that matter.

Third: I'm not going to sell you anything or encourage you to sign up for webinars or coaching sessions. You've already invested in this book and that means a lot.

What I *will* do, is tell you about the stuff between the lines. You know, the things you wish they'd told you before you started reinventing the wheel. A lot of that stuff happens to be business-related and is highly practical. A lot of it has to do with what's going on between your ears and it's based on over thirty years of experience. It's the stuff they usually don't teach you in voice-over school.

So, is this just another book for (aspiring) voice actors?

Definitely not.

In essence, it is a book for freelancers.

Whether you're a copywriter, a graphic designer, a photographer, or you're making money with your mouth, freelancers have a lot in common.

Even though I'm writing from the perspective of a voice-over professional, much of what I'm about to share applies to anyone who is self-employed. Things such as:

- Should you turn your hobby into a profession
- How to promote your business
- How to turn potential customers into clients
- How to put a price on your services
- How to make sure you get paid
- What to do when business is slow
- How to stand out among colleagues

TELLING STORIES

That being said, in one way voice-overs are different from other free-lancers. Voice-overs are part of an ancient tribe. The tribe of story-tellers. That's why, rather than bombarding you with dry factoids, I often use stories and real world examples to get my points across.

The structure of this book suggests a specific order in which these stories should be read. That's one way to do it. Although I have grouped my pieces around certain topics, most of them can be read separately and out of order.

The contents of this book are reflections of my personal interests and expertise. Most of what you're about to read, started as a blog post. By definition, a blog doesn't deal with undisputed scientific facts. It revolves around personal opinion. The opinions stated are subjective and mine, unless otherwise indicated. I tend to live by the advice I give to others, and I strongly encourage you to take away what you find useful. Don't take my word for it, though. Try it out and see for yourself what makes sense.

OVERVIEW

From the outside, a voice-over career seems almost ideal. You talk into a microphone and you get paid. In **Part One** of this book, I'll debunk the most prevalent myths that unscrupulous sales people use to try to sell you expensive voice-over trainings and demo-packages.

You'll also get a much better idea of whether or not a voice-over career is for you.

Part Two deals with self-guided learning, coaching, and voice acting. I'll tell you what producers and agents are listening for when they're evaluating auditions, and how you can learn to let a script speak to you. I will also reveal my number one trick to get rid of loud breaths and other mouth noises that can mess up your recordings.

In the next part we get down to business. Most newcomers to voice-over will give up within a year because they don't know anything about freelancing. **Part Three** prepares you for the road ahead by learning from other people's failures and successes. That way, you don't have to start from scratch. I'll also talk about selecting the right gear and about home studios. If you are serious about voice acting, you're going to need both.

Having a pleasant voice is nice if you want to become a voice-over, but it's not essential. Making sure that clients can find you is crucial for your career. In "Spreading the Word" (**Part Four**), you'll learn how to market yourself through your website and social media, and by developing a personal brand. It's the story of "telling, not selling" any freelancer can benefit from.

If you want to build a long-term career, you'll need your colleagues just as much as you need your clients. In **Part Five** I'll tell you how to separate the pros from the con artists, and I will introduce you to some of the colorful characters you're bound to meet in this crazy business.

Whether or not you are going to make it as a pro, will depend as much on your ability to read scripts as on your ability to read clients. That's what **Part Six** is about. I will show you what you need to know before you start bidding on projects, and I'll share my experience with one of the most popular voice casting sites.

Part Seven is about money. It doesn't matter what you do as a free-lancer, but if you don't learn how to manage your money, you are sabotaging your success. I will spend a good deal of time discussing what you're worth so that you won't ever sell yourself or your colleagues short. And if you've ever been short-changed by a client, the chapters on collecting money are a must-read.

And finally, I'll talk about the secret ingredient that can make or break a freelance career: *Attitude*. **Part Eight** is called "The Inner Game."

Life as a solopreneur can be a roller coaster ride. Some months you'll feel on top of the world. Other months you may feel like hanging up your hat. How do you deal with that, emotionally? Well, you're about to find out.

At the very end I will share something you'll want to print out and put on your wall: *The Freelancers Creed*.

Making Money In Your PJs contains a number of hyperlinks. Since you are reading the print version, please refer to the link library on the website MakingMoneyInYourPJs.com.

The hyperlinks in the print version you are reading, are indicated by the triple star*** symbol. Click on the icon with the three horizontal lines in the upper-right corner of the website to open up the menu, and click "Links."

Now that you know what to expect, I suggest you put on your PJs and let's get started!

Paul Strikwerda

Spring, 2014

[1]

Turning Your Hobby into a Business

It often starts with a compliment:

"I just love your voice. I could listen to it for hours."

"Wow, you take great pictures."

"Your jewelry is absolutely amazing."

"You're a born writer."

Followed by:

"Have you ever thought of doing this professionally?"

For a moment you feel flattered, but then you quickly dismiss the compliment and say:

"Thank you so much. It's just something I like to do for fun."

But after hearing the same comments from different people, your brain starts playing with the possibility. Someone planted a seed in your mind and it's definitely growing!

One day, you wake up in the middle of the night with this question:

"What if?"

"What if I were to turn my hobby into something I could do for a living? Why shouldn't I get paid for something I love doing? What could be more fun than that?"

And that's where the trouble begins.

THE SLIPPERY SLOPE

Before you give up your day job and spend a ton of money on a fantasy, take one step back and ask yourself:

What do these "admirers" actually know about running this type of business?

Do they know what it takes to make money as a voice-over? Do they have any idea how much a photographer needs to invest before he can open a studio? Can they tell the difference between fine art jewelry and a design from a dabbler? How can they be sure you're destined to win the Man Booker Prize a few years from now?

Advice from friends, family, and other nitwits, no matter how well intended and pleasing to the ear, is probably the worst advice you can get.

If you want to know if you have potential, go to a pro without a hidden agenda.

By that I mean: Find someone who's not intent on selling something to a sucker. This world is filled with unscrupulous characters who will tell you what you want to hear in order to make a sale.

You need someone who tells you what you don't want to hear. Someone who has nothing to lose and nothing to gain by being brutally honest.

Once the verdict is in, you have to find another pro and then another, before making a decision that could change your life and the lives of those that are near and dear to you. And if those pros confirm what others have told you, it's time to do some serious research to really understand what you are getting yourself into.

There is a reason why so many startups fail. Twelve months from now you don't want to be in over your head, heavily in debt and hating your hobby.

ONE STEP BACK

Before you take further action, there's more homework to do. Ask yourself:

What is it about this hobby that I enjoy so much? What does it do for me?

Someone I know is a pretty successful home brewer. His Pale Ales have won several prizes, and for some reason his friends always want to meet at his house. At one point he thought of setting up shop and asked me if he should go for it. I told him:

"I can't give you an answer because I know nothing about the market and very little about beer. Let me ask you a question instead:

What do you like so much about making your own brews?"

He opened one of his bottles and said:

"When I go down to the basement to play with my hops, I leave all the worries of work behind. There's nobody looking over my shoulder. I take as much time as I like. I can pick the best ingredients and I never have to compromise quality. There's no pressure to perform. If one of my brews doesn't turn out right, who cares? I'll just try again. I'm telling you, it's the most relaxing feeling in the world."

He took another sip of his beer and looked at me, knowingly.

"Thank you," he said, after a short pause.

"For what?" I wondered.

He put the bottle down and smiled: "I think I just answered my own question. I love my hobby so much, I'd never do it for a living!"

"I'll drink to that," I said. "L'Chaim!"

THE NOT SO SECRET INGREDIENTS

Just as every beer is based on a recipe, there is a recipe for those who want to turn their hobby into a business. These are the three basic ingredients:

Talent, Time and Money

If one of them is missing, you might as well forget about it. If you have talent and money but no time, you'll never accomplish anything. If you have time and money but no talent, who's going to hire you? If you have time and talent but no money, how are you going to cover your costs?

It's simple. You need money to make money. As far as the taxman is concerned, money is the main factor that separates a hobbyist from a professional. Business consultant and writer Paul Marsden said:

"Business is all about solving people's problems at a profit."

The IRS presumes that an activity is classified as a business if it makes a profit during at least three of the last five tax years, including the current year.

In my field of voice-overs, there is an ongoing discussion about when someone may call him or herself a voice-over professional. Some people get really agitated about it. I think the answer is simple.

Show me your books and I'll tell you!

PRICE FOR PROFIT

If you want to be considered a professional, you have to price for profit. That's a lesson many hobbyists never learn.

A very talented woodworker with lots of time on his hands sold his carefully crafted bowls way too low, hoping to attract customers. His product was unique but his business never took off. Last time I checked, there weren't too many self-made millionaires on Etsy or Fiverr.

As a business owner, you need to mind your money by tracking what's coming in and what's going out. Hobbyists hate that. They usually spend discretionary cash and don't have to worry about covering expenses.

Hobbyists turned professionals will jump for joy when they get a hundred-dollar check. "Look," they say, "I just made a hundred bucks. Isn't that wonderful?"

"Excuse me?

How much did you spend to make that amount and how much of it is yours to keep?

Oh, you have no idea?

Don't you know know the difference between revenue and profit?

And you consider yourself to be a pro?"

IT'S ABOUT TIME

In order to determine whether you are enjoying a hobby or you are running a business, the IRS looks at other factors as well. Uncle Sam wants to know if you have the necessary knowledge to succeed in your field. You also need to put in time and effort to turn a profit.

For most hobbyists, that's tough. Their hobby was never a priority or a moneymaker. It was just something they did on the side. In general, hobbyists completely underestimate how much time it takes to run a for-profit business.

Most freelancers I know once had a dream of making more money by doing less. Some traded a corporate nine-to-five culture for a never-ending workweek that includes weekends. The first years of a new business are the most demanding, exhausting, and frustrating for the freelancing entrepreneur and his or her family. That is, if you take it seriously. Even then there are no guarantees.

For the self-employed who are working from home there are other challenges. It is very tempting to take the afternoon off. The movies are cheaper and so is lunch.

Back home you might as well do some laundry. A friend you haven't heard from in ages finally calls. You've got to pick up the kids and drive them to their piano lesson. Be sure to have dinner ready at six! Before you know it, it's dark outside and you haven't done a thing for your so-called business.

Now, if this were a hobby, it wouldn't be a big deal. But you wanted to do this *professionally*, remember?

CONFLICTING PRIORITIES

It's even harder for those who try to start a new business while they are working full-time or part-time. After all, bills need to be paid and without money to invest you have no business.

If you can't prioritize and set boundaries and you're running out of hours to get things done, your dream job is doomed. In contrast, a hobbyist does not have to be disciplined, organized or accountable. A hobbyist just gets to have fun.

Megan Auman is a designer, educator, and entrepreneur. Her blog *Designing an MBA**** is an inspiration. She had to learn to carve out time for her business. Megan:

> *"I've got a new mantra. I'm trying to stop saying "I didn't have time for something," and switch to "I didn't make it a priority." Because often, lack of time is really lack of prioritization."*

If you're thinking of turning your hobby into a business, there's one more problem you have to face. It's the problem of perception.

If you don't perceive yourself as a business owner, others won't either and they'll run all over you. You have to tackle this on two fronts.

First you have to be completely honest with yourself and answer the question:

Do I really, really want this?

I know plenty of people with talent, money and time who are much happier working for someone else. Their lives are more structured and predictable, and at the end of the day they get to go home, put their feet up, and relax. Some of those jobs even come with benefits!

Should you decide to go ahead and become your own boss, you better make sure your significant other, your family, and your friends know that you mean business when you say you're running a business. You have to reorganize your life to support your new venture, and they need to support you unconditionally, night and day.

It's only fair, don't you think?

After all, weren't they the ones who encouraged you to "do this professionally" in the first place?

So, really think about it before you decide to turn your wonderful hobby into an ordinary job.

Do you have the talent, the funds, the time, the guts, and the support it takes to succeed?

Do you have a plan in place?

Otherwise, the only money you'll ever make is...

Beer money!

[2]

Head over Heels

"I LOVE my job."

"It's a dream come true"

"Doing voice-overs is absolutely amazing!"

Not a day goes by without someone shouting from the rooftops that life has never been better since they joined the tribe of semi-professional voice talent hoping to make it big.

They want all their Facebook friends to know how exquisite their existence has become after they got married to their microphone.

"I wouldn't trade it for anything else," they say. "For the first time in my life I do what I love and I LOVE what I do!"

If that's how you feel, I'm happy for you. Really.

I'm also a bit worried.

You see, love does weird things to the brain.

It beclouds our judgment. Lovestruck people see the object of their affection not for what it really is, but for what they believe it to be:

Flawless.

Magnificent.

Irresistible.

Love is obsessive. Love is possessive.

Love is a double-edged sword.

Without passion and desire we don't have the drive to take a chance and change course. But it also makes us vulnerable because we're more likely to make emotional decisions instead of rational ones. These emotional decisions could cost us dearly.

Friends of friends fell in love with a gorgeous lake house they could not afford. They bought it anyway. Now they are paying over fifty percent of their combined income to the bank and they owe more than their home is worth.

Every month they are nickel-and-diming to pay the bills. No more eating out. No more vacations. They're only one payment away from going under. And did I mention they started hating their home?

A colleague was crazy about a certain Italian sports car. It had to be red, of course. He searched the web for months and months, until he found a dealership that happened to have one on its lot.

As soon as the salesman sensed how much my colleague wanted this car, he knew he could name his price and he got what he asked for.

A week later the car broke down and it has been in and out of the shop ever since. "This car should have been yellow," my friend joked. "It's a lemon. The most expensive one I ever bought."

Here's the mistake these people made.

They fell in love with the idea of owning a nice home and a fast car without thinking it through. They imagined what it would be like to live in the perfect property or drive the ultimate Italian hot rod.

To put it differently: They were head over (w)heels and couldn't wait to get married. But as soon as the honeymoon was over, they discovered that there's a big difference between romance and reality.

Reality is raw and unforgiving. It doesn't care about your dreams and aspirations.

Reality isn't fair and doesn't play favorites either.

If anything, it is a teacher. If you need to learn a lesson, it will present you with one. Some lessons can be pleasant. Others are painful. And they tend to keep on repeating themselves until you get the message.

Loving the idea of becoming a voice-over (or any other freelance profession) is not enough to launch a career. It may seem blissful but it cannot be a basis for a long-term relationship.

It doesn't prepare you for what life as a solopreneur really is: tough, uncertain and without instantaneous rewards. Sometimes it may even feel like a real job!

It has been said many times that if you do what you love, the money will follow. If that were true, pretty much every voice-over actor I know would be loaded, yours truly included.

Sadly, I know too many colleagues who are struggling right now, even though they are very talented and their hearts are in the right place.

So, if you're thinking of becoming a voice-over professional, do me one favor.

Don't change careers solely based on what gives you a warm and fuzzy feeling.

That's how you pick a hobby.

It's not a way to plan your life.

Life passionately rewards these four things:

Preparation, planning, effort and persistence.

[3]

Fifteen Reasons

The Holidays are always a great time to meet new people and to catch up with folks we can only stand to see once or twice a year.

This last season I noticed a new trend. I'd be quietly munching on a Christmas cookie, and a relative of a friend of a friend would come up to me with a glass of eggnog in his hand.

"I hear you do voices, right?"

"Well," I said, "I'm a voice-over, if that's what you mean."

"You do books for the blind?" he wanted to know.

"No, not really. I...." And before I could finish he continued:

"Because everyone's been telling me that I have a great voice and I should be doing what you're doing, if you know what I mean. No offense, but it can't be that hard. I bet you make some pretty good money. I said to the wife: "I talk all day long. I might as well get paid for it.""

"I wish someone would pay him to shut up for a moment," said the wife, who had been listening to the conversation.

No matter where I went, I'd always run into guys with eggnog, ready to show off their terrible Sean Connery impersonation or some version of a movie trailer man voice.

All of them had three things in common:

1. They knew as much about a voice-over career as a rodent would know about the art collection at New York's Museum of Modern Art.

2. What they did know was based on misinformation and unrealistic expectations.

3. They all wanted me to tell them how to "break into the business," preferably in two minutes or less.

Where do people get these weird ideas about my line of work? Who's been feeding them false information?

It's quite simple. There are lots of coaches and companies that will tell you how easy it is to get started in this business. All you need is a computer, a microphone, some free recording software, and a credit card.

When you sign up for their site and service, they'll show you all you need to know to become the next movie trailer man or award show announcer girl. What's your card number and expiration date? Enroll today, and you'll receive a free booklet with tongue twisters you didn't realize you just paid for!

But before you fork over a small fortune, have an umbrella ready. In the next few paragraphs I'll make sure that realism will rain on your parade by popping a few voice-over balloons filled with hot air, empty promises, and unrealistic expectations.

Mind you, I'm not on a mission to destroy your dreams. I just want you to wake up!

REALITY CHECK

In a way, the idea of a voice-over career is like a microwave meal. The picture on the box looks great, but what's inside does not come close to what you see on the outside. That's why I would like to share some inside information with you. But why should you even listen to me?

First of all: I don't want more of your money. You just bought the book. Let's leave it at that. All I'm asking for is a few minutes of your time.

Secondly: I've been behind the mic since I left high school, and I've learned a few things along the way.

I got my big break at seventeen, when a Dutch public radio and TV station asked me to produce and present programs for teens. This was the beginning of an international career in broadcast journalism that eventually led me to Radio Netherlands International, the BBC and American Public Radio.

If you're interested in what I'm up to these days, go to my website. I'm at nethervoice.com and you'll see that I work for many clients in major markets on all continents.

I'm an expert-contributor to VoiceOverXtra, The International Free-lancers Academy, and recordinghacks.com. I coach privately and for Edge Studio, headquartered in New York. Thousands of people like you read my blog every month.

In all modesty, I think I know what I'm talking about. Hey, I'm a voice-over pro. Even if I don't know what I'm talking about, it's my job to sound like I know what I am talking about!

By the way, I'm not asking you to agree with everything you're about to read. Please keep an open mind and remember what resonates with you. This applies to the entire book, by the way.

Here are my fifteen reasons why you should not become a voice-over pro yet.

1. People have told you that you have a great voice.

Take it from me: It's not about the voice. Having a nice voice certainly helps but it's such a small piece of a big puzzle. Owning a Steinway does not make you a pianist. It's what you do with it that matters. Being able to play a few notes doesn't make you a musician. Only a few musicians will ever make it to Carnegie Hall. Once you're ready for Carnegie Hall, you still have to beat out the competition.

2. You don't need any training. How hard can this be? Anyone can read!

The very best performers make what they do look effortless. Please remember that we only see and hear the end result of years and years of practice.

Would you jump into the ocean without knowing how to swim? Can you learn how to swim from reading a book or listening to a recording? Even the best swimmers need constant training from a top-coach.

3. You can hone your skills on the job. Auditioning is great practice.

Practicing the wrong things over and over again makes you even better at what you're not good at.

Practice prepares you for Carnegie Hall, but people aren't paying to hear you do scales. They expect you to be ready and give the performance of a lifetime, night after night after night.

Bottom line: Practice precedes performance. Period.

4. You don't need solid business skills. You want to be a voice-over Artist, not an entrepreneur.

Fine-tuning your talent is essential for doing the work. Being business-savvy is crucial to getting the work and turning a profit. If you don't treat it as a business, it will never be one.

5. You hardly need any money to get started.

It's easy to buy a car with no money down, but you can't buy yourself a voice-over career, especially if you barely know how to drive.

Some budding voice-overs go broke breaking into this business. Even some experienced voice actors can't make ends meet anymore. If you wish to compete with the pros, you need professional gear and a professional recording space. That alone can set you back thousands of dollars.

6. You don't need to know how to market yourself.

Being outstanding doesn't make you stand out. If people don't know you exist, don't expect them to hire you. If you really want to play the trumpet professionally, you better learn how to toot your own horn.

7. Voice casting sites and agents will get you work.

It seems like every week a new voice casting website opens its doors ready to take your money to promote your pipes. Talent or experience not required.

Here's the thing. A temp agency funnels leads. *You* have to nail the job interview and do the work. And even if you nailed that interview, the client might give the job to someone cheaper.

8. It's easy money.

These two false assumptions in one sentence could cost you dearly. The big names make the big bucks and easy never does it. If you think that one hundred dollars is nice for a two-minute script, you must be confusing gross income with net profit and that's an expensive mistake you can't afford to make. It can take years of practice before something sounds seamless. The current market is saturated with talent. Only a few make it to the top and are making a good living.

9. It's a great part-time job.

If you're just starting out, it is wise to keep your day job. Get your feet wet and see if this really is the dream job you never knew you always wanted.

Don't expect to earn a full-time income on a part-time basis. The results you get are not always equivalent to the energy you put into your new career. With rates going down steadily (and the cost of living going up), even established talent is struggling these days.

10. You love cartoons and you can do some mean impressions.

Being a character and creating a character are two different things.

If you decide to focus on impersonations, you better be amazing and check in with a lawyer. In some states it is now illegal to pose as someone else promoting a product or service. It's seen as a form of deceit.

It's nice that you can sound like a celebrity. It's even nicer if you can make a career out of being YOU. There's certainly less competition.

11. You used to work for a local radio station. You know how to work a mic.

Writing news bulletins and writing novels are two different things. Reading the news and narrating an audio book are just as unrelated.

Many presenters find it nearly impossible to get rid of that dreaded announcer voice they have cultivated over the years. These days, many clients prefer talent to sound as natural as the girl next door. Even though learning things is easier than unlearning them, some radio jocks are now enjoying a successful voice-over career. They already have the perfect face.

12. For once in your life, you'd like to do a job where people will appreciate you.

As a VO-pro, it is your job to fulfill your clients' needs, not to have people massage your ego.

Most jobs you audition for you'll never get, and you'll never know why. Given the right incentive, people will applaud anything. It's the caliber of your performance that matters. Fame fades fast. Quality lasts.

13. You crave variety. Voice actors never know what the next day will bring. How exciting is that?!

Perhaps you think stability is boring and you happen to love a life of uncertainty. Perhaps you don't need a steady paycheck, benefits, and a nine-to-five schedule. Know this. The rest of the world expects you to pay your bills on time, every time.

14. You can make money in your PJs.

Here's what you should know about working from home.

Your "dream job" will never leave you and distraction is always around the corner. Go tell your kids to stop fighting because their Mommy has a Fortune 500 client on the line.

Go tell your neighbors to silence their lawn mowers, weed whackers, and snow blowers. Stop all ground and air traffic. Spend thousands of dollars soundproofing the basement.

Congratulations!

Now you are ready to audition for that fifty-dollar Craigslist job!

15. You honestly think that you're the next best thing since Don LaFontaine, the king of movie trailers.

Big egos don't make amigos.

If your hollow balloon is filled with hot air, people will be happy to pop it. But if you're really that good at what you do, others will sing your praises.

Ready for some more eggnog?

[4]

How to Break into the Voice-Over Business

"I did stand-up comedy for eighteen years. Ten of those years were spent learning, four years were spent refining, and four were spent in wild success." **Steve Martin**, *from his memoir "Born Standing Up"****

As the writer of a popular blog, I receive a lot of questions from my readers.

This is the question I get asked the most:

"How do I break into the voice-over business?"

Questions are interesting things.

One can often tell how the person asking the question thinks the world works or should work.

Questions contain spoken or unspoken assumptions that reveal a lot about someone's beliefs and values.

Most people just answer a question without challenging those hidden assumptions, unless they've been trained to do so.

QUESTION THE QUESTION

A question like "How do I break into the voice-over business?" has at least three assumptions. Before I attempt to answer it, I need to know more about what is presumed.

Assumption number one: It is a business.

Now, I'd be the last person to deny that, but it's a very superficial statement that doesn't tell me much. What I really want to know is this:

– What do you mean by business?

– What do you think is involved?

– What makes a voice-over business different from other businesses?

– How would you run such a business on a day-to-day basis?

Asking these questions does two things. First, I get to know how the other person defines "business." If I don't do that, it is likely that I will respond using my definition of the word, which could be very different from theirs.

Secondly, if it turns out that the person hasn't really given it any thought or has a very unrealistic idea, I need to address that. Why?

Because many newcomers will never make it – not due to a lack of talent – but because they lack a fundamental understanding of what it takes to run a for-profit business.

Just look at the many voice-over groups on LinkedIn and Facebook. People advertising themselves as professional voice talent ask all kinds of basic questions about marketing, sales, auditioning, setting rates, and so on.

What's wrong with that, you ask? I'll tell you.

If you want to set yourself up for success, you figure those things out in advance, whether you're selling bread, flowers, software, or your voice. Otherwise, don't call yourself a pro.

The last point I usually make is that there is not "one" voice-over business. It's very diversified. Some voice actors specialize in audio books, others in video games or animation. Some make most of their money in e-Learning. Which segment would you like to break into?

WHO ARE YOU?

Then there's the word *I*. That's the next assumption.

I do not, personally or professionally, know 95% of the people asking me "How do I break into the voice-over business?"

I've never met them. I've never listened to their demos. They might not even have demos. Perhaps all they have is a dream... and I'm supposed to tell these people how to make it in the voice-over business? What I really should be asking is this:

– Who are you, and why would you even contemplate a voice-over career?

– If I don't know anything about you, how do I know you're even remotely talented?

– Are you trained? Do you have any experience? Do you have a business plan?

– Do you have a website, decent equipment, and can you provide studio quality audio?

– Can you handle daily rejection, financial uncertainty, and constant pressure to perform?

– If I were a loan officer at a bank, why would I give you any money so you could start this so-called business of yours?

All these questions might sound a bit harsh and needlessly confrontational, but if you can't answer them, you live in La-La land.

The truth is, a lot of people asking "How do I break into the voice-over business?" are either only vaguely interested, they have an inflated sense of self, or they want me to hand them the golden formula to instant success.

How do I know? Because when I ask people why they want to be a voice-over, they tell me:

"It seems like a fun thing to do."

"I'm special."

"It's something I think I can pick up pretty quickly."

Let me ask you this: "If you are doing it for fun, why not keep it a hobby? Just because you enjoy taking pictures, doesn't mean you should become a professional photographer."

If you believe you're special, I'd like to introduce you to lots of other people who think they're the next best thing since sliced bread.

How do you know you have what the current market wants? Did you pay a company to research that for you, or have you been listening to friends and family?

PATIENCE BELONGS TO THE PAST

This brings me to assumption number three. The notion of breaking into something. What exactly does that mean?

Here's what I've noticed.

Years ago, breaking into something simply meant: "to start doing something." These days, the expression has gained more urgency, as in "to start having success." It must be something of the "I want it and I want it NOW"-generation. A typical email starts:

> "Paul, I've been auditioning for a few months without any luck. Tell me, how do I break into this business?"

> "I just finished an introduction to voice-overs with company Such-and-so. How do I start getting the jobs that were promised?"

> "I spent a few thousand dollars on a home studio and some demos. Agents don't seem interested. What the heck do I do to begin making some money?"

So, what do I tell these people?

OVERNIGHT SUCCESS

Especially in the creative field, it's so easy to focus on the end product and ignore the long road to get there.

We see the pianist play. She seems so seamless, and part of us is tricked into believing that we, too, could play like that. Never mind the many years of practicing eight hours a day, the fierce competitions and all the sacrifices she made to make it to the top.

We admire the downhill skier. His rapid descent looks so gracious and effortless. We don't even notice his flawless technique, based on years and years of being on the slopes, great coaching, tons of talent and a very disciplined lifestyle.

We watch as the actress arrives at the Golden Globes. Her last movie was a box office sensation and we wonder what it must feel like to be her right now. It's easy to forget how many times she failed to land a part, and how hard it was to stay afloat when no one was interested in hiring her.

We want the glory, but are we willing to pay the price?

We long for recognition, but are we ready to do the work?

We wish to break into the business – preferably yesterday – but do we know what it takes?

How about this:

Ten years of learning.

Four years of refining...

... for years of wild success.

[5]

Bursting the Audition Bubble

If you want to get work as a voice-over, you have to audition. Some of my colleagues audition ten to fifty times a day. If they manage to book one of those jobs, they consider that to be a success.

I once asked a few of my voice acting friends if they felt they were wasting their time running after jobs they would probably never get. This is the answer I heard the most:

> "Auditioning is great practice! Even if you don't get that job, at least you're honing your skills."

This answer is echoed by many voice casting sites and coaches. Let me take you to a crowded conference room in a New Jersey hotel to get some perspective.

WORDS OF WISDOM

At the end of a two-day "voice-over intensive," the trainer looked at her students one last time. By the expression on her face they could tell she was about to say something significant.

Her velvet voice had sold millions of sheets of the softest bathroom tissue known to mankind. Anything that came out of her mouth was as good as gold. Star-struck, the students all listened carefully, like attention-deprived orphans, waiting to get one last bit of tough love.

"People," she said, as she took stock of her class, "this weekend was just the beginning. Now it's up to you to go out there and break a leg. Make me proud! Audition as much as possible. It doesn't matter what for. If you can't make it, fake it. It's a numbers game. The more you audition, the greater the chance you'll eventually get hired. If I can do it, you can do it!

Never in my wildest dreams could I have imagined that my biggest achievement would come from the smallest room in the house. But didn't the Romans coin the phrase: *Pecunia non olet*? Take it from me: Once you're on a roll, you just keep on rolling, wherever your destiny leads you.

Now, before you go, be sure to check out the table with my products. Only today they're 15% off. And if you sign up for the next seminar, you are eligible for an early bird discount. All credit cards are welcome."

TRAINING TALENT

Business was booming. As the U.S. economy went down the drain, enrollment for voice-over trainings was up. Kindergarten teachers, homemakers, librarians, retired car salesmen, call center assistants... all of them had a dream: to become the next Don LaFontaine, the King of voice-overs.

Don had it made. Working from home or being chauffeured from studio to studio in a limo. That's the life! There's no need to learn lines. A glorious set of vocal cords was all that was required. And a membership to one of those online voice casting sites, of course.

A few months after the training, things were not going as advertised. Take John, for instance.

John used to work for a local radio station, until a fund drive didn't go so well. "But," said John, "at least I have a background in broadcasting. I know how to talk to invisible people. I'll just transition to voice-overs."

John sent out about twelve to fifteen auditions a day, and hadn't had one single bite. He'd spent a small fortune on the setup of his home studio, and it was about time he got some return on his investment. When he called his trainer for some advice, he got an assistant on the line.

John explained that he hadn't been so lucky lately, and asked her what he should do.

"Sir," she said, "How about I sign you up for our next seminar? It's called 'Winning Auditions' and it will really take you to the next level. But if you can't make it, you should definitely buy the CD, recorded at a live training in Vegas. It's powerful stuff and it's even on sale! We take all credit cards."

IT'S A MYTH

John's story is not uncommon. He had fallen for a fallacy. It's the idea that you should audition as much as you can if you want to break into the business. And if things don't work out, no problem.

Doing demos is great practice!

Really?

I'm not buying it.

It reminds me of the exit of one of the participants in a conducting competition. He was a young guy who already had spent a great deal of time in front of various symphony orchestras. Yet, after the first round of the competition, the jury decided to send him home.

"How is that possible?" the young conductor wanted to know. "I probably have more experience than the majority of the people in this contest."

"Experience, yes" said the chairman of the jury calmly. "But there's good experience and bad experience. I'm afraid your experience wasn't very good. Have a nice day."

In my mind, you practice to audition; you don't audition to practice.

Take the Olympics. If you've been glued to the TV as much as I have been during the last Games, you've noticed that competitions usually start off with qualifiers. Some athletes will tell you that these initial qualifying rounds are actually more stressful and demanding than the real thing. It's during these qualifiers that you have to prove to the world that you're worthy of a top spot.

That's not where you learn it. That's where you earn it!

What would happen if a top athlete would go into a qualifier with an attitude of:

"It doesn't really matter if I make it or not. I can at least look back on some great practice rounds."

It's a totally different mindset. A very different energy. It will never get you on the podium.

NUMBERS DON'T ADD UP

The secret to winning auditions does not lie in how many you can crank out. Anybody can record ten to twenty a day, even a talking parrot.

Ultimately, it's a matter of quality, not quantity. And in order to deliver quality, you need to be qualified and that's where practice comes into play. Practice and training.

No one would dare to audition for a Broadway show after taking a two-day tap dancing seminar, no matter how famous the teacher might have been in his heydays. It's ludicrous. But that's exactly what happens if you start sending demos to every producer who's posting a job that vaguely meets your criteria, when you're not ready and when you're not really going for it.

If you can't nail it, you will fail it.

Now, that's not something they taught you at that two-day voice-over class, was it?

It gets even worse.

In a weird way, it's often easier for us to remember the bad, the bizarre and the outrageous. One stupid mistake in one race can haunt an athlete for years. One dumb demo can ruin your chances for a long time. That's why it is so important to be selective, to be prepared and to give it all you've got.

THE NEXT CHAPTER

Radio Station-John didn't buy that voice-over seminar CD recorded in Vegas. He didn't sign up for the next training either. Instead, he had a professional critique his demos and he worked one-on-one with a coach to get rid of his "announcer voice."

He no longer auditions for every job on the voice-over planet. In fact, something very strange happened.

The pickier he became, the more success he had. And instead of spending most of the day recording demos, he actually had time to develop a solid business plan.

John's a smart guy.

He gave himself a second chance to make a first impression.

PART TWO: COACHING AND VOICE ACTING

[6]

Your Biggest Blind Spot

Do you remember the first time you heard a recording of your own voice? Going back to that moment now, what went through your mind?

Were you shocked or pleasantly surprised? Did you expect you'd sound like that?

Most people respond the same way. When they hear themselves on tape, they get a bit uncomfortable and will tell you:

"Did I just say that? That does not sound like me at all. Who is that person?"

People tend to become very self-conscious and self-critical. Why? Because most of us don't have a clue how other people perceive the sound of our voice. How could we?

We hear ourselves from the inside 24/7. We're locked into our own little world thinking that – because we perceive ourselves a certain way – others hear what we hear and will respond accordingly.

Let me break the news to you: They do not.

CONFRONTATIONAL CAMERAS

As a media trainer, I spent many years coaching influential people on how to prepare for interviews on radio and TV. My favorite part was taking a CEO to a studio and putting him or her in front of a few cameras and blinding lights, while I would ask innocent questions.

When the interview was over, I'd say to them: "Well, how do you think you did?"

Nine out of ten times, they would tell me: "Pretty good. You know, I run a multimillion-dollar business. I'm used to speaking in public. I don't really think I need any media coaching, but my PR people talked me into it. What's for lunch?"

Then I'd play the tape back to them, without sound.

I would watch them closely as they were watching themselves. I could see the color fade from their faces. Some people would turn away. Some were utterly embarrassed. Others would tell me:

"That's so mean of you! This is unfair."

Staring at that person on television, it was as if they were watching themselves naked. The unforgiving camera exposed every micro muscle movement; every time they unknowingly scratched their nose or rolled their eyes; every drop of sweat; every clenched fist and every nervous tic.

After these two minutes of terror, I'd ask them again: "So, how do you think you did?"

At that very moment, I could see the penny drop, as these high-level executives became aware of the huge disconnect between how they thought they came across, and they way the rest of the world perceived them to be.

Things they'd never noticed before became a big deal: a silver button missing from a striped shirt, a small stain on a preppy tie, dandruff, nose hair, noisy jewelry, clogged mascara... rendering what they were saying utterly irrelevant.

Body language always overpowers the words we speak.

When we hold up a big mirror, it is interesting to see what happens. Seeing oneself through the eyes of someone else can feel like a cold morning shower. It's refreshing. It wakes you up, but it's not necessarily enjoyable.

THE PASSIONATE PURSUIT

As voice-over pros, we think that we have a big advantage over the rest of the world. We listen to ourselves day in day out. It's a very self-indulgent profession and some of us have become our own worst enemies.

Take the perfectionists, for instance. They're never happy with what they hear. They keep on twisting and tweaking their audition until they're last in line when sending out the demo. But even then, they're not satisfied. They keep on listening back to the tape, spotting yet another breath or mouth noise that should have been edited out.

For the flagellating perfectionist, nothing's ever good enough and every audition becomes an almost impossible mountain to climb. The stress and anxiety of this process alone, usually sucks the lifeblood out of any performance. It's a self-defeating strategy of those who believe they never, ever measure up... until they realize that it's only human to be perfectly imperfect.

Perfectionists are over-aware of their own flaws, but most of us are wired differently. In a way, you and I are much more like that CEO coming to my media training. Most of the time, we think we're doing alright, and we don't get why we didn't get that job after we delivered yet another stunning demo. Why is that?

THE BREAKFAST OF CHAMPIONS

Writers have editors. Translators have proofreaders. Advertising agencies use focus groups to gather feedback. Comedians test their material during try-outs. And what do voice-overs do? We stare at ourselves in the big talent pool, falling more and more in love with our own reflection, cheered on by fans, family and friends who can only see and hear a fully-clothed emperor.

As masters and commanders of the home studio, we've become a one-person multitasking band. We annotate the script, we read the lines as we self-direct and take on the role of recording engineer, before we edit everything unwanted out and sweeten the sound.

By that time, we're thoroughly emotionally invested in the fruits of our labor. We've played back the tape a thousand times, making us immune to what probably could be so much better.

There must be a reason why the Greek "Narkissos" is seemingly derived from the word "narke," meaning sleep or numbness. We're numb like a lover, incapable of seeing the flaws in the object of our adoration.

GNOTHI SEAUTON

In 1750, Benjamin Franklin wrote the following in his Poor Richard's Almanack:

> *"There are three Things extremely hard, Steel, a Diamond, and to know one's self."*

What do you think: Can a psychoanalyst effectively analyze himself? Can we really know how we come across? Is it humanly possible to separate ourselves from ourselves and listen to our own voice the way others do? Or are we our own, biggest blind spot?

It gets worse.

Some people don't even realize that they're blind and lost. Take the radio jock who's utterly unaware of his announcer voice, or the priest who has no clue he's preaching even when he thinks he's not.

Others do know that they are lost, but they have a very hard time admitting it publicly. Out of those who do admit it, some will wander off, wondering where to find their destination. They usually end up getting farther away from where they want to be.

Some will blame others for getting lost in the first place, and if it's someone else's fault, it's really someone else's problem. You don't have to change a thing.

But by far the biggest group is made up of those who keep on running around in circles because they refuse to ask for directions, and this group is not only made up of men!

Bad habits are very effective strategies for consistently getting undesired results. But as Dr. Phil tells us: "You can't change what you don't acknowledge." Here's what you do about it.

STEP ONE:

If you insist on pulling yourself out of the swamp, you first need to admit you're in deep sh*t, and get a clue of how deep it really is. What are some of the signs?

- Your booking rate has gone way down
- Your agent is ignoring you
- Return business isn't returning

- Your income has dropped dramatically
- You feel tired, uninspired, and don't care if you're hired

STEP TWO:

Be brave enough to revisit some of last year's auditions, preferably the ones that you can't even remember you did. Take those skeletons out of the closet and listen to them with fresh ears. You'll be amazed at what you'll hear. The passing of time helps us disassociate and notice things we'd otherwise never notice.

The next phase is critical.

STEP THREE:

Write down your observations and not your interpretations.

A sensory observation is something you can smell, touch, hear or see, such as:

– I can clearly hear the hum of my computer in the background
– The company name did not stand out
– There was an obvious edit 29 seconds into the demo

An interpretation is a label we attach to those observations:

– This audition totally sucked.
– I am such a loser. I might as well give up.

An observation refers to facts. An interpretation is an opinion, based on those facts.

In order to learn, grow and move forward, I strongly suggest you focus on facts (unless you're a masochist. In that case, you deserve a good spanking).

STEP FOUR:

For every audition, write something you specifically liked and wish to keep.

For instance: saying "I sounded pretty good," is neither specific nor helpful. Get the details! What exactly was it that you liked? What did you *specifically* do to get to that result? What can you do to replicate and reinforce it and possibly teach to others?

Why is this step necessary? Because I believe that we can learn just as much from the things we do well, as from the things that we're not so good at.

STEP FIVE:

Once you've listened to a number of old auditions and have compared notes, I predict that you will discover patterns. If you keep on repeating your mistakes, you have become better at what you're not good at.

Look at those patterns and pick the one that – if you were to change it – would have the greatest positive impact on your performance.

Ask yourself:

– What do I need to improve upon?

– What can I specifically do to make those improvements?

– Do I need outside help?

– To whom should I turn?

– What's one step I can take right now to get the ball rolling?

STEP SIX:

Take immediate ACTION!

Postpone your procrastination. Talk is cheap. If you're a voice-over, you already know that.

If you want to go off on your own and try to fix things by yourself, be my guest. But realize that the hardest way to learn is through trial and error. Experience is a slow teacher, especially if your experience is not very good. Best-case scenario, it will lead to more of the same, or you'll spend years reinventing the wheel.

Reading a book or a blog isn't going to cut it either. Information has never changed a single soul. It's what you do with it that makes the difference.

Why not take a shortcut?

Let me ask you a question:

How much can you realistically learn from someone who knows just as much as you do?

Even your greatest successes are limited and limiting examples of how much more you're actually capable of.

That's where a coach comes in.

WHEN THE STUDENT IS READY

A coach not only sees your blind spots, senses your insecurities, and takes apart your rusty routines. A good coach does more than teach an old dog new tricks. Rather than create a clone, a good coach taps into your unique potential and draws things out of you that you never even knew were there.

Bad coaches turn students into shadows of their teachers. Great coaches help you rekindle the fire that's burning inside of you, and inspire you to step into the light and shine like never before.

Great coaches want the best for you, because they see the best in you. They are never threatened by your talent. Instead, they are proud of your accomplishments.

If you want a great coach, don't look at his or her credits.

Great performers can be lousy, self-absorbed, power-hungry teachers in need of adulation.

If you want a great coach, look at their students instead.

Their students are their best credentials.

THE TEACHER WILL APPEAR

A coach can lead the way and give you tools to further your development and speed up your growth. But a coach can't run the race for you. You have to do the work.

Ultimately, it doesn't matter what potential a coach sees in you. You have to see it yourself. It doesn't matter if a coach believes in you. You have to believe in yourself.

Last but not least, if you wish to grow, you have to relax and cut yourself some slack.

Be passionate, be persistent, and be patient.

Take a clue from nature. It takes a while for a tree to mature and grow deep roots that can weather a storm before it bears fruit. That's not a popular message in a culture of instant gratification.

Back in my days as a reporter, I once asked a brilliant sitar player how long it had taken him to master his instrument.

As the camera was rolling, he looked at me meaningfully and said:

"Several lifetimes...

... and I'm still learning!

[7]

Playing Hard to Get

It's time for an apology.

Yes, I'm truly sorry, but I can explain.

If you are one of the people who asked me to be your voice-over coach, chances are that I turned you down. Not that I don't enjoy coaching. I've been coaching professionally for the past twenty years.

You already know that I used to prepare people to meet the press in my role of media coach. Later on, I became what people now call a "Life Coach," helping clients overcome obstacles and reach goals. I also taught two-week certification trainings centered on personal growth and development, and I loved every minute of it.

Even though the FAQ page*** on my website will tell you that I still offer voice-over coaching services, I'm not shouting it from the roof-tops.

WHY I KEEP COACHING QUIET

First of all, my clients are keeping me pretty busy, so I don't have much time to be a coach. Secondly, it's a matter of focus. If you try to do too many different things at the same time, you're spreading yourself too thin. You cannot build a full-time career on a part-time schedule. It just doesn't work.

Before I became a full-time voice-over, I used to do a lot of translations. I'm a native Dutch speaker with a good knowledge of German. The work was boring, uncreative, and repetitive. It became something I was okay at, that prevented me from doing something I was good at; something I actually enjoyed.

Most days, as I was rushing to meet yet another midnight deadline, I resented it. Bad attitude isn't exactly a client magnet.

However, when I decided to transition into voice-overs, something weird started to happen. My inbox began to fill up with translation projects! I'd never had so many offers in my entire life. It was as if my resolve was being tested. Had I accepted all those offers, I would have never had the energy and time to obsessively pursue a new career.

Tempting short-turn opportunities often prevent us from reaching long-term goals.

If you are determined to make it in any field, you have to be prepared to say NO to distractions and keep your eye on the prize.

MOTIVATION METER

That same determination is another reason why I only coach a handful of people. Theoretically, I could sell my services to hundreds of interested folks who want to explore the possibility of perhaps maybe talking into a microphone every once in a while. That's not my crowd.

I choose not to work with people who are merely interested. It's a waste of my time and their money. I want my students to be totally committed. Strong commitment will increase their chances of becoming successful, and it increases my chance to be successful as a coach. So, how do I know that someone I've never met even has "the right stuff?"

Believe it or not, I take my first cues from religion.

Traditionally, Judaism has not sought out converts. In fact, by tradition, a potential convert is supposed to be turned away by the rabbi – three times. If the person then persists past that third rejection, it is assumed he or she is adequately motivated.

I don't want to compare myself to a rabbi, but rabbi means "teacher" and that's what a coach really is. So, if you were to ask me to become your voice-over coach, chances are that I would turn you down. And if you can't handle rejection, perhaps you're not cut out for this profession.

AUDIO EVALUATION

Once you've proven that you're positively persistent, I will ask for some samples of your work and I will evaluate them for a fee. At that stage, some will politely thank me and move on because they're not willing to spend the money. To me, that's a clear sign. If you don't think my time is valuable now, why would you value my advice once the coaching process has started?

The quality of the audio samples I receive can be quite revealing. You'd be surprised how many "interested" people don't own any tools of the trade to make a decent recording.

There's still this myth that one can make good voice-over money on a shoestring budget. If a potential student is not willing to make a serious investment in his or her career, why should I? Besides, with that microphone that's built into your laptop and Garageband, we're not going to get anywhere.

Next, I will evaluate the audition. I call it that, because people are in fact auditioning for me. Most of the time, they think I'll be listening to the actual sound of their voice. Is it warm and welcoming? Is it boomy? Is it seductive?

Even though I listen to the timbre of their instrument, I'm much more interested in whether or not they're using it to make music. I'm not expecting a perfect performance. Otherwise they wouldn't need me. I am listening for *potential* and *authenticity*.

Are they capable of keeping me interested for more than fifteen seconds? Do they reveal something that is uniquely theirs, or are they pretending to be someone they're not?

Every day, people sign up for voice casting sites with high hopes and big dreams. They'll submit demos that sound like what they think a voice-over should sound like. Mark my words:

The industry is not looking and listening for more of the same. They want more of YOU!

THE VERDICT

The next thing I'll do is send the potential student a detailed critique of their demo. I have to warn you: I think I am fair but I'm not always diplomatic. Even though I don't subscribe to the school of "break 'em down before you build them up," I will give you an honest opinion. Then I wait.

Not everybody is happy with what I have to say. Expectations can be high and egos are fragile. Sometimes, I will receive a response filled with explanations, excuses, and justifications as to why they did what they did. Sometimes they flat-out disagree with me. That's fine. All I want to know from them is this:

How open are you to feedback? Are you sure you can handle constructive criticism?

If you're going to fight me tooth and nail from the get-go, what will our coaching sessions be like? You don't hire a coach to have someone massage your ego. You hire a coach to kick your butt. You hire a coach because you don't have all the answers and you need new tools and a new direction. You say you're open to my suggestions, but tell me:

How can I pour water into a cup that's already overflowing?

WRITTEN AGREEMENT

Those who make it past the refusal and audition phase have two more hurdles to take before we begin.

First, they have to go over and sign a four-page Coaching Agreement, which is all about managing expectations and setting boundaries. That's necessary because some people still believe I own a magic wand and that I am able to miraculously make them successful. If that were true, I would probably be sitting on a sunny, tropical island enjoying early retirement.

The keyword in coaching is empowerment. I can help you become a better driver. I'm not going to be your chauffeur. Bad coaches make their students dependent. My goal is to make myself redundant. Bad coaches take credit for their students' successes. I want my students to take credit for their own accomplishments.

INVESTED IN GROWTH

The last step to secure people's commitment requires an investment of time and money. I don't allow my students to sign up for single sessions. That's like going to the gym once or twice, expecting major results. You can't change old habits and learn new ones by taking a session whenever you feel like it. Quite often, old patterns are established over many years and change doesn't happen overnight.

One recurring issue for most of my students is the lack of structure and discipline in their professional life. It's one of the curses of being self-employed. You can do whatever you want whenever you want, and get nothing done. So, task number one is to schedule these coaching sessions and bring some structure to the workweek.

Initially, I'll ask my students to commit to at least five sessions. In my experience, it works best to do a minimum of one or two sessions a week via Skype. After those first five sessions, both of us will have a much better sense of where we will be going and at what speed.

JUMPING THROUGH HOOPS

I realize that putting up those barriers might sound a bit over the top. But being my own boss, I can choose whom I want to work with.

I refuse to take money from untalented hopefuls and milk them for every penny until they record a demo that needs be doctored in order to sound somewhat acceptable.

My standards are as high as my expectations. My commitment to my students is as great as their commitment to the coaching process. In my book, that's the only way to do it.

So, if you didn't hear back from me after you asked me to be your coach, you now know why.

It was "just" a test.

There's one last reason why I don't feel the need to take on many coaching clients.

You're looking at it right now.

Why hire me if you can buy this book? It's packed with practical information.

I know, I know.... it's not the same, but still.

Some people believe it's a pretty good deal.

Who am I to disagree?

[8]

Are You a Cliché?

His name is Jake Foushee and he's an online voice-over sensation.

Over one million people have watched his short movie trailer man impersonation on YouTube. If you haven't seen the video,*** you may wonder: What's the big deal?

Well, even though he sounds like he's in his fifties, Mr. Foushee was actually fourteen years old at the time he shot the video. It's creepy. Fortunately for Jake, we like creepy. Regular Joes rarely make the headlines, but we all love the bizarre and the eccentric, don't we?

Next to the bearded lady we now have a fourteen-year old who sounds a bit like Don LaFontaine. It doesn't get any better than that.

Ellen DeGeneres had him on her show and like a docile puppy, Jake eagerly showed off his tricks.

That's a good boy!

And because good boys deserve a reward, Ellen announced that the renowned Abrams Agency was eager to introduce him to the voice-over business. I am sure a little bit of showbiz pressure and the prospect of free publicity didn't hurt.

GOLDEN PIPES

Remember all the companies that were lining up to jump on the Ted Williams bandwagon (the homeless man with the golden pipes)? When Ted got back into his bad old drug-related habits, the job offers melted away as fast as snow on a hot summer's day.

We like to be associated with a feel-good story, especially if we can dangle our brand name in front of television cameras. But when a humble hero falls, we leave him on the side of the road, right where he came from.

Mind you, I don't wish to deny Jake his two minutes of fame, but does he really deserve to be coached by one of the nation's premier talent agencies? Come on! I can think of a number of colleagues who can do a far better movie trailer man impersonation, and for whom access to the hallowed hallways at Abrams has always been a distant dream. Their problem: They're no longer fourteen... and creepy.

There's one consolation.

I predict young Jake will be forgotten before he turns fifteen, because he is making two mistakes many aspiring voice-overs make:

1. He's starting too early, thinking that owning an okay instrument makes one a professional musician;

2. His reputation is based on imitation.

FAKING FOR FAME

Now, don't give me that "imitation is the highest form of flattery" nonsense. It's called making money off someone else's unique talent and creativity. It's a gimmick. A party trick. Not exactly something you can build a career on. Granted, a few brilliant impersonators are making good money doing one-man shows around the world, but these guys can do many voices to perfection.

Not only that, as they "do" the voice, they actually become the character. It's an acting tour de force!

Even though I predict that Jake's success will be short-lived, I think many voice actors can relate to him.

So many of us started out imitating cartoon characters, family members,   teachers   and   celebrities. I certainly did and still do, even though I stink at it (my wife and daughter can attest to that). You should hear me try to speak with an American accent. It's pathetic!

There's nothing wrong with stretching one's voice acting muscles, but there's a big problem with impersonations. Most of them are nothing more than a caricature built out of mannerisms. There's no depth to it. It's just a bunch of clichés.

Regrettably, some folks who are trying to break into the voice-over business are trying to jumpstart a career by copying mannerisms. Sadly, some veterans have never grown out of that habit.

When you listen to their demos, you do not hear a natural, original interpretation. What you hear is an impression of what the talent believes a voice actor should sound like. Instead of pure sincerity and individuality, you hear a stereotype.

This goes to the heart of what acting really is.

WHAT IS ACTING?

The art of acting is about creating a unique character.

It is not about recreating a cliché.

Acting has little to do with clever imitation... unless the role requires it.

Great actors are phenomenal at pretending not to pretend.

In a way, voice acting can be even more demanding than on-camera acting.

When narrating a novel, a voice actor has to create many characters and keep them consistent throughout an entire book. Most of the time, a stage or screen actor only has to play one role.

The audio book narrator cannot fall back on body language, fancy costumes, or on make-up to set a character apart. All of that has to be done with pitch, timbre, tempo, inflection, and accent. In order to be convincing, nothing can come across as contrived. It has to sound spontaneous and real.

On top of that, today's audio book narrator often works without a director, a technical crew, a PA, a publicist, a personal chef, trainer, and nanny.

Of course most voice-over work is far removed from Shakespeare, Spielberg, and Harry Potter. Medical narrations, e-Learning programs, and corporate presentations call for a very different approach. Yet, I hear many voice-overs make the same mistake.

They start imitating a certain sound they believe to be appropriate for the read, very much like a radio announcer. One moment you're having a normal conversation with them in the studio, but as soon as they're on the air they flip an internal switch and out comes the announcer voice.

Here's the crux of the matter

When you're imitating, the focus is always on someone or something else; on the sound you're trying to recreate. It's disingenuous by definition.

Great painters, architects, scientists, and writers are not great because they're trying to emulate someone else. They are great because they are who they are and there's no one like them.

Painters and poets who try to rip off someone else's work engage in plagiarism.

So, I'm happy for you if you can do an amazing Morgan Freeman impersonation or you can sound just like Christopher Walken, but we all know that's not you.

It might get you a job here or there, but most agents and producers aren't looking for something we already have.

It took me years to find out that most clients hire me for who I am and not for who I can pretend to be.

Of course there's a difference between the Paul in the studio and the Paul enjoying a cappuccino in his favorite coffee shop. The Paul in the studio is more polished, articulate, and prepared. Every now and then I still do character voices, but that's just part of being a versatile voice actor.

After decades of searching, I can honestly say that I'm okay being me, and I'm happy with the way I sound.

And you know what?

As soon as I started accepting myself for who I am, I was overcome by a relaxed kind of confidence. I could feel it in my bones and it came out through my mouth. That's when it happened:

I found my sound.

It is the inimitable sum of all my life experiences, the languages I speak, the people I have met, and the countries I have lived and worked in.

It is that Northern European sound most of my clients select and pay me for.

And what about fourteen-year-old Jake?

Well, if he plays his cards right and starts working with the right voice-over coaches, one day we might actually hear the real Jake Foushee, instead of Movie Trailer Man.

That's when he will find out if he really has a future in this business.

Now, let's forget about Jake and talk about you.

Have you found your voice yet?

[9]

Ways to Win an Audition and Nail the Job

On paper it sounded so easy.

> "You have been hired to record the voices of five different guys for a new interactive game."

After I had signed a contract and a comprehensive non-disclosure agreement, I took a moment to reflect on what I had gotten myself into.

I had wanted to break into this segment of the voice-over market, but there were at least three minor complications with this assignment.

One: I had to play all five characters.

Two: These guys were supposed to be teenagers.

Three: At the time I was 49 years old.

As soon as I signed the papers, I started having second thoughts. Could I pull this one off? Was I really the right person for this project?

Who was I kidding?

I always tell my students: "Never to accept a job you think you can't handle." Why did I choose to ignore my own advice?

Then there was this.

Part of me believes there's something creepy about a guy my age pretending to be a thirteen-year old. Shouldn't I be going through male menopause, instead of trying to relive my teenage years?

On the other hand, the director had selected me based on my demo, so, if he was convinced I could do this, why should I worry about my acting abilities?

Self-doubt never leads to a solid performance. That's a given. If anything, it sabotages it.

To cut a long story short, I decided to bite the bullet and go ahead with the recording. Looking back, four key elements helped me get the job and do the job:

Timing, **Pricing**, **Preparation** and **Direction**

Let's start with timing.

Quite often I listen to something a voice-over colleague recorded and wonder:

"How the heck did he or she ever land that job? I know at least ten people who could have done that so much better!"

Well, here's a not so secret "secret."

We live in a world where "okay" is often good enough. Producers under pressure only have time to listen to the first ten to twenty submissions and must make a choice. Those who win auditions aren't necessarily perfect for the part, but they got their demo in before the rest of the pack. Take my advice:

Be fast but don't hurry.

If your custom demo sounds too rushed, you won't be considered. If you take too much time to perfect every second, you'll miss the boat. More on timing a bit later.

KA-CHING!

In an ideal world, money should never be an issue, but it always is. The difference between winning and losing an audition has just as much to do with your quote as with your qualities, especially when you're responding to one of those online cattle calls.

I've compared the auditioning process to playing darts in the dark. Some clients expect us to hit the bull's-eye while giving us a minimum of information and listing the budget as "undefined." It is a stupid strategy.

Ideally, your price should give the client confidence that he's not hiring an idiot and confirm that you're not ripping him off.

ARE YOU READY

The best way to increase your competence and calm your nerves can be summarized in one word: preparation. Obviously, there's not much time to prepare for those last-minute auditions, but once you've got the job, remember this:

Don't wing it. Bring it!

Going back to my story for a moment, I made sure to get the script and the specs on my five characters a few days before the recording session. I was lucky. The producer sent along five pictures of the teens I was supposed to voice, as well as a few lines about each character.

With this in hand, I started experimenting.

To me, this is not just a mental exercise. It's very much a physical process.

Think of your body as an instrument. As soon as you transform the shape of that instrument, you transform the way it sounds.

I need to step into a character's skin and imagine what the world looks like through his eyes. I don't have to know everything about the character. I only have to pretend I know.

When I do that, my posture changes, my breathing changes, and my facial expressions start to change. Only then do I dare to open my mouth.

This, however, is not enough.

Once I'm in character and I've practiced my lines, I need to hear myself the way other people hear me. I need to record my voice in order to fine-tune my performance. Here's what still amazes me:

The way I think I sound is very different from the way I actually sound. That's what makes self-direction so tricky!

I also discovered that the best time to record these five characters was around 3:30 PM. I'll tell you why.

TIMING IS EVERYTHING

In order to sound like a teenager, my voice needed to be about an octave higher. Being a tenor, I am already comfortable with the upper register, but I would still have to pick the right time of day to read my lines.

I usually get to my studio around 7:00 AM. Early in the day, the voice isn't warmed up yet and the lower register comes naturally. Factor that in, the next time you need to sound older or more authoritative. Plan these recordings for early in the day.

As the hours pass, our voice gets progressively lighter and higher. Because this is a gradual process, we don't notice it, until we try to match a morning recording during an evening session. It usually doesn't work, does it?

When we're just out of bed, our facial muscles aren't as flexible either, and until we have completed our warm-ups, our morning face isn't always willing to bend to our will.

Then there's the food-factor.

BAD EATINGS

I don't like to record before breakfast because my stomach behaves like Audrey II from "The Little Shop of Horrors."

It yells: "FEED ME!"

I don't like to record right after breakfast either, because my digestive system always insists on making a guest appearance on my audio.

Right before and after lunch this drama repeats itself again, and if I don't plan my recordings carefully, I end up wasting tons of time editing all kinds of stomach noises out.

So, for me, the ideal time to record is from 3:30 to 4:30 PM. My voice is sufficiently warmed up, lunch is out of the way, and my body isn't craving for dinner yet.

I'm not a big fan of post-dinner recordings. After talking all day long, my voice usually isn't at its best anymore, and I also value my downtime.

A SENSE OF DIRECTION

If I have a choice between a low-tech, cheap solution or some high-priced gadget, I am very frugal. So, when the director joined me for the recording session, we used Skype to stay connected.

I cannot emphasize enough what a delight it is to have someone on the other end of the line to give you immediate feedback. Assuming the director knows what he or she wants, you no longer have to guess what you think a client might hope to hear.

At some point in time, all of us have heard back from a client after we'd completed a recording, and we've received a new set of instructions. "Could you do it a bit faster? Could you read the second line a bit slower? Make it more conversational and less of a hard sell."

Back to the drawing board you go, knowing this could have been avoided if only the client had been more specific in the first place.

In the end, a directed session always saves time and leads to a better result. Besides, it's fun to hear someone respond and cheer you on when things are going well. It helps to have a real person to talk to. You stop acting and begin interacting.

That's exactly what happened during my session.

We made sure I recorded at least three different takes of the five teenagers. That way, the client had something to choose from. Once we were done, I cleaned the audio up, separated the files, and I uploaded them to a Dropbox.

It was invigorating!

You see, that's one of the things I love about this job.

It keeps me young.

In spirit, at least.

[10]

Shut Up and Listen!

The two women were sitting opposite each other in the ski lodge. Their kids were out on the slopes, so they had all morning to catch up.

I usually don't mind other people's business, but these two were very hard to ignore. Their nasal voices were as loud as the bling they were wearing. Even though they were dressed in the latest ski apparel, I don't think either of them had any intention of ever going down a snowy hill.

This morning they seemed to be discussing their favorite topic: family illness.

"My father just went in for a double bypass," said the one closest to me, as she was digging deep into a Boston Cream doughnut. "The doctor had told him years ago that he should start exercising, but he just wouldn't listen. You know how men are... I guess I shouldn't be worried about him, but I am. I couldn't sleep all night."

"My cousin is starting dialysis this week," said the other woman who was sipping on a soft drink. "Her blood sugar level was way up there, which is no surprise if you know how much soda that family is drinking. I read somewhere that one soda a day equals fifty pounds of sugar a year. Imagine that!"

"The doctor told me it was a routine operation, but that's easy for him to say," said her friend. "It's not his dad we're talking about. What if my papa wakes up while they're cutting him open? I swear to you, that's my nightmare! And have you heard about this hospital super-bug that's resistant to everything?"

"Oh, Brenda, tell me about it," her friend responded. "You know I was in the hospital a few years ago to get that 'thing' removed. I never felt more miserable in my entire life. It's the worst place to get better, I swear."

"What if my dad doesn't make it?" asked Brenda. "I wouldn't know what to do without him. Mom's gone. Jim's parents are both dead. Who's going to cut the turkey on Thanksgiving?"

"We had the best turkey, last Thanksgiving," said her friend. "Those guys at Boston Market really know how to cook a bird. It was lean, it was juicy, and it was huge. We ate leftovers for three days straight. Have you ever had their mashed potatoes? They're to die for!"

Then the phone rang. Brenda picked it up. She looked at her friend and whispered: "I've got to take this call."

A minute or so later it seemed as if a tremendous weight had fallen off her shoulders. Then she took a deep breath.

"It was the hospital," she said with the biggest smile on her face. "They say he's going to be alright! I can come and see him this after-noon."

"The hospital?" her friend asked perplexed.

"Who's in the hospital?

You never tell me anything, do you?

And I thought we were friends..."

DEAF EARS

I have heard this kind of conversation a million times, and I'm sure you've heard it too. The topic isn't really important. It's about communication or the lack thereof.

On the surface it may seem that these two women were engaged in a lively dialogue, but in reality, both of them were caught in their own monologue. One was reaching out to the other. The other was reaching out to her soda.

You don't have to be a keen observer to notice a trend these days:

Everybody is talking and no one is listening.

If you don't believe me, I challenge you to do three very simple but revealing experiments.

1. Watch a few interview shows on TV or listen to them on the radio. It could be a talk show or even a short interview on the news. I want you to pay attention to three things:

One: Does the person being interviewed actually answer all of the questions?

Two: Does the interviewer ever ask a follow-up question based on what's just been said? In other words: Is he/she really listening to the answer or is he/she ticking off a box?

Three: Is the interviewer asking neutral questions, or is he/she using the interviewee to validate his/her own viewpoints?

Here's your next assignment:

2. Be a fly on the wall as you overhear other people's conversations. Look at the body language first. Then listen to the tone of voice. Next, concentrate on what's being said. Based on that, what can you tell me about the focus of the two people talking?

Are they focused on themselves or on the person they're talking to? Do they interrupt each other? How can you tell if someone's a good listener?

The last thing I'd like you to do is probably the most revealing.

3. When you are talking to someone, notice how many times you're tempted to start your response with the word "I." How many times are you using what's just been said as a springboard for something you want to say? How strong is your tendency to want to shift the attention back to you?

LEARNING TO LISTEN

You may remember that I spent a great part of my professional life as a broadcast journalist. When I was being trained to be a better interviewer, we did an experiment that blew me away. Our coach played a two-minute answer taken from a real interview. He asked us to write down what had been said, and to come up with a new question for the interviewee.

It was embarrassing because we all got it wrong. We couldn't even get simple facts straight. Most of us had written down what we thought we had heard. Not what was being said. We'd been too busy thinking of what to say or do next.

The following day we worked on retention as we were interviewing each other. Before we were allowed to ask a new question, we had to correctly summarize what had been said, using the other person's words. We were not allowed to paraphrase because that would mean we were using our own words, shifting the focus back to ourselves.

Believe me, it's not as easy as it sounds. Active listening is not something they teach you in elementary school. I can still hear my interview trainer say:

"If you only take away one thing from this training, I hope it's this:

The secret to active listening is to be in the moment and forget about yourself. Forget about what you just did or what you are going to do. Forget about what you were going to ask, because then you're not even listening to what's being said. Be in the NOW. That's all that matters."

When we were getting better at retaining information, he continued:

"Now that you can actually remember what was said, ask yourself this question: What does it mean? Do I understand the answer? If not, what's missing that prevents me from understanding it? That should be the basis for your next question and not number two on the list you jotted down when you were preparing for the interview a few hours ago.

If you do not understand the answer, your audience is likely not to understand it either. So, why on earth would you move on to the next question? Let me give you an example.

Let's say the person you're interviewing uses the word 'frustrating' when she's telling you about her experience. You can do one of two things: assume that you know what 'frustrating' means and move on, or you can ask her about it.

Most people, when they say 'they understand,' have no clue what they're talking about. All they do is project their personal experience onto someone else. They automatically assume that their sense of frustration equals the other person's sense of frustration. Isn't that frustrating?

Life doesn't revolve around you. I hate to break it to you, but you're not that interesting. Otherwise, someone would be interviewing you."

BRINGING IT HOME

When I came home that day, I was eager to try out my new skills.

"How was your day, honey?" I asked my wife.

"Exhausting," she said.

"Exhausting?" I asked. I paused for a moment and said: "In what way?"

"Do you really want to know, or are you just asking?" my wife said.

"No, I really want to know," I tried in my most sincere tone of voice. "By the way, what's for dinner? It smells delicious!"

"Now that's exhausting," said my wife.

"What is?" I asked.

She looked at me knowingly and said:

"YOU are!"

LISTEN TO THE TEXT

Even though my career has since shifted from interviewing people to telling stories, the skills I learned as a journalist and broadcaster are vital to the way I approach my work as a voice actor.

Before I hit record, I begin by imagining that I am talking to a real person, even if that person looks remarkably like a script on a monitor or a microphone. That's exactly what I did in the radio studio.

It is my job as narrator to make the information I'm about to present easy to absorb and to retain. In order to do that, I first have to analyze and understand the text, and decide which words need emphasis. So, I let the text speak to me first.

As I'm reading, I look for certain keywords and phrases I want my listeners to remember.

These words work like hooks.

If the listener can remember those keywords and phrases, they should be able to remember the gist of the story.

As I start reading, I lift those keywords and phrases up in a deliberate but hopefully natural way. It's like using a highlighter in a textbook. If I were to stress too many words, the listener wouldn't be able to tell which ones are important and which ones aren't. If I do the opposite, my read ends up being flat, boring and unmemorable.

SERVING THE SCRIPT

The next thing I do, is to move myself out of the way. My job is to serve the script and the intentions of the client or author to the best of my ability. How do I know what the intentions of the client are? By listening carefully, by asking questions, and by leaving my ego at the door. Who cares if I think the script is better served by reading it like Sir Patrick Stewart, if the client wants me to sound like Kevin Spacey or John Goodman?

Sometimes, listening to the script means getting into a character that's far removed from who I am in real life. It involves studying the backstory and reading up on a certain time period. I might have to learn a new accent or a few words in a foreign language. If I would only draw from my limited life experience, I would be painting with a very limited color palate.

Acting begins with allowing the part to speak to you.

Sometimes, I am fortunate to work with other actors in one studio. I remember recording a PSA for the U.S. Census Bureau. Imagine five voice actors cramped into a rather small booth.

When we started recording, I was so focused on getting my own lines right, that I often didn't hear what the others were saying. I was glued to the script, waiting for my turn, just like the woman in the ski lodge who couldn't wait to bring the conversation back to herself.

Because I was too busy with my own lines, I was completely out of the moment. A million things were racing through my head: What would the director think? Which words should I emphasize? Where in the sentence should I breathe? Did I need to fill up the parking meter again? How come my mouth is so dry? Why is the woman next to me wearing so much perfume?

I had yet to learn this lesson:

Acting is reacting.

It requires the studied recreation of a moment, bringing it to life as if it is completely new and spontaneous. Acting is as much about active listening as about a deliberate delivery of lines.

A LOST ART

Some communication experts fear that we have lost the ancient art of listening. There are simply too many distractions around us. We are forced to multitask at home and at work. Our collective attention span is getting shorter. Children are conditioned to crave constant stimulation. A good conversation is often interrupted by a piercing ring tone of a stupid smart phone.

When we're entertaining guests, the TV stays on and we don't even notice it. We pump out music in shopping malls, waiting rooms, and even on the ski slopes. Objects need to make noise so we know they're working. Many of us don't know what absolute silence sounds like. Quietude even frightens people.

On top of that, we live in the age of individualism where the focus is on "ME" instead of on "WE." As long as you and I get our personal needs met, everything will be alright. That's what all the ads want us to believe. In conversations, we're like strings in need of a sounding board. We're not looking to play music together anymore.

Does it have to be like that?

Absolutely not.

We can choose what we focus on. We can direct our interests. We can decide to get rid of distractions, turn off the television and put our cell phones away for an hour or two.

The world won't come to an end. I promise.

If you own a business in this fragile economy, it is vital that you relearn how to listen to – and connect with – your customers. Don't assume you know what they need. Stop shouting about how brilliant your products are.

Open your ears.

Dale Carnegie once said:

> *"You can be more successful in two months by becoming really interested in other people's success, than you can in two years trying to get more people interested in your own success."*

I wonder what would happen if we would tame the urge to talk.

It's easy.

All we need to do is shut up and listen.

Did you hear me?

[11]

Why You Suck and What To Do About It

Small things can annoy me big time:

Loud neighbors past midnight.

People who believe the earth is their trash can.

Zigzagging drivers who don't signal before changing lanes.

Folks who chew gum with their mouth wide open.

Lowballing "colleagues."

I could go on forever but I won't because I'll end up annoying you.

A while ago, I was in my car listening to a popular current affairs show on the radio, and something else bugged me. It wasn't their angle on the news or their choice of topics. It was something more subtle.

I found myself criticizing the loud breaths both presenters were taking. When I pointed it out to the passenger next to me, she acted surprised.

She hadn't noticed a thing. Once I had mentioned it though, she heard it too. Isn't that the way it always works?

One function of our brain is to quickly filter out the things that are not immediately relevant to our survival. That's actually very useful. Think about it.

Every second of every day, you and I are bombarded with sights, sounds, smells, and tactile impressions. If we were to pay attention to every single thing, we'd rapidly reach sensory overload and go mad.

So why did my brain choose to have me focus on something as useless as the presenter's breath?

CONDITIONED RESPONSE

Well, as a voice actor, I suffer from professional deformation. Some people prefer to call it "job conditioning."

Just as a music critic can't help but analyze any performance instead of simply enjoying it, I find myself constantly critiquing colleagues, including their noisy intake of oxygen. But it gets worse.

When it comes to my own performance, I am absolutely merciless.

Because I listen to myself in close-up all day long, I hear every little detail and have lost the ability to hear my voice the way other people hear it. It's become my biggest blind spot.

One of the things I'm obsessed with is my breath. You may think it's no big deal, but some days I can't stand it.

I have this unwritten rule in my VO-studio. If a breath distracts from the message I'm trying to convey, it gets cut or I camouflage it in post-production. That takes time.

Mind you: not all breaths distract. Some can actually add drama to a read. There's the scared breath, the surprised breath, and the

"I can't believe I just said that" breath...

Removing all breaths sounds unnatural.

Being mindful of our breath brings up something else.

UNCONSCIOUS CONNECTION

For one, the way we breathe immediately reveals the physical state we're in.

If we are in bad shape, our breathing will give us away. Secondly, our breath is closely linked to our emotional state. It's that mind-body connection.

When we are anxious or tense, our breath tends to be a bit faster and shallow. When we're relaxed, our breathing is deeper and slower. It's one of those amazing autonomic, automatic connections.

I especially notice this interplay between mind and body when I'm distracted and stressed. My breathing becomes irregular and I can clearly hear it when I listen back to what I've just recorded. When I'm that unfocused, I do my worst work. This – in turn – annoys me even more, making the situation worse. I know I need to step out of it, but how?

Indian musician Ravi Shankar once said:

> *"The mind is like a kite, flying here and there, and the breath is like the string of the kite, generally bringing the mind back into the present moment. The breath brings the mind, which is all over the place, back to its source, a natural state of peacefulness and joy."*

As soon as I became aware of the connection, I realized that I could actually influence my state of mind by changing my body. One of the quickest ways to do that is by changing my breathing. That's nothing new. Yogis have been doing it since the dawn of time.

Good breathing starts with good posture. The kneeling chair I use in my studio not only prevents lower back pain, it helps me sit up straight and it allows the diaphragm to move freely and efficiently, thus promoting better breathing and blood circulation.

I also started practicing diaphragmatic or abdominal breathing.

Babies are natural abdominal breathers, but somehow we nervous grown-ups have forgotten how to do it.

Diaphragmatic breathing comes from the stomach area, rather than from the chest (thoracic breathing). When done properly, the entire torso expands, starting with the belly and followed by the ribcage. It's often mentioned as an easy way to reduce stress and increase mental focus.

From a voice-over point of view, there are more advantages to belly breathing. Because we're taking in more oxygen, we can read longer passages without having to gasp for air.

Abdominal breaths are also much more quiet than those coming from the upper part of our body.

WHY YOU SUCK

Thanks to shallow chest breathing, most of us are suckers.

We literally suck the air into the upper part of our body, past our vocal folds, as if we're filling up a vacuum tank. This distracting suck-ing sound is usually enhanced because we don't open our mouth fully before we breathe.

For most of us this is a completely unconscious process and we don't even hear the sound we make as we breathe in.... until we play back the audio.

I don't know about you, but I'd rather prevent these annoyingly loud breaths rather than having to edit them out.

So, before you take your next breath, sit up straight, open your mouth wide like a singer and take a nice, deep, r e l a x e d breath from the abdomen.

This should dramatically reduce the sound you make while filling your lungs with more oxygen.

Most teachers of abdominal breathing will tell you to slowly breathe in through the nose and breathe out through the mouth. There is a good reason why I am asking you to breathe in with your mouth open. Not only is it quieter, it prevents those nasty smacks that are the result of you parting your lips.

I take it one step further.

OPEN UP

Not only do I open my mouth at the beginning of a sentence, I keep it open at the very end and for the very same reason. As your lips close, chances are that they make another unwanted sound.

Even though this "technique" sounds like a no-brainer, you are basically relearning something that you've done "wrong" for most of your life. I am asking you to become mindful of something you've been unaware of and have done almost naturally.

Be soft on yourself as you practice abdominal breathing. It's okay if you're not perfect at it straight away. Give yourself a breather.

If you start feeling light-headed, you're doing it too quickly and with too much effort.

Be gentle.

Relax. It's good for you.

Personally and professionally.

And remember: There's no quick fix for being out of shape.

The sooner you start to take care of yourself, the better it is.

PART THREE:
IT'S A BUSINESS

[12]

Failure is Always an Option

A few years ago, entrepreneur and New York Times contributor Jay Goltz*** asked owners of failed small businesses what had gone wrong.

Guess what?

Most of them didn't really have a clue.

To a certain extent that's not surprising. Had they known what the problem was, they might have been able to fix it.

Some owners were in denial. Instead of acknowledging their own responsibility, they blamed the economy, the current administration, the bank, or an idiot partner.

Never themselves.

In many cases, Goltz noted that (ex)-customers had a much better understanding of what went wrong. The owner still had his stubborn head in the sand.

Over the years, I've counseled quite a few struggling voice-overs who were almost ready to give up. Without exception they were sweet, well-intentioned, and hard-working people. Some of them were even talented. And like the folks Goltz interviewed, they were wondering why their new career was going down the drain.

TAKE LARRY

Larry called himself a victim of the recession.

At 45 he was out of a job and he was looking for possible things to do. People had often told him he had a nice voice, and he thought he'd "give this voice-over thing a try." That was his first mistake.

Just because people say you're such good cook, doesn't mean you should open a restaurant. Besides, some of the best chefs make some of the worst managers.

Successful entrepreneurs don't start a business to explore options or to enjoy a hobby. They don't "give things a try." Opening up shop is not an experiment. It's a calculated risk.

Larry lacked what most owners of a failed business lack: knowledge, skills, and experience.

Those who make it are well prepared, have a plan in place, and can pump a sufficient amount of money into the business to survive the first years. Goltz calls it a "cash cushion."

MEET JESSICA

Jessica was a dreamer. As a child she fell in love with cartoons, and all she wanted was a career in animation. Her parents pushed her to get a "real job" which she did. Working as a dental hygienist, Jessica always had a willing audience for her cartoon voices.

One day, she had enough of making money off other people's mouths, and decided to pursue her passion.

"I just know I'm gonna make it," she told me. "I'm one of the most optimistic people I know, and a positive attitude is something they can't take away from me."

Jessica is right. Self-starters have to have a strong inner drive in order to succeed. They have to believe in themselves, even when no one else shares their dream. It's what propels them, and it's what makes them vulnerable. As Jessica found out, there's a huge difference between dreaming of a career and building one.

For one, Jessica completely underestimated the competition. She quickly learned that the same voices were booking all the jobs. A-list celebrities with zero voice-over experience were hired on the spot. After a year of knocking on lots of doors, Jessica was ready to go back to her old job, entertaining her clients. Her favorite quote is from Steve Jobs:

> *"Follow your heart, but check it with your head."*

POOR JESSE

Jesse has a voice I could listen to for hours. When I first met him, he told me he was keeping himself pretty busy as a voice actor.

"That's great," I said. "But are you making any money?"

"Well, that's the problem," said Jesse. "I don't. You see, when I first started doing this, I accepted all these low-paying gigs just to get into the game. Now I can't seem to make any serious money. Am I pricing myself out of business?"

Jesse made some common mistakes. For one, he didn't know the market. He accepted jobs for anywhere between $25 and $50; jobs that could have made him hundreds of dollars if not more.

Secondly, he was focused on the short term.

"Fifty bucks today is fifty bucks I didn't have yesterday," he used to tell himself. Unfortunately, these fifty-dollar jobs couldn't pay the bills.

Short-term small gains will never sustain a profitable long-term career. Competing on price is a losing strategy.

Third, Jesse had trained his current clients that his low rates were perfectly acceptable for the work he was doing. They weren't willing to pay him a dime more. Clients with bigger budgets didn't take him seriously because of how little he charged.

BLESSED BOB

Bob's problems were similar to Jesse's. He showed me a long list of satisfied clients and told me he absolutely LOVED his job. He had so much fun doing voice-over work that he really didn't care about the money.

"Being able to do this for a living," he said, "is a huge reward in and of itself. The Creator has blessed me with this voice. Life isn't all about getting filthy rich."

"I'm glad you love your work," I said, "but how are you going to pay off your credit card debt, Bob? Do you even know how much you owe? And don't you need to have health insurance?"

It turned out that Bob didn't really have a sense of how little money was coming in and how much was going out. His stressed-out wife had tried to talk to him, but Bob wouldn't listen. "I want to surround myself with positive energy," he told her.

Small businesses don't fail because the owner has no dreams, talent, or ambition. Even businesses with plenty of clients close their doors every day. Why?

Because they're not making any money!

Unless you're running a charity, the bottom line is the bottom line.

CASH-IN CARL

Some business owners are their own worst enemies. Carl was one of them. He loved getting the latest gear. Unfortunately, all that new equipment didn't get him any new clients. Preamplifiers are really bad at marketing.

What Carl really should have done is amplify the promotion of his business. His freebie website had "amateur" written all over it; he had no social media presence and virtually no professional network. I told him: "If you want to make it as a voice talent, a solid website, word of mouth, and strong connections are essential to your success."

On top of that, Carl often dipped into his business funds for personal use. He used part of a business loan to pay for every day expenses. His accounting was such a mess, it got him into trouble with the IRS. Eventually, Carl had to sell most of his gear on eBay. At a huge loss.

SAD REALITY

Here's what's so tragic about all these stories. Carl, Bob, Jesse, Jessica and even Larry have potential. They are motivated. They're willing to work long hours to pursue what seems to be an amazing career. But becoming your own boss is more than following a dream. It's more than doing what you love.

It takes passion, but also preparedness, patience, and persistence.

New York Times contributor Jay Goltz has this to add:

"In life, you may have forgiving friends and relatives, but entrepreneurship is rarely forgiving."

Being in business means that you have to do a lot of stuff that's not necessarily fun or fulfilling. Stuff you're not necessarily trained for or good at. And because you are the boss, you have to know your limitations.

Either outsource what you can't handle, or get up to speed as fast as you can.

If you believe you can do it all and do it well, you are mistaken.

Being in business means spending money before you can make any money. And when you start making money, you have to learn how to manage it.

By the way, it's not how much you make that matters, but how much you get to keep.

In America, we have a tendency to glorify those who have made it and use their success stories as anecdotal evidence. While that can be useful, I believe there's much to learn from those who have failed.

As long as we keep learning, those failures were not in vain.

[13]

The One Word that Saved My Freelance Career

No, I'm not going to tell you what it is just yet.

Let me begin by asking you a simple question:

Do words have power?

When you think of it, aren't they just letters, arranged in a certain order? Or are there words in our language that are so potent, that they have the potential to transform our life and our livelihood?

Now, before you think that I've gone all philosophical instead of practical, just STOP for a moment and think about it.

In the past few days I've asked some of my friends about words they feel have had (and still have) a profound impact on their professional lives. Here are some of the words they came up with:

- Faith
- Fear
- Confidence
- Creativity

- Luck
- Love
- Play
- Passion

As for me, the one word that has been my guiding light in the past thirty years as a freelancer, is neither grand nor deep. Yet, I believe it to be one of the most powerful words in our vocabulary. Without it, my career certainly wouldn't be where it is today.

It consists of two letters.

It is the word **NO**.

NO is the ultimate reflection of where I draw the line in life. It is the line between what I am willing to accept and what I must reject. Right now I can honestly say that I owe most of my success as a solopreneur to this word. It's quite simple:

In order to give yourself a leg up, you sometimes have to put your foot down.

That's why I am going to offer you seven suggestions for shaping your freelance career by using the power of what author William Ury calls a "Positive No."

1. SAY NO TO MOST FREELANCE JOBS

In this recession it seems that many freelancers function in survival mode and operate out of fear. They jump on every job opportunity that presents itself because "you never know what tomorrow will bring." They're like a mad batter who's hitting at everything the pitcher's throwing at him.

Although you might consider yourself to be a versatile voice-over pro, web designer, or copywriter, even the famous Swiss Army knife has its limitations. It is humanly impossible to be everything to everyone.

Like a batter, you have to wait for the perfect moment. The moment where preparation meets opportunity to hit that ball out of the park.

KNOW when to say NO.

It's early in the day as I am writing these words, but I've already said NO to at least fifteen voice-over jobs that didn't meet my criteria. Why waste time applying for work I'm not totally qualified for?

I could get really ticked off by colleagues who subscribe to the "more is more strategy," telling me: "It's a numbers game. The more I try, the more chances I have to land a job." Even though it might look that way sometimes, it is not a lottery. It is a business.

And why am I not ticked off? Well, we all have our life lessons to learn, and some people just prefer to learn things the hard way. And because they can't...

2. SAY NO TO DIY

If you're running your own business, it's probably safe to say that you're wearing many hats: CEO, CFO, Head of HR, Advertising, PR, Acquisition, Marketing, IT, R & D, Quality Control... Are you tired yet? And guess who's delivering the goods?

Just because you're self-employed doesn't mean that you must do everything yourself. You shouldn't, because you'll burn out before you've even lit up the place.

KNOW your strengths.

A realtor decided to shoot his own real estate video tours to save some money. As he was taking his shaky camera through a million dollar property, I could hear him do his own narration. The result was cheap, unprofessional and embarrassing. When he watched the footage, he quickly decided that he was not going to be the new host of the hit show *House Hunters*.

So, here is your assignment of the day. Ask yourself:

What is the number one thing in my business that:

1. Is an essential part of my job
2. I'm not good at
3. I hate to do
4. Takes up way too much time

Now ask yourself two questions:

1. How much more *productive* would I be, if I would outsource this to an expert?
2. How much more *profitable* would I be, if I would outsource this work, especially if I...

3. SAY NO TO LOW RATES

In a society where most of us still equate value and quality with price, low rates are the trademark of an amateur. This strategy might bring you a few short-term gains, but you'll end up a long-term loser.

KNOW the value of your work and the effect of your pricing on your bottom line and on your market.

Then take the next step and...

4. SAY NO TO LOW STANDARDS

The Greek philosopher Mediocrates gave us the Law of Averages:

"Average standards lead to average results"

Look around you. Despite all the self-help hoopla that is sold as the "psychology of excellence," the best most can hope for is mediocrity. Otherwise, "average" wouldn't be the most common denominator and Walmart would have no customers.

KNOW that you have the privilege of not having to live by other people's rules. You're an independent contractor.

Look at your role models. Did they achieve success by following other people's standards, or by setting their own? Become a non-conformist. Be utterly un-average and totally inimitable.

Be younique and...

5. SAY NO TO BLAME

The Law of Causality deals with the relationship between an event and the consequence of that event. This interplay of Cause and Effect is reflected in our language as in: "My business isn't doing so well because...."

We all know people who aren't where they want to be in life, and they're absolutely convinced that it is someone else's fault. If only all the other people on this planet would change, they would be so much happier! Those are the folks who blame the fast food industry for the obesity crisis and the tobacco industry for turning them into helpless, brainwashed chain smokers.

Blame makes people lame and seemingly dependent on things they have little or no control over. Mind you, I am definitely not denying the devastating role some external circumstances can play in some-one's life. Neither am I trying to guilt-trip people for having been dealt some terrible cards.

I am talking about people who – rather than take responsibility for the things they have control over – expect others to fix them for them. Those are the people who'd rather complain about something than do something about it.

KNOW the difference between making things happen and letting things happen. It's fine to subscribe to an online job search service.

However, if you adopt a wait-and-see approach and blame the website when you're not landing a new position within a week, you are giving them way too much credit. You also have effectively disempowered yourself.

I firmly believe that we're not helpless leaves in the wind. I believe that we can harness the power of the wind and adjust our sails by the virtue of the choices we make.

One of those choices is to...

6. SAY NO TO UNCONTROLLED SPENDING

Why did the venerable New York Times*** write that "one of the world's most successful photographers essentially pawned every snap of the shutter she had made or will make until her loans are paid off?"

The Times cited as one of the reasons, that Annie Leibovitz has had a "long history of less than careful financial dealings."

In the ideal world, you always have a pipeline full of projects, but in reality, work can come in waves.

When you finally hit that freelance jackpot and you're starting to make some serious money, nothing is more tempting than to go on a spending spree. After all, you deserve it, don't you?

Yes, you totally deserve to reap the rewards of your hard labor, today, tomorrow.... and in a few months when that big project is done and the money is no more. It's not fun to be brilliant but broke.

KNOW that when it rains it probably pours, and when it doesn't, you must set money aside for a rainy day.

Your bills don't care whether or not you were lucky to get a nice chunk of cash in July. There's always August, September, and –dare I mention it – the day you hope to retire.

The book "The Millionaire Next Door"*** is not about big spenders. It is about people like you and me who live well below their means.

Those folks are likely to...

7. SAY NO TO TAKING INSTEAD OF GIVING

"What's in it for me? I want it for free!" seems to be the mantra of the new millennium. This narrow focus on personal gain, often at the expense of others and our planet, is an egotistical and eco-destructive philosophy.

Yet, some self-styled entrepreneurs have made the following three words the cornerstone of their business:

Gimme, gimme, gimme.

With the rise of social media, this new group of predators is all about getting instead of giving. They want to befriend you in order to milk your network, so they can slam your contacts with overt or covert product- and self-promotion.

These vampires seldom contribute to an online discussion, and when they do, it's mainly to get their contact information in the comment field. They ask for referrals. They don't give referrals. They want a sample of your work... and run away with it.

KNOW that the way to build and grow a freelance business is to become a contributor, by giving back.

Over the years, countless generous people have given me their time and expertise free of charge, just because they wanted to help.

The best way to honor the gifts they have given me, is by passing them on to someone else. That's one of the reasons why I started writing, and that's why you might find me answering someone else's questions on a networking site.

When you start paying it forward, amazing things will happen.

One last thing.

Should you choose to adopt these seven suggestions and become a no-sayer, expect to be tested!

We live in a culture of YES and instant gratification. People don't want to hear the word no.

They'd rather cut off their no's to spite their face.

When they're putting pressure on you to cave in, remember this:

The best students usually get the most challenging tests!

So, stick to the program and keep on saying "yes" to saying NO.

[14]

The Yin and Yang of Freelancing

Impossible clients.

We know who you are!

You're searching for a specialist who can handle almost anything.

Isn't that a contradiction in terms?

Does your family doctor make a great brain surgeon?

Can a novelist write irresistible advertising copy?

Yet, some clients are looking for a be-all, do-it-all freelancer with young, fresh ideas and years of experience.

Is that too much to ask?

Some psychologists say that the fact that we humans are able to hold two diametrically opposed ideas in our mind at the same time is a true sign of intelligence. Part of me wants to believe that this is indeed correct.

The other part thinks it's utter hogwash.

Does this theory imply that we have to develop a split personality in order to be perspicacious? Well, I'm more than torn about that too.

On one hand it seems kind of dim to define intelligence in such a limited way. On the other hand, aren't most eternal truths simple and succinct in nature?

Let's pause for a moment and reflect on the dichotomies of freelance life. Day in day out, we're dealing with seemingly contrary forces that are connected and interdependent, that –somehow – give rise to each other.

Taoists already know what I'm talking about: the ancient concept of Yin and Yang.

Here's an example of two concepts that seem mutually exclusive or at least contradictory:

1. SPECIALIZE or GENERALIZE?

Marketing gurus tell us that you can't be a Jack-of-all-trades. Don't do what everybody else does. Find your niche. Create, don't imitate. Lead, don't follow. Distinguish yourself.

The problem is this. By narrowing your niche, you could potentially be narrowing your market and run the risk of becoming a one-dimensional, one-trick pony. However, if you don't differentiate yourself from the rest of the pack, you could become a dime a dozen. Why should a client hire Mr. or Mrs. More-of-the-Same?

This is your challenge. You have to find your own voice and yet be flexible. Great inventors come up with a product that:

- solves a common problem
- is totally unique and
- appeals to a wide audience

2. FAMILIAR OR FOREIGN?

Most people embrace the familiar and fear the unknown. But if you wish to grow on a personal and professional level, you must step into uncharted territory and invite the unpredictable.

During one of my voice-over coaching sessions, I asked a rather stuck-up student to read part of the Declaration of Independence in a pirate voice. I ran into resistance from the get-go.

"I can't do a pirate voice," he said emphatically.

"Why not?" I asked.

"First off, it's disrespectful. Secondly, I'm not going to make a fool of myself," he replied.

I said: "You want to be a voice-over actor, don't you? Actors have the ultimate excuse to be ridiculous. How are you ever going to expand your range, if you're not willing to try something new? Were you one of those kids that only ate Mac & Cheese?"

Reluctantly, my student became Bad-Rum Ronny and started:

"Arrrr... When, in the course of human events..."

And just as he was getting more comfortable with his newfound identity, I said:

"That was fantastic! Now, please take it from the beginning, but this time, I want you to be a female pirate. Pretend you're Johnny Depp's big sister..."

My student looked at me as if I had lost my sanity.

"You're really pushing the envelope," he said.

"Oh, come on," I pleaded.

"The Founding Mothers would be so proud of you. And if you do it, I promise to write about it in my new book."

That apparently worked because this time he sounded more like Geena Davis in the movie *Cutthroat Island*.

"Wow," he said. "I never knew I had that in me. That's kind of scary..."

"Here's what I learned," I said to him. "Some people avoid taking risks because they're afraid of what the world might think of them. But playing it safe won't get you very far. One day, you will have a producer who will ask you to do something you've never done before. Something that might scare the living daylights out of you.

Do it anyway.

You have to be comfortable with who you are in order to allow yourself to break out of your comfort zone. In other words:

Be comfortable being uncomfortable.

It means you're growing!"

3. ACT NATURALLY

As a professional performer, this is another oxymoron you have to live with. You have to learn how to be natural in unnatural situations. It comes in different variations:

> – Act, but don't make it look like you're acting.
> – Read but don't sound like you're reading.
> – Deliver a meticulously prepared and polished performance that seems totally spontaneous.
> – Give it your all, but make it seem effortless.
> – Don't try it. Just do it. Be yourself.

It's great advice, but nobody ever tells you how to get there, right?! It all goes back to the "Four Stages of Learning." It's a theory posited by psychologist Abraham Maslow. Maslow coined four psychological states involved in the process of progressing from incompetence to competence in a skill:

1. Unconsciously incompetent: you're not aware that you can't do something
2. Consciously incompetent: you know that you are incompetent at something
3. Consciously competent: you're developing the skill, but you constantly have to think about what you're doing
4. Unconsciously competent: you've become so good at it, that it has become second nature

All of us go through these phases when we're learning how to drive, how to talk, and how to walk. Only when we've reached the level of unconscious competence, are we able to act naturally.

In a world that revolves around instant gratification, quick fixes, easy answers, and immediate results, this is a very unpopular four-step process.

We want it all and we want it NOW!

4. EXPERIENCED OR EXCITING?

Do the following scenarios ring a bell?

a. You're trying to break into the business, but you don't want to come across as an absolute beginner.

b. You have years of experience, but you don't want them to think of you as yesterday's news.

It's an impossible situation, isn't it?

Here are a few more stereotypes:

– Seasoned pros are old school and too expensive.
– Rookies are wild cards and need a lot of handholding.
– Veterans are rigid, arrogant, and demanding.
– Newbies are unpredictable and have yet to hone their skills.

This black and white thinking is nothing but a distortion of reality. Do not fall for these false dilemmas. Challenge them instead.

You might have years of experience, but does that mean that you have lost your Mojo? Is a beginner by definition always new, fresh, and exciting, or is he just a copycat? Are clients paying more because your rate is higher, or is it more expensive to hire an amateur?

A BALANCING ACT

As a freelancer and solopreneur, you have to be able to deal with two diametrically different ideas at the same time. Don't worry. You're intelligent. You can handle it!

Let me leave you with some more freelance Yin and Yang:

– Have a strong backbone, but dare to be vulnerable.
– Be personable and keep things strictly business.
– Be spontaneous, but bite your tongue.
– Be proud of your accomplishments and stay humble.
– Be confident, but doubt yourself enough to evaluate your performance.
– Set the highest standards, but cut yourself some slack.
– Be available and accessible, but balance work and play.
– Sell yourself, but don't sound like you're selling yourself.
– Be passionate about your work, but know that it's a means to an end.
– Keep your head in the clouds and your feet firmly planted on the ground.
– Be able to multitask and stay completely focused.

– Be in the moment and plan for the future.
– Admire without feeling threatened.

A NEW YEAR

At the beginning of the new year, one of my friends asked me:

"Paul, what are your plans? You have published a book and you're turning down work. Are you going to focus more on your writing or on voice-overs?"

I thought about it for a moment, and then I said:

"Either way is better."

[15]

My 10,000-Dollar Mistake

I was in a rush. I wasn't thinking.

And it almost cost me ten thousand dollars.

The lesson I learned that day has been one of the cornerstones of my success as a freelancer and a voice talent. Before I share that lesson with you, let me ask you this:

Have you heard of the Calimero complex?

It is named after an Italian/Japanese cartoon character named Calimero, and many freelancers seem to suffer from it.

Calimero is the only black chick in a family of yellow chickens, and he still wears half of his eggshell on his head. It is as if he never really made it out of the nest.

Calimero is the archetypal underdog. He often gets in trouble and believes the whole world is out to get him. When the show reaches a dramatic climax, Calimero usually utters the following catch phrase:

"They are big and I am small and that's not fair, oh no!"

That's the Calimero complex.

I get why some freelancers can identify with him. Operating a small business in a big world is not easy. We might not wear an eggshell on our noggin, but we certainly wear many different hats.

ARE YOU INTIMIDATED?

Unlike bigger businesses, we don't have huge marketing budgets, top-of-the line facilities or people to do the work we don't like doing. As solopreneurs we do it all, and quite often we seem to be at an unfair disadvantage.

Being self-employed can be invigorating, liberating... and terribly intimidating.

Some of us thrive under pressure. Others cannot stand it and they eventually chicken out.

Personally, I believe that small is beautiful. I love being my own boss. As a solopreneur I have worked with many corporations on extended contracts. I was glad I could join them, and most of the time I was even happier to leave.

Think of the endless bureaucracy, the boring bean counters, the silly pencil pushers, dirty office politics, and the untalented, uninspiring people being promoted to the level of incompetence, clocking in and counting the hours till the next coffee or lunch break. Not to mention the endless meetings that never lead to anything.

And have you ever wondered why big businesses spend so much money on advertising and PR? Why do you think they hire movie stars to voice commercials to convince us that their products are so special?

Because they're not!

Name one big brand that is not bland.

GENERIC RULES THE WORLD

We live in a culture of more of the same. Generic companies produce generic products using automated processes, backed by generic quality control and careless customer service.

Some corporations may pretend they are passionate, but you know that's only on paper. It's not something you can fake. Intangible things like passion, imagination and originality cannot be imposed by means of corporate policy.

That's exactly why I as a small business owner do not suffer from the Calimero complex. I'm not afraid of the big guys because I know I have something to offer that big businesses can never compete with, no matter how hard they try.

I'm not a chain, a franchise or a branch. I personify my product and there's nothing generic about that.

I might not have offices on five continents, but I do business with people from all over the world.

I don't build brands. I build relationships.

My customers don't have to jump through a million hoops to speak to someone from management. My clients have direct access to the CEO. And when they send me an email, they won't get an automated response. They receive a personal message, usually within the hour.

I don't outsource quality control and customer service. I am quality control and customer service. I don't dictate to clients what to do. I listen to what they need.

And most importantly: I don't do more of the same. I customize. I localize. I personalize based on the unique requirements of the job.

It's a lesson I learned the hard way.

One day, an audio book publisher asked me to audition for a 1,200-page biography. He didn't send me a demo script. He only told me what the book was about. His request came at the end of a very busy day and I was ready to leave my studio to meet a friend.

I usually answer these types of emails as soon as I can, and on my way out, I wrote the publisher that I was interested in the project and I attached a generic demo to my message.

BIG MISTAKE!

A few days went by before the publisher emailed me back. He said he'd continue his search for a narrator because my demo sounded "too commercial." He needed an international storyteller. Not someone doing a sales pitch. He was right.

I could have left it at that, but my inner voice told me I should try to turn things around. Perhaps I could get a second chance and nail the audition.

I went online to find the book in question and picked a paragraph or two to read. This time I recorded a custom demo, showing off my multilingual narration skills.

That same day I received some great news. My new and improved audition was a big hit. The job was mine and I ended up recording (and getting paid for) over 32 hours of audio. A few months later, the same publisher asked me to narrate a second book.

THE MAGIC OF CUSTOMIZATION

These days, I hardly send out generic demos anymore. When no script is provided, I look at the subject matter and (if available) the name of the client. Then I go online and find a press release or an article about the product or service the client is associated with, and use that for my audition. This does two things.

It is my way of telling clients that I do my homework and that I'm willing to go the extra mile.

Secondly, clients get the opportunity to hear me say the name of their company and product and "try on" my voice in a context they can relate to. All of a sudden, a simple demo becomes relevant.

Of course I don't win every job I audition for. Far from it, but I do know that customization sets me apart from the rest of the pack. It makes my entries more memorable and as such, it enhances my chances. And when I ask my clients why they picked me, the custom demo is often cited as the difference that made the difference.

It does take extra time and effort to do the research and record something special. But that's an investment well worth making.

Customers are the lifeblood of your business.

Why give them a hotel chain treatment, if you can give them a customized bed-and-breakfast experience?

Being small in a big world can be a huge competitive advantage.

Please tell that to Calimero!

[16]

Learning on the Job

It happened again.

On one of the many LinkedIn groups for working voice actors, the discussion had turned to ACX***, the Audiobook Creation Exchange. This site brings authors and narrators together to produce spoken books.

Of course we all want to know whether or not people are booking jobs through this site, and if it's worth their time and effort.

The answer to the first question is YES and to the second one: a very definite MAYBE.

It's a fact that most best-selling authors don't have to go to ACX to get their books published in audio format. Celebrities will do their own narration, and a league of ten to fifteen distinguished gentlemen and women will read the rest, skillfully assisted by an audio engineer and a director, hired by Harper Collins or Hachette.

With the might of a marketing machine only a big publishing house can muster, the spoken version of an immensely popular vampire trilogy is bound to become a resounding commercial success. That's the way it works.

THE MINOR LEAGUE

In contrast, I think that ACX is the home of the small potato. It's a sanctuary for vanity publications, second-rate writers, mediocre scholars, and those rejected by Simon and Schuster. It is a place where many try to break a leg and hope to break even.

People are joining ACX in the hopes of making some money, but think of it this way. If the book you've been narrating is only vaguely interesting to a niche audience and the budget for marketing is zero, what kind of sales figures can you expect?

Is it really worth your effort? Is a royalty share (that's getting smaller and smaller) going to pay the bills and solidify your status as a VO-pro?

Now, whenever I bring this up, eventually someone, somewhere will tell me:

> "Okay, I might not make boatloads of money, but it's such great experience. Everybody's got to start somewhere!"

Oh, please...

BAD PRACTICE

I totally disagree with the notion that working on an ACX title is a good way to get one's voice-over feet wet, learn from mistakes and gain experience. The same myth is perpetuated when people refer to regular auditions.

Colleagues who take part in online cattle calls are often told:

> "Hey, even if you didn't book the job, at least you gained some experience, right? That alone makes it worth your time, energy, and money!"

That's complete nonsense. Every audition is a job interview.

You don't apply for a permanent position if you barely qualify for an internship.

If you've ever recorded a spoken book, you know that this is one of the most demanding and underestimated areas in the entire voice-over industry. Not only do you need to know what you're doing from an acting perspective, you also have to know what you're doing as the chief audio engineer.

Is this really where you want to get your feet wet? Are you sure? Why don't you start by learning how to swim before you try to cross the English Channel? Or do you wish to drown in your own misery for a stupid stipend? (a stipend is a bonus payment on selected titles)

THE BIG BOYS

"Not so fast, my friend," said a beginning colleague to me. "Playing in the minors such as ACX, really helps me hone my skills. That way, I can get myself ready to play with the big boys."

Forgive me, but that's not how I see it.

We can't excuse our lack of skill, experience (or even talent) by telling ourselves: "It's just ACX. It's the minor league; a place to start out and if you're good enough, move up in the business."

If you believe that you are good enough to get paid for narrating and recording a novel, you must be held to certain minimum standards, whether you're doing something for ACX or for a major publishing house. You owe it to the author, to the audience, and to yourself, to deliver the finest product possible.

In my book, every client – big or small – is paying for my professionalism, and that is exactly what they get.

There is no major or minor league. There is only major or minor talent.

LEARNING OR REFINING

As a voice-over professional, you will mature and get more refined, but you don't get hired so you can learn on the job. Ever.

You are supposed to know your job.

As long as you don't have a minimum level of expertise, you keep on training with a reputable teacher until you do. That's how it works.

You can never be your own coach because you'll only get as far as the level of your inexperience. If that's true in pretty much any profession, why should it be different for voice-overs?

Here's the hard part.

Getting ready to record your first audio book will take time, but I can tell you one thing.

Learning through trial and error will take even longer.

Putting out the products of those trials and errors is not exactly smart advertising, is it?

The work you produce is going to be a testament to your talent for years and years to come. People will probably be able to access it well into the next century. It's going to be part of your artistic legacy.

So, do yourself and your community of colleagues a favor.

Only take on what you can handle.

Don't use your clients' time for your own practice.

You will hurt yourself and the reputation of our profession.

[17]

Winning an Audition and Losing the Job

She jokingly called her students "germ bags" and described school parents as "snobby" and "arrogant."

On Facebook.

As a result, this Massachusetts math and science teacher*** lost her $92,636-a-year job.

A waitress at a pizza restaurant in uptown Charlotte was fired after making derogatory remarks about customers who'd made her work an hour past the end of her shift and only left a small tip.

On Twitter.

Comedian Gilbert Gottfried*** lost his job as the voice of the Aflac duck, after the insurance company found out he was tweeting "jokes" about the devastating tsunami in Japan.

Free speech is a wonderful thing, as long as you understand who's listening. Big Brother is following you. He might even be a Facebook friend or a Google Spy-der.

The website Digital Inspiration*** discovered that:

> "Googlebots, or the spiders that crawl web pages, are now reading Facebook comments on websites just like any other text content and the more interesting part is that you can also search the text of these comments using regular Google search."

Many sites allow you to use your Facebook profile to leave comments. It's easy and it saves time. But when you do that, your remarks are linked to your user name, profile picture and they link back to your Facebook profile.

As CNET's Sharon Vaknin*** warned:

> "A Google search for your name may reveal your comments. Since your Facebook account is tied to your (presumably) real name, anyone googling you may stumble upon your political, religious, or general views expressed in comments you've left across the Web. Consider this when leaving comments using the Facebook Comments platform."

And it's not just your comments that could get you in trouble.

One of my European colleagues had landed a voice-over job for a high-end electronics company. She was thrilled to be associated with such a big name, and she liked the video she had voiced so much, that she put a link up on her blog.

The next day the phone rang. The legal department of the electronics giant asked her to read the fine print in her contract. It stated that she was not allowed to publicly associate herself with the company and that she could not use any material for promotional purposes.

Even though she removed the link immediately, she never heard from this client again.

Later she told me: "It was just a link to a video that was on the company website. It was in the public domain. What's the big deal?

The way I see it, I was creating some free publicity for this company."

What really amazed me was how quickly the legal department had discovered the link on a blog that wasn't exactly popular. It goes to show that you never know who is watching over your shoulder.

This week, one of my agents received the following message from a casting director:

> "Agents – it has come to our attention that many actors excited about their auditions, will post notices on Facebook and Twitter. This weekend, an actor lost a job because the tweet got back to the client on a product that had not been announced. Please ask your actors to not tweet/Facebook the products for auditions."

My agent immediately sent an email to all talent:

> "We know you get excited about auditions and bookings, but please do not tweet, Facebook, blog, or share in any way before the finished media is out.
>
> The safest sharing rule for the entertainment industry: only share information on your project AFTER the date of first insertion. No exceptions.
>
> DO NOT announce clients or products for auditions, callbacks or bookings.
>
> DO NOT check in on Facebook.
>
> DO NOT use social media on set."

Remember:

You have the right to remain silent.

Anything you say can and will be used against you.

[18]

Good Enough Is Never Good Enough

Dear voice casting agencies, you are being deceived!

People pretending to be professionals have infiltrated your talent pool. People who can barely swim. It's happening on your watch and you probably have no idea what the heck is going on.

Why?

Because you don't know or you don't care.

You're too busy trying to make a buck in this competitive market, and you have no time or money for decent quality control. Or you are aware that you're accepting and advertising third-rate "talent," but this is simply a reflection of your standards.

AVERAGE HAS BECOME ACCEPTABLE

Let's talk about those standards for a moment. We live in a world full of crap where things aren't made to last. Intentionally. Mediocrity has become the norm. Our shelves are filled with knock-offs made in far away places by poor, powerless people who get paid dirt to work long hours in unsafe conditions.

We buy it. We try it. We trash it.

After all, the price is right, so who cares about sustainability? It's a free market, folks! What would you want instead? Fair pay? Worker's rights? Socialism?

As long as a product meets some basic regulations and doesn't poison babies or explode in your face (unless it's a gun), good enough is good enough.

Things are expendable. People can be replaced.

This mentality has not only permeated the manufacturing of today's consumer products, it also runs rampant in the service industry where cutting corners has become a commendable quality.

Ironically, the worst offenders are the so-called customer service centers. How many valuable hours of your life have you wasted so far, trying to get through to someone named James whose only job it is to read an unintelligible script back to you with a thick accent?

Need I say more?

WHAT ABOUT VOICE-OVERS?

That same corner-cutting mentality can be found in the happily unregulated voice-over industry where there's no official standard or professional code of conduct. Anything goes and it certainly shows!

That's why uneducated and inexperienced talent can pose as pros and profit from the ignorance and/or carelessness of casting sites.

Thankfully, there are still people who care and think that quality is critical. People like Delphine. The other day she sent me the following message:

> "Hi Paul, I wonder if you can help me. I'm a collaborator of a French agency and they have a Dutch voice talent in their database.

A Dutch colleague that isn't in the team told me that this girl has a not native accent. Someone else listened to her and told me that she's okay. Can you help? Thanks so much."

Here's part of my response:

"The girl I just listened to is from the Netherlands, but she's not a professional voice talent. The first clue is the quality of her recording. Her voice-only demo is in stereo. Since we only have one voice, it makes no sense to record in stereo. Mono is the norm, unless you're sending out a studio-produced demo, embedded in music.

Secondly, I can clearly hear flutter echo in the room, which means her recording space is poorly treated. Lastly, I can hear a lot of mouth noises such as clicks and lip smacks. Pros deliver clean sound without pops, loud breaths, or clicks. If they do stumble upon the occasional click, they edit it out.

Then there's the issue of the read itself. The talent puts too much stress on too many syllables, making her sound unnatural. She allows the English words in the script to influence her Dutch pronunciation, making her Dutch sound a bit English at certain points. Voice-over pros know how to keep the languages separate.

Listening to her accent, I can tell you that she does not have a neutral, standard Dutch accent but a northern twang.

If what she's going to record is only meant for that specific, regional market, this might be appropriate. If it's meant for the Dutch market as a whole, her accent is a distraction and it will not appeal to a wider audience."

In my experience, people like Delphine are an exception. She just avoided the embarrassment of connecting a client with a subpar talent by asking an expert for a second opinion. To me, that's a sign of professionalism. Because she cared, she wanted to know.

Doing things the right way is not cheapest or the fastest way. With thousands of voices in an online database, some companies believe they can't afford to carefully scrutinize every talent that signs up, especially foreign talent. Some feel it is the client's responsibility to screen voice-overs, and not the job of the middleman.

If I'm totally honest, neither the voice caster nor the client bears all the blame. It's also too easy to point at sliding standards in the world around us. Ultimately, quality control begins with each individual talent. It starts with you and me.

THE ESSENCE OF EXCELLENCE

So, let's take a moment or two to talk about quality. It's one of those illusive buzzwords that means different things to different people. I believe that quality is more than a combination of talent, skills and experience. Yes, you have to be qualified to produce quality work, but above all it's an attitude based on the three Cs:

Craftsmanship, **Consistency** and **Care**.

Quality is relentless.

Quality knows no compromise.

Good enough, is never good enough.

Ultimately, it should have nothing to do with the standards of the people you work for or work with. It should come from inside. From you. You and you alone should decide how high you set the bar. The quality of your work is your most important unique selling point.

Quality has to do with paying attention to details that no one notices. It requires being able to step outside of yourself and look and listen with the eyes and ears of your most critical customers. It's more than delivering a stellar product on time. Quality is about being a class act.

Quality is a matter of personal integrity and truth. It means aspiring to be the best. Not the cheapest.

Here's the most amazing thing about it.

Quality work is instantly recognizable. It needs no accolades.

It speaks for itself.

The bitterness of poor quality remains long after the sweetness of low price is forgotten.

If you wish to build a business that lasts, you have to offer a quality product or service that lasts, and you should not be ashamed to charge a good and fair price for it.

It's the most reliable strategy for sustainable success.

[19]

There's No Crying in Voice-Overs

Every once in a while, we make a fool of ourselves.

Thanks to the powers of social media, we can now do it publicly.

Those who have hurt and humiliated themselves, vent their frustration on Facebook and start fishing for some sympathy:

"Life is so unfair! Look what just happened to me. Client X did this. Colleague Y said that. My agent doesn't love me anymore... Woe is me!"

Yes, you're a miserable son of a gun. Let's have a pity party and invite some friends. Shared suffering is double the fun, but don't expect me to join in.

I don't want to borrow your sorrow and smooth it over with a cheap platitude and a positive attitude.

Stop being such a crybaby. Person up to your problems. Get a backbone, will you?!

There's no crying in voice-overs.

I don't want to hear you complain about the voice-over fee being too low and this annoying client being super high-maintenance. I have warned you ahead of time, didn't I? Did you listen?

You agreed to the terms and no one forced you to sign on the dotted line. Now you're stuck with your own stupidity. Wise up or get used to it.

If that novel you are narrating is so poorly written, why are you moaning and groaning about it when you're halfway into the project? Did you even bother to read the first chapter before you decided to attach your name to it for eternity?

Don't blame it on the author. There was a reason why no reputable publishing house was interested in this second-rate piece of pulp fiction. You just had to jump on this "golden opportunity," didn't you? I'm sure it will look great on your portfolio.

Yesterday you said yes to this massive e-Learning project and today you've come across weird terminology and foreign phrases that are impossible to pronounce. In a panic you are asking your online community to do the homework for you. That's the mark of a true professional!

Did you ask the client to provide you with a pronunciation guide ahead of time; the same client who happens to be on a two-week vacation when you need him most?

That company you had never worked for before, thanked you for sending three hours of audio ahead of schedule. Nice job! Five months and ten emails later you're still waiting to get paid. Their website is state of the art. They sounded so friendly on the phone. The project manager even promised you more work.

You proclaim that you do business based on trust. That's why you have nothing in writing and why you are willfully ignored.

It's a sad, sad situation and it's getting more and more absurd. Just don't expect me to feel sorry for you. Next time, get paid first before you hand over the goods, okay?

You auditioned for a documentary and the producer loved your voice. Now you have one day to record a fifteen-page script, just as the neighbors are digging in the dirt to install a backyard pool. After two paragraphs you realize that the walk-in closet you use for voice-over work doesn't protect you from the noise the hydraulic excavator is making. And this is only the beginning.

"I want a Studiobricks vocal booth.*** I want it NOW," you tweet in sheer exasperation... "before I strangle the folks next door!"

Don't point your fingers at the neighbors. Every handyman knows not to take on a project without having the right tools. What made you think you could handle this job?

You started narrating a long corporate training program and you figured that if you record for three hours a day, you can meet the tight deadline. After the first sixty-seven minutes, your throat feels sore and your voice sounds raspy. Why? Because you've never done long-form narration before and your vocal folds aren't properly prepared.

Next thing, you go online asking your colleagues for a quick fix, wondering why a sprinter can't just run a marathon. Are you really that naive?

Your drama teacher said that you are "a natural" and you should seriously think of getting into voice-overs. Based on that advice, you've bought some equipment, you recorded your own demos and you've signed up for a few voice casting sites.

A thousand dollars and two hundred auditions later, you wonder why no one is listening.

You've listed yourself as a professional, but you know as little about voice acting as you do about marketing yourself.

"I've been tricked," you cry out on your Facebook page. "People told me I could do this, but I found out they had no idea what it takes to succeed. Can anyone please help me?"

Dry your tears, young lady. With so much online information and professional training available, ignorance and inexperience are no longer acceptable excuses. Always judge the quality of the advice by the quality of the source. If you haven't learned how to swing a bat, don't expect to join the Major League any day soon.

Now, if you're new to the biz and you're wondering why this grumpy writer is dishing out tough love today, I have one answer: Because you need to hear this!

Listen, I could easily fill this book with the pleasures of using my voice professionally. That might inspire you, but it's not going to help you. I don't want you to make the same mistakes I made when I began establishing myself as a voice-over. Things I wish I would have known in advance.

Any coach wants to see his team succeed. He/she knows that the things that seem to be easy, are often deceptively difficult. They may take years of practice before they become second nature.

Dumb mistakes can easily be avoided, so don't make me tell you "I told you so." And please don't go online to start sobbing about your misfortunes. Things go right and things go wrong. You're gaining experience. Learn from your mistakes and move on. It's all in the game.

The only tears I want to see are tears of joy when you finally hit that home run.

[20]

Work for Free for Charity?

The other day, one of my colleagues posted the following message on Facebook:

> "Now offering FREE voice-overs for charity and animal rescue organizations. Please spread the word."

When I first saw this message, my reaction was mixed. At first glance, it looked like a noble thing to do. Times are certainly tough for charities, so why not help them a little? The less they have to spend on advertising, the more money is left for the cause. What could possibly be wrong with that?

Yet, another part of me said: "Wait a minute... Being the voice of a charity, that's a paying job for people like you and me who have to make a living talking into a microphone. If we'd all start giving our services away, we'd undermine our own business. It's also unfair competition."

Of course this isn't something that's only affecting voice-over professionals. If you're designing websites, why not give one away to the local animal shelter? If you're running a print shop, why not donate a few thousand brochures to promote the food bank? If you're a professional musician, why not do a benefit concert for your church?

It's better to give than to receive, right?

In the past few days, my entrepreneurial side vigorously debated my philanthropic side like two presidential candidates who are running for office. One of the questions my inner moderator came up with was this:

Are all charities created equal and do they need and deserve a break?

To answer that question, let's start with another one.

What do you think of, when you hear the word Charity or Non-profit? What's the first image that comes to mind?

Are you thinking of a small, struggling, idealistic organization run by volunteers on a shoestring budget, or of a multimillion-dollar, well-oiled machine with sleek media campaigns and celebrity endorsers?

Let's take a closer look.

The Chronicle of Philanthropy*** publishes surveys on giving, foundations, and executive salaries. Get this. According to the Chronicle, more than twenty non-profit groups paid their top executive more than $1 million a year in 2010 and 2011.

SWEET CHARITY

The highest-paid professional in the survey was Herbert Pardes, executive vice-chairman of the New York Presbyterian Hospital Board of Trustees, who had a 2010 compensation of $4.3 million, including a $1.71 million salary.

American Cancer Society CEO John Seffrin ranked fifth with a 2010 compensation of $2.08 million. This included $1.49 million in deferred compensation and retirement.

Boys & Girls Club CEO Roxanne Spillett ranked eighth with a 2011 compensation of $1.81 million.

In spite of a recession, top executives at the largest U.S. charities and foundations received a median pay increase of 3.8 percent to $429,512 in 2011, according to the Chronicle's survey of 132 of the biggest organizations.

One-third of the non-profits in the survey provided bonuses to their executives in 2010. The median bonus was slightly over $50,000.

Do you even make $50,000 a year recording voice-overs or running another type of freelance business?

PROFITING FROM NON-PROFITS

Please don't get me wrong. In order to attract top leaders, non-profits need to offer top salaries. I'm sure that most of these executives work really hard to advocate the cause they're representing. Some of them do a much better job than others, though.

Charity Navigator*** is the nation's largest evaluator of charities. The organization has examined tens of thousands of non-profit financial documents and uses this knowledge to develop an objective, numbers-based rating system to assess over 5,000 of America's charities.

On its website you'll find a list of 10 Highly Paid CEOs at Low-Rated Charities.*** Despite receiving more than $200,000 in annual pay, these CEOs run U.S. organizations that devote less than 60% of their budgets to their programs and services.

Number one on the list is the CEO of the American Heart Association, with a salary of $602,529.

Where does all this charity money come from? From frail old ladies writing checks to save puppies from being euthanized? From school kids washing cars for cancer? From volunteers holding up buckets (and traffic) at a busy intersection?

THE PINK RIBBON EFFECT

Successful charities increasingly rely on the commercialization of their cause. October is breast cancer awareness month,*** and I'm sure you've seen pink ribbons on practically anything, from cereal boxes to smoothies to shower gel. Companies love to be associated with charities to boost their public image... and their bottom line.

The official name for plastering the world with pink and other charity related paraphernalia, is *cause marketing promotion*.

You'll often see that a company will donate a certain percentage of the sale to the charity featured on the product. But did you know that charities are not required to specifically disclose how much money they generate via cause-related marketing projects?

When asked, Sheila Brown, Director of Development and Special Projects of the Breast Cancer Fund, told Charity Navigator that twenty percent of the Fund's $3.9 million budget comes from business support. According to the same article,*** forty percent of the Breast Cancer Research Foundation came from cause-related marketing.

MONEY WELL SPENT?

Charity Navigator looked at two dozen of the largest charities that are working to fight and prevent breast cancer in America. Together, they raised nearly $1.7 billion annually in contributions.

The website concluded:***

> "The good news is that several of these charities efficiently utilize donations to pursue their mission of curing and preventing breast cancer. However, others will astound donors with their inefficient operations and low marks for Accountability & Transparency. For example, one charity spends less than 2% of its budget on fundraising expenses, while another spends nearly 98%!"

So, let me ask you again:

Are all charities created equal and do they need and deserve a break?

I don't think so.

Now, I didn't write this chapter to bash charitable organizations. Many of them provide important services, but most people do not realize how large charities have become, and how much funding flows through them each year.

According to Charity Navigator, their operations are so big that during 2011, total giving was more than $298 billion.

I know there are quite a few charities that have trouble staying afloat. Some of them are managed very well. Others are not. Some make millions through clever partnerships with big businesses. Some are lucky and hit the jackpot.

In 2012, the non-profit Central Park Conservancy in New York received a $100 million donation*** from hedge fund manager John Paulson. He made an estimated four billion dollars by betting the U.S. housing market would slump.

Charities come in all colors, shapes and sizes. Given this diversity, is it wise to make a blanket statement such as:

> "Now offering FREE voice-overs for charity and animal rescue organizations."

Wouldn't it make much more sense to evaluate each charity and non-profit on a case-by-case basis, before giving your work away?

I have three questions for you:

1. If some of them can afford to pay their CEO more than this nation pays its president, should we really be offering our services for free?

2. If some charities are generously compensating celebrities to make a brief appearance at a fund-raiser, why should we work pro bono?

3. If some charities choose to waste donations or take huge sums of money from corporations without full disclosure, should we still be providing our services and not charge a penny?

I greatly value the work most non-profits do, but I want them to value my work as well. I am not a charity. I am in business to turn a profit. At the end of the day, that profit allows me to make charitable contributions, quite possibly to the organizations I've worked for.

Before I write out those checks, I do my research. I want to know how my money is going to be spent. I only give to organizations that are transparent and accountable, and that can show clear results. Charity Navigator.org offers plenty of tools to objectively evaluate thousands of charities, non-profits, and foundations.

EPILOGUE

Today I finished narrating a documentary highlighting some of the work of Handicap International.*** This is a non-governmental organization, known for its fight against anti-personnel mines and cluster munitions. It also helps the victims of these unexploded devices. The film focuses on the people of Laos, the most bombed country in the world.

I could have offered to do this project pro bono, but I'm charging my regular fee without feeling the least guilty. You see, this documentary is not funded by some desperate, cash-strapped, small charity in a developing country.

It is entirely paid for by the Ministry of Foreign Affairs of the Grand Duchy of Luxembourg.

In 2013, tiny Luxembourg took second place on the list of the world's richest nations.

I'm more than happy to help them spread the wealth!

PART FOUR: SPREADING THE WORD

[21]

Why Your Website Stinks

Are you happy with your website?

Does it represent who you are and what you do?

Does it convert visitors into customers?

How do you know?

My very first website was based on a rather generic template, and to tell you the truth: it was just okay, and "just okay" doesn't cut it. That's why I had to rebuild it from the ground up.

It turns out that I'm not the only one.

Whether you're redesigning or starting from scratch, there are some important dos and don'ts you have to keep in mind.

In the following, I will assume that you have your own domain name. If you don't own the name, you don't own the site.

First, let's talk about what makes a website work.

Number One: In times of microwave meals and high-speed internet, people have become impatient. An effective website is easy to find, easy on the eyes, easy to navigate, and it loads fast.

Number Two: A website is as effective as its home/landing page. If the window to your shop doesn't catch people's attention and isn't inviting, it's time for a make-over.

That was the good.

Now it's time to look at the bad and the ugly.

Mistake #1: Designing a site based on what you want to share instead of on what the client wants to know.

A winning website is not about you. It's about your customers.

What are they looking for when they're searching the web? What questions do they have that need to be answered? What do they want to do once they've landed on your site? What will scare them off? What will keep them interested for longer than four seconds?

If you don't have the answer to these questions, chances are that you're designing a site to please yourself, and you'll end up being your only customer. It's an exercise in narcissism.

Mistake number #2: Not making a value proposition.

A value proposition answers the question:

Why should your ideal prospect buy from you rather than any of your competitors? If you can't explain why clients should hire YOU, you're encouraging them to shop elsewhere.

It's vital to describe the benefits of hiring you from the viewpoint of your clients.

You are a solution to their problem and the pleasure to their pain.

Mistake #3: Having static content.

Having a website is one thing, but search engines have to learn to like it. Don't stuff your site with strategic keywords just to please Google. That is so yesterday. Think of your visitors first. Give them a reason to spend time on your site and come back for more.

Web crawlers (the internet bots that systematically browse the World Wide Web for the purpose of web indexing) love fresh and relevant content that drives lots of traffic. There's a reason why my blog is an integral part of my site!

Mistake #4: Having a site that's not mobile responsive.

More and more people access online information on mobile devices. Ineffective sites are designed for computer screens and can be hard to navigate on smart phones and iPads.

If you decide to use a template to build your site, make sure that it automatically adapts to allow your visitors to view your content – whether from a desktop, laptop, smart phone, or tablet.

Mistake number #5: Not establishing credibility and professionalism.

In order to hire you, the client has to have faith that you can handle the job. But how do you get someone to trust you who doesn't know you ?

The way I see it, you have two options:

One: Toot your own horn really loud.

Two: Let others do the tooting.

Nothing you say about yourself will be as credible as what others say about you. That's why I am a fan of incorporating short testimonials and logos of companies you've worked for. There's one condition.

Don't make things up. If you fake it, you won't make it.

Remember: Everything you put out into the world is a reflection of your professionalism: your demos, your pictures, and your website. First impressions matter. If your site looks unprofessional, you look unprofessional.

Mistake #6: Too much text and uninterrupted paragraphs.

Some freelancers don't know the difference between writing the next Great American Novel and a few webpages.

Yes, you want to answer your clients' questions, but you must leave something to talk about. Don't you want them to contact you?

- People don't read anymore. They scan.
- Long pages and paragraphs scare your visitors away
- Bullet points get their attention
- Winning websites have lots of blank space and
- Eye-catching images

And please, check your spelling and grammar. Have someone else proofread your copy. Errors undermine you're cridibility.

Mistake #7: Make clients jump through hoops to get to important information.

Easy does it. Things like "Client list and testimonials upon request" require busy visitors to do extra work. Not a good idea.

Are you still secretive about your rates? Isn't that one of the first things clients want to know? Don't make them fish for it.

Why don't you tell your client where you're located? If that French director wants you to come to his Paris studio, shouldn't he know that you live near Montreal? Visitors expect contact information at a prominent place.

By the way: a Gmail, Yahoo or Hotmail email address does not look very professional. Get a proper business address, but use a spam-proof contact form on your site. Listing your full email address on a website is an open invitation to spammers.

Next: Can clients download your demos or do they need to ask you to send them to you?

We're creatures of convenience. If you were a producer and you needed a demo NOW, what would you do? Would you go to talent A and take a few seconds to download it from her website, or write an email to talent B and ask for it?

Mistake #8: Flash landing pages and automatic audio.

Flash animation slows down the loading time of your website and it forces people to watch something they might hate. What a way to greet your customers! What's more, Apple devices don't do Flash.

The same applies to background music or an automated welcome message. I have a demo on my landing page, but visitors have to click on it to hear it. People want to be in control.

Another no-no is a Doorway Page. You know, the one with a button that says: ENTER. It might as well say: LEAVE.

Mistake #9: No call to action.

Do you leave your visitors all dressed up and nowhere to go? That's a big blunder. You put all that effort into crafting a core message in a neat online package.

For what purpose?

What do you want your visitors to do?

Download your demo? Buy your audio book? Get in touch with you?

You tell me.

Then you tell your visitors.

I mean it!

Mistake #10: You can't update the website yourself.

There's a testimonial you'd like to add. You have a great new demo that needs to go on your site. Your latest audio book is on the shelves. Do you want to wait a few weeks until your webmaster gets his act together?

I have three words for you:

DIY!

With a platform like WordPress, there's no need to learn complicated codes anymore. There is a wealth of affordable, snazzy templates that can be easily customized to create a unique, clean look.

Updates install at the click of a button. New plugins are developed every day. Many WordPress templates are already search engine optimized. It doesn't get any easier.

I'm not saying you must design your own website, but you should at least learn how to update your virtual store. It's cheaper too.

There is absolutely no reason why your online presence should have a sign saying:

SITE UNSEEN

[22]

What Makes People Click?

On June 8th of 2009, something occurred that had never happened before in the history of mankind.

Hyères, the oldest and most southerly resort on the French Riviera, was the scene of an attempt to break the world record in Static Apnea. That's the discipline in which a freediver holds his or her breath for as long as possible.

The old record of ten minutes and twelve seconds, set in 2008, was held by Tom Sietas of Germany.

The challenger, Frenchman Stéphan Mifsud, was determined to destroy it. Some called him a hero. Others thought he was a suicidal lunatic. Few believed that he could do it.

AIDA is the International Association for the Development of Freediving. Their website offers a lot of in-depth information about various disciplines, such as "free immersion," "constant weight," and "dynamic with fins." However, it does not answer one fundamental question:

Why do seemingly normal people do these crazy, death-defying things?

After all, no one is forcing them to risk their lives in the pursuit of....
what exactly?

THE ETERNAL QUESTION

Whether we realize it or not, as (voice) actors we are constantly
struggling with the very same issue: What motivates people? What
motivates us?

Day in day out, we're analyzing dead words on a piece of paper. As
we're attempting to breathe life into lackluster letters, we wonder:

– For whom is this written; what drives them; why would they listen
to me?
– What character am I portraying; what is making this character tick?
– What's the ultimate purpose of this message?
– How can I infuse that purpose into my performance?

We have to ask ourselves similar questions when it comes to our own
writing. Take the copywriting we do for our website or blog. It's easy
to say that, in order to bring visitors to our site, we need to serve
them a fresh meal of mouth-watering content. But tell me who has
the recipe? Gordon Ramsey?

TIME IS TICKING

Every day, all of us have a limited amount of time at our disposal. For
others to spend some of that precious time on our website, we need
to give them something special. It has to be something relevant and
new that you can't get anywhere else. It boils down to this: we have to
feed a need.

In order to tap into our reader's needs, we have to ask ourselves:

– What's our audience hungry for?
– What pains and problems do they have?
– What issues do they care about?

– What solutions are they hoping to find?
– What am I passionate about?
– What do I have to offer that's unique and applicable?
– Why should people trust me?

If you can answer all of these questions, you are well on your way to create what professional communicators call "sticky content."

Sticky content gives users a compelling reason to come to a site, spend time on that site and come back for more.

Things that stick make people click.

Websites that are able to improve how long they can keep visitors engaged, are enjoying improvements to their search results in only a matter of months.

A FRAMEWORK

In 1947, Percy H. Whiting published *"The Five Great Rules of Selling."* In it, he came up with a simple 4-step structure that can turn content into something sticky. All you have to do is to remember the acronym AIDA:

1. Attention
2. Interest
3. Desire
4. Action

Let's break it down into bite-sized pieces. The first thing you need to do is...

Grab the attention of your readers with a HEADLINE that gets your readers hooked. Be provocative. Ask a controversial question.

A while ago, I had a chance to test this out. I was writing a piece on what happens to all the custom demos we upload to online voice casting sites (also known as Pay-to-Plays). A majority of them seem to disappear without a trace.

My headline could have read:

"Where do all your custom demos go?"

That's pretty tame. Instead I wrote:

"Are your auditions sucked into a black hole?"

In a matter of hours my readership skyrocketed to unprecedented levels. Apparently, my heading had hit a raw nerve.

Once the reader is hooked by a headline, it's time for you to describe the PROBLEM (step 2). This is where you share some experiences, facts, or your personal struggle. It is your chance to bond with your reader, to show the extent of the problem and the need for a solution.

Once you have created an interest in that SOLUTION, it's time for step 3. Here's where you write about what you have to offer and where you describe the benefits of your product or service.

This part should answer the age-old question: "What's in it for me?" It's a good idea to throw in compelling reasons as to why what you have to offer actually works. Think of adding testimonials and real world examples.

If you've done your job, your readers should be all dressed up by now. But where can they go? No sales-cycle is complete without a call to ACTION. Whether you want your visitors to email you, subscribe to your newsletter, or buy your latest audio book, you have to let them know what the next step is.

Tell them:

"Download my free eBook." "Subscribe to my blog." "Sign up for my training." "Contact me today."

Of course there are many techniques to arrange your writings in ways that will get the attention of your readers. And we haven't even addressed what you should write about. But all of that is completely irrelevant if you don't do one thing: Get started!

YOUR CHALLENGE

There are approximately 152 million blogs on the internet today. Every half second, someone creates a new blog somewhere in the world. Blogs are represented in the top ten web site lists across all categories. Businesses that blog at least twenty times per month generate 5 times more traffic. Blogs help to influence customers' buying decisions and purchases.

Here's the big question:

With so much info to choose from, how do you cut through the noise and get heard?

Lewis Green, the CEO of marketing firm L&G Business Solutions, puts it this way:

> "To break through and get noticed, we really need to understand who we are writing for and exceed their wants and needs. Not much different from running a business, and if we are a business blog, we better write for the readers, not for ourselves."

As a freelancer, you might not be a freediver, but now is the time to get your feet wet and to start creating sticky content.

Don't expect overnight success, though. It takes preparation, time, and imagination to become a blogger people want to follow. But with the right motivation and training, you can get there, as long as you're willing to take the plunge.

This brings us back to the town of Hyères, France, and the world record in static apnea.

BREATHTAKING

Just imagine sitting stationary underwater, holding your breath.... for an eternity.

After a while you can hear your blood pumping, and the pounding of your heart becomes almost deafening. Your lungs are about to burst and yet you have to stay still as sheer panic is taking over every single thought.

Could you do it?

Would you?

On June 8th, 2009, Stéphan Mifsud did not break the world record in static apnea.

He absolutely shattered it.

His mind-blowing record time of eleven minutes and thirty-five seconds still stands today.

[23]

Eight Ways to Increase Web Traffic – guaranteed

Just about every week I publish a new blog post on my website about the world of voice acting and about issues that involve many free-lancers. In only a few years time I managed to attract thousands of subscribers and my stories are shared, discussed, and reprinted. It's proven to be one of the best ways to promote my services.

If you're wondering how I got to this point and how you can get there too, stay tuned. But before I tell you what worked for me, I have a confession to make.

To me, blogging is not a numbers game. It never was and it never will be.

Having lots of subscribers is nice, but I see it as a side effect and not as a goal. A bigger platform simply gives the author a bigger bullhorn, but it does not make the message any better. In fact, right now there are thousands of blogs with tons of subscribers that are pumping out a constant stream of sponsored bullsh*t we could live without.

I sometimes compare playing the numbers game to the marketing strategy of a well-known fast food chain. Just because they've served billions of customers doesn't mean their food is any good. I usually try to avoid those places.

SOCIAL PROOF

Having said that, big numbers seem to be an indication of social proof, although I know my readers are more intelligent than that. They realize that social proof is nothing but assumed influence, mostly based on shallow observations and hearsay.

So, while I am really happy that my readership is growing, I look for other indicators to find out if I'm on the right track with my blog and my website.

It's one thing to get people to visit your corner in cyberspace. Having them hang around for a while is something else. That's why I always look at the average length of a visit.

We live in a strange culture of impatient, overstimulated, and easily distracted internet users. Most visitors spend about two minutes on my site. That may not seem very long, but the average time people spend on a webpage is between ten and twenty seconds. One of my goals for this year is to increase the average length of a visit to my site.

Next, I look at the *Bounce Rate*. That's the percentage of visits that go to only one page before leaving the site. Home pages are known to have the worst bounce rates with 70-90% of visitors going somewhere else. Blogs do slightly better with an average bounce rate of 40-60%. At the moment, my bounce rate is below two percent. No complaints there.

VISITORS & ENGAGEMENT

Another metric I track is the number of unique visitors to my website. Those are all the people who are visiting my site for the first time. Of course I love every single visit, but having a growing number of unique visitors means I manage to attract a new audience for my blog and for my services. On average I have at least 4,000 unique visitors every month in a niche market.

Even though I'm quite happy with these numbers, there's one thing I value even more. It's the level of engagement. I know it's a buzzword in the online marketing industry, but to me it's crucial. One indicator of engagement is the average length of a visit. I also look at what type of response I elicit in the social media. How many "likes" does a particular post attract? How many times is a story shared and by whom?

What I particularly value are the responses to my blog posts. Those who care to comment go beyond just passively reading the words on the page. It takes time and energy to come up with a thoughtful remark. Mind you, just because you don't see a lot of comments at the bottom of the page doesn't mean that people have nothing to say. Some prefer to share their remarks on LinkedIn or on Facebook. Others send me an email or a tweet.

By the way, did you know that one of my voice-over colleagues was actually hired after a client read his comments on one of my blog posts?

Now, for the 64 thousand dollar question: How do you get all this traffic and interaction going?

ATTRACTING AN AUDIENCE

1. The easiest way to attract tons of engaged visitors is by offering them something, preferably for free. Everybody loves freebies.

One of my blog posts got an unprecedented number of comments because I raffled off a CEntrance MicPort Pro to one lucky reader. Companies do it all the time. "Sign up for my free webinar." "Download your free eBook today." "Just enter the sweepstakes and you'll be eligible to win a cruise to the Caribbean!"

Of course there can only be one winner, but boy does it increase traffic!

I know what you're thinking. That's not earning an audience. That's bribing an audience. Anyone can do it. Just dangle a nice carrot and the masses will come. It works, but it's not how I operate.

2. The most valuable and legitimate way to earn an audience is by offering quality content. I know it's a cliché, but most clichés are true. The trick is to have a unique point of view and to write about things a wide audience is interested in. Of course that's easier said than done. You also need to sell your story with a powerful headline. Headlines are the hook.

LOOKS MATTER

3. You need to present your content in an attractive way: clear fonts, short paragraphs, and lots of white space. Adding a great picture or a video is a huge plus.

4. Make sure your content can be read on any device. There's no excuse for having a website that is not mobile responsive. When I made that change, I pretty much doubled my audience in a week.

5. Encourage people to stay on your site by adding internal links and by having external links open in a new page. Display a top-ten of most popular blog posts and lead the reader to other related posts. That's the purpose of the "Keep on reading" section at the bottom of my blog. It works like a charm!

6. Make social sharing super easy and promote your posts on other platforms. Don't just focus on your colleagues. Dare to step outside of your trusted circle to find new readers.

7. If you're hoping for audience involvement, you have to be involved yourself. Allow people to get to know you, not just through your blog or website, but through your participation on other platforms.

If you like to be "liked" on Facebook, you have to lead by example. If you want people to comment on your post, you must leave comments yourself. Give, give, and give (instead of gimme, gimme, gimme).

8. Now, even if you take all these tips to heart, please realize one thing. I started blogging back in 2009, so it took me a number of years to build up an audience. You've got to be in there for the long run. You can't expect the same results if you're only blogging when you feel like it. You have to develop a steady rhythm and stick to it.

9. The last thing I discovered brings me back to beginning of this part of the book where I talked about how many subscribers had signed up. What I learned sounds completely counterintuitive, and yet it makes perfect sense:

If you don't make it about the numbers, your numbers will grow.

Quality attracts quantity.

Be honest. As a reader, you don't really care about how many people subscribe to a particular blog, do you? And do you really order a book just because a number of other people bought it? I don't think so.

The first thing you look for is *relevance*. The only way a site, a blog or a book will speak to you is when the information offered is interesting, applicable, and meaningful. But there's more...

What really counts is a meaningful *connection*. A connection you have with the author through his or her writings. That's what ultimately connects a community of readers.

If you find a way to connect, your audience will follow.

Here's the last tip to increase traffic to your website:

10. Always underpromise and overdeliver!

[24]

Cold Calling is Dead

Is there a cure for the common cold call, or should we just let it rest in peace?

Before you start reading, let's do a quick experiment. In a moment I am going to list four things.

As soon as you see number one, simply label your very first response as either positive or negative and move on to the next word.

Are you ready? Here we go:

- Telemarketing
- Cold calling
- Do-Not-Call Registry
- Networking

So, what's your score?

Do you think your reaction is unique or universal?

I've just subjected a few of my friends to this unscientific test and – surprise, surprise – the numbers 1 and 2 elicited a strong negative response.

Telemarketers are among the most hated professionals on the planet. Most people would rather have their wisdom teeth extracted without sedation, than make a couple of cold calls.

In essence, cold calling revolves around fear and loathing!

Some commentators call cold calling "an abusive and masochistic process that damages your brand as well as your personal reputation." Others still believe that playing the numbers game (100 calls leading to 10 appointments resulting in 3 sales) is a foolproof system for the thick-skinned. They claim that cold callers who piss people off just aren't very good at their job. In reality, the most successful telemarketers have a 96% chance of being turned down.

NAMES, NOT NUMBERS

Consultant Mahan Khalsa*** founded the Sales Performance Group of FranklinCovey. He's the co-author of *Let's Get Real or Let's Not Play: Transforming the Buyer/Seller Relationship.****

He writes:

> "When sales is a numbers game, people are numbers and each one of the numbers tends to get treated equally. After all, we don't know which one out of ten will even want to meet with us, so we can't afford to do the research and preparation necessary to customize the call to their company and to them as a person. And that's exactly what it feels like on the other end. You don't really know me, don't know my company, don't know what is important to us and yet you feel you have something we want."

John Jantsch*** is a leading small business expert and author of *Duct Tape Marketing*** and *The Referral Engine.**** Both books are highly recommended.

Jantsch heard Khalsa speak at a conference and shared the following statistic in his blog:

"Cold calling results in about a 1-3% success rate for getting an initial appointment and it's generally abusive to both parties. When that same call is made with a referral, the rate jumps up to 40% and even higher when that referral comes from within the company."

There you have it. As far as I'm concerned, Jantsch and Khalsa just killed Cold Calling. I don't think we'll have too many mourners at the funeral, do you?

DRUMMING UP BUSINESS

As Jantsch points out, there are much more effective ways to find new customers. I must warn you, though: the strategies are neither for the passive nor for the aggressive. They are not for the introvert, the modest, the lazy, or the 'what's in it for me' and 'wait-and-see' types.

If you want to dig up potential clients, you have to become a miner. You most certainly will have to get your hands dirty and take the time to delve deeper. Here are a few gold mines that are surprisingly close to home:

1. CURRENT CLIENTS are a phenomenal resource. So: mine your own business! Satisfied customers are your best credentials and walking billboards. Please promise me to never conclude business without asking for:

– A testimonial
– Referrals

Tell your client:

"I really enjoyed working on this project with you. You must know a lot of people in the business. Who else do you think could benefit from my services?"

Always ask:

"Can I let Mr. so-and-so know that you referred me?"

Most of us enjoy buying stuff, but we deeply distrust salespeople. We will, however, trust colleagues and friends. That's one of the reasons why under the radar marketing is so effective.

2. NETWORKING works, as long as you get off your behind. Don't expect people to come to you. Anywhere and everywhere that you can meet other businesspeople face to face is better than cold calling.

Local networking groups like your Chamber of Commerce offer many opportunities to meet and mingle. Here's how to make the most of these types of meetings:

– Be unconventional! Seek out events where you might be the only expert in your field. Don't waste your time and money talking to sad colleagues sharing horror stories at so-called conventions that are crammed with colleagues.

– Spend 80% of your time asking questions and listening to the answer. It's priceless market research!

– Be sincere. Be positive. Pay people compliments. I know you're good at that sort of thing. They will remember you.

– Realize that this is about building relationships and never about selling.

– When you receive a business card, write a few key words on the back that will jog your memory. After the event, enter the info into your database and add your personal impressions.

– Select a few people who could benefit from what you have to offer and with whom you have good rapport. Then take the next step.

3. SOCIAL MEDIA offer a convenient way to follow up with your new contacts. Connect on LinkedIn:

"Steve, it was nice meeting you the other night. Good luck with that new project. When I drove back I had to think of that charity you're involved in. I can help you with a logo. I'd love to contribute."

Don't just send someone the "I'd like to add you to my professional network on LinkedIn" message. A network is often the result of years of careful relationship building. Do you think you can just tap into that treasure by sending me an automated message? I know you can do better than that!

Give me a reason to connect. Have the decency to respond to someone who was kind enough to open up his or her network to you. If you can't take a minute or two to say "thank you," what does that tell me about the way you usually do business?

OLD VERSUS NEW

In the old sales model, the focus was on closing a deal ASAP. The new paradigm is: "How can I help you?" It's not about getting. It is about giving. Don't expect to get any referrals if you're not prepared to give any referrals.

The old model was built on dialing rates and on breaking through respondent resistance. In the new model you would never force a relationship. Be patient. You can't expect to reap the rewards if you're not willing to sow the seeds and tend to your crop.

Use social media to get to know your contact as a person, not as a prospect. Once you're connected, they'll get to know you too.

4. FREE PUBLICITY is a perfect way to introduce yourself to the community.

Your neighborhood paper is starving for copy. How often have you seen the headline:

Local author signs new novel at Barnes & Noble

How about: "Local voice talent lands gig on national TV?" These types of stories don't come out of a hat. You have to create that BUZZ. How do you do that?

– Write a press release about your latest accomplishment. Make sure it's written in the third person. Otherwise it comes across as self-gratifying.

– Fax your messages. Unlike emails, a fax can't be deleted or filtered out. Snail mail doesn't have to be opened immediately. A fax shows urgency.

– Get in touch with the host of a radio show highlighting businesses in your area. You could be her next guest.

– Hold or sponsor a contest and make your service the prize.

– Prominently participate in your community by donating time and expertise. Don't settle for a behind the scenes job. Be the spokesperson!

– Always follow up with a call.

5. BECOME A KNOWN EXPERT by offering free talks or by writing a blog or a column in your paper. Get your name out. If people don't know that you exist, they will never hire you. A few pointers:

– Make sure that what you have to say is relevant to your audience. Come up with a catchy title for your talk. Instead of "Creative Writing 101" try "How to Sell Your First Short Story."

– Speak no longer than twenty minutes and stay away from Power Point; then take questions. Engage your audience.

Don't bore them with a sleepy slide show!

– Give everyone a freebie at the end with your contact information; put out a mailing list and follow up.

6. PEOPLE YOU DO BUSINESS WITH don't need to warm up to you. Your car dealership, your accountant, your lawyer, that studio you work with, even your hairdresser, caterer, and photographer are all part of huge networks. Why bother grooming a business in Baltimore when you have these resources in your back yard? Unless – of course – you live in Charm City.

Here's the key: Start sending these people some business today, but don't do it because you expect something in return. Do it because they deserve it. And remember: make sure the friends and colleagues you refer to that business drop your name.

What if nothing happens in the next few weeks? I'd say this to you: Delays are not denials. This is not instant oatmeal. Besides, the old-fashioned type tastes better and it will give you more sustenance.

You can't manipulate people and turn them into your puppets. What you can do is model certain behavior, hoping it will rub off. If you're a parent or a teacher, you already know that this works. If nothing happens, nothing's lost. You've gained valuable feedback that allows you to fine-tune your approach. Focus on finding businesses that share your philosophy.

THE PROOF AND THE PUDDING

Old paradigms are like dragons. They are hard to kill. Once you cut off its head, a new one appears. People who have bought into the presumed strength of one sales system, aren't easily sold on some-thing they aren't even willing to try.

I know for a fact that I can't convince you of anything. I don't even want to. Make up your own mind, but do me one favor.

Don't diss these strategies out of hand. Try them out. Experiment, knowing that no system in the world works one hundred percent, all the time.

Don't even treat it as a system. Before you know it, a system becomes a formula, a procedure, and a routine, taking us right back to square one.

Allow me to share one last story with you. This time, it's personal.

LOVE AT FIRST SITE

I love my wife dearly. Not only is she beautiful, wise, warm, intelligent, witty, strong, creative, a fabulous musician and teacher... she also puts up with all of my quirks. People always ask me: "You are so lucky! How did you meet her?" The honest answer is: Online!

Looking for love online is no easy thing. Right now, there are millions of lonely hopefuls longing for some eHarmony or the perfect Match. And all of them will tell you they like long strolls on the beach, someone with a sense of humor who loves kids and has a steady job.

What would you do to find Mr. or Mrs. Wonderful among millions of internet singles?

Would you type a zip code into a matchmaking search engine, pick a 100-mile radius, and start calling every single prospect within that area?

You'd probably face verbal abuse, accusations of harassment, and maybe you'd go on a couple of first dates. Still, how would you know these people are a good fit for you? Yet, this is the old cold callers way of (mis)conducting business.

Instead, why don't you begin by asking yourself these questions:

– Who am I?
– What's important to me in a relationship and why?
– What do I have to offer?
– What kind of person would be a good match for me and why?

Based on these answers, it will be much easier to come up with a unique profile and zoom in on people with potential.

At the end of the day, it all boils down to this precious platitude:

It's not about finding the right partner.

It is about being the right partner.

One last thing.

Before I put my online profile up, I did some serious soul-searching and I answered the questions above to the best of my ability.

The end result?

I did not find my wife.

She found me!

[25]

Want More Clients?
Go Undercover!

Clients don't grow on trees. We all know that.

We can't expect them to find us if they don't know we exist. In order for them to discover our needle in the online haystack, we have to make noise. Lots of noise. But what kind?

Some say the answer lies in Massive Marketing.

The truth is, most voice talents are pretty good at doing someone else's marketing. That's what they get paid for. But when it comes to tooting their own horn, a lot of them are as clueless as a hamster in outer space.

If marketing is not your forte, you're not alone.

Recently, the online magazine VoiceOverXtra polled its readers and asked the following question:

> "As a newcomer to voice-over, what is your biggest challenge at this moment to starting or growing your VO income and career?"

A quarter of respondents answered: *Marketing for jobs.*

Because different people mean different things when using the same words, here's my definition of marketing:

> Any activity that helps you find clients and helps clients find you.

> It's about understanding your clients' needs and connecting your product or service with customers who want it.

> Effective marketing is a compelling, engaging conversation. It's about building profitable relationships and creating an amazing experience around your brand, product, or service.

That rather long interpretation might not be approved by the famous Harvard Business School, but it works for me.

Before we delve into that a bit deeper, let's make one thing clear. It all starts with what you have to offer.

If your product or service sucks, no marketing campaign – no matter how brilliant – is going to help you make millions, or even a decent living.

Stinky flowers don't attract a lot of bees.

Most manufacturers know that they should not bring a product to market that is not fully developed. Many budding voice-overs have yet to learn that lesson. They'll pay a demo-factory good money to make them sound alright, until the client finds out that the Emperor has no clothes.

That's not marketing.

That's misleading the customer by offering something you can't deliver.

Marketing starts with creating the right product, letting the right people know you have it, and making it easy for others who don't yet know you to find you. But there's more to it than that. Much more.

As a seller, you still have to convince the interested party that you can be trusted and that the value of what you offer exceeds the asking price.

How do you do that?

For one thing, trust needs to be earned.

You need to give people the feeling that you understand their needs and that they're in the right hands.

Every single interaction you have with a potential client is a chance to prove yourself. Every interaction is a marketing opportunity. That's why I'm always marketing.

In fact, I'm doing it right now!

Writing a book or a blog is a form of content marketing. It's about offering relevant and valuable information to attract and engage a specific audience. Blogging is a way to establish yourself as a likable, knowledgeable, and trustworthy partner.

At this point I can already hear you say:

"But I'm not a client. Just a colleague. I don't hire voices. You don't need to market to me."

You're wrong!

Since a great part of my work is based on referrals from people like you, wouldn't it be beneficial to let my fellow-professionals know I've been around the block a few times when it comes to voice-overs?

People don't refer people they don't know and don't like. This book and my blog are both opportunities for you to find out who I am and what makes me tick.

Secondly, my publications are read by lots of other people: graphic designers, copywriters, videographers, people in advertising, agents, and so on. Some of these people do hire voices or know someone who does.

To most people, reading a blog or a book doesn't feel like they're absorbing marketing information. Quite often, the writer is just telling a story.

I call it *Covert Marketing*.

Now, *Overt Marketing* is all about pushing information down someone's throat, whether they're hungry for it or not, and whether or not we've established relationship.

Covert Marketing is making people aware of what you're offering so they become hungry for your service.

Overt Marketing revolves around what you want to sell.

Covert Marketing is about what people want to buy.

Overt marketing is about you.

Covert marketing is about the customer.

Overt Marketing is giving people direct messages:

HIRE ME

BUY MY SERVICE

SIGN UP TODAY

I AM THE BEST

Covert Marketing is suggestive and under the radar:

You answer a question posted on an online forum.

You write a (relevant and semi-intelligent) Facebook comment. You write a blog in which you share some of your expertise. You help out a colleague. You're a guest speaker at a seminar.

Here's a critical distinction.

At no point do you ask people to buy from you.

Overt Marketing is sending a mass mailing to all your contacts. It is a general message telling the world how great you are and what you have done for other clients.

Covert Marketing is targeted. It is relevant. It's almost always personal. There is a connection. There is a reason why you are contacting someone.

Overt Marketing is you doing the talking (and we all know that voice-overs are good at that).

Covert Marketing starts with you doing a lot of listening and asking a lot of questions. You identify a need or a problem. You find out how valuable meeting that need or solving that problem would be for your contact. Only then can you connect what you have to offer to meeting the needs of your client.

Overt Marketing is a sales pitch. It's about getting. It's driven by the "What's in it for me?" question.

Covert Marketing is about giving. It is about being of service. It is reciprocal.

If you want information, you need to give information.
If you want people to contact you, you need to contact people.
If you want people to refer you, you need to refer people.

Treat people the way you want to be treated.

In the end, Covert Marketing goes even further than that.

B.L. Ochman, president of *What's Next*, said it best:

> *"Marketing is everything a company does, from how they answer the phone, how quickly and effectively they respond to email, to how they handle accounts payable, to how they treat their employees and customers. Done right, marketing integrates a great product or service with PR, sales, advertising, new media, personal contact. In other words, marketing is not a discipline or an activity – it is everything a company is – at least if the company wants to be successful."*

Now, that's what I'm talking about when I say you're in the business of creating amazing experiences for your clients.

Once you start doing that, something unexpected and delightful will happen.

You can stop marketing.

Your clients will do it for you.

You just keep on wowing them!

[26]

Are You Talking To Me?

Dialogue or Monologue?

That's the question I ask when I read other people's blogs.

Is the author talking to me or to him or herself?

Dialogue or Monologue?

It's a question I ask myself every time I'm writing a new blog post or a chapter for this book. Am I really talking to my readers, or am I involved in a narcissistic exercise?

Ideally, I want my stories to be the start of a conversation with you. I absolutely love it when readers share their experiences and offer additional insights. That's why the comment section is my favorite part of my blog. For a book, it's a bit harder to organize, but you can always send me an email or find me on various social media (on the last page of this book I'll tell you how we can stay in touch).

People email me almost every day, and I do my best to get back to each and every one of them. Sometimes they tell me very personal stories that move me to tears. Other times they just want some practical advice.

Lately, I have been getting a lot of questions about blogging. That's no surprise because so many colleagues started blogging or are thinking about it. Let me answer a couple of the most popular blog-related questions. Let's start with one I get asked all the time.

How do I know blogging is for me? I'm not much of a writer.

It really depends on what you mean by "writer." Some people think of Tolstoy, Hemingway, or Steinbeck. That's quite intimidating. Most bloggers will never be nominated for the Nobel Prize in Literature. That's not the goal. There's one thing successful bloggers have in common with giants like Capote, Faulkner, and Irving: they are good storytellers.

You might not see yourself as a writer, but we all have stories to tell. Start there. Often, the more personal stories tend to have universal appeal. There's no need to construct complicated plots or introduce a plethora of characters. Stay close to home. Keep it simple. Some of the best blogs read like a conversation that's written down.

If you feel that that's something you're interested in, go for it. Too many people give up without even trying. The operative word is "feel." If you look at blogging as something you "must" do, it becomes another chore and it will show.

What do I write about? Where do I find ideas?

Blogging is more about opinions and not so much about unearthing new facts. A blog is an opportunity to put your spin on something your community is talking about. Social media makes it really easy to tap into that. Not everything can be discussed in 140 characters. Sometimes, a short Facebook comment can grow into a full-blown article.

I often write about things I run into myself as a freelancer: how to market my business, how to determine my rates, what to do about clients who pay late, what equipment to buy, et cetera. If it's something that concerns you, you can bet it concerns others as well. I can't tell you how many times my research resulted in a story.

Don't underestimate your own expertise. For many of us, being a voice-over is a second or third career. Some of you came from sales, others were educators, and many of you did something in media. What you've learned there is a gold mine. It has colored your take on "the business." Draw from that experience and translate it to the world of voice-overs. That's going to be your unique perspective.

I find myself staring at a blank page. How do I get started?

It's a myth that writers look out of the window, waiting for a wave of inspiration. It rarely happens. Most authors have to work at it. Every time I get a snippet of an idea, I write it down. If I don't record it, it will disappear. At that stage I find it helpful not to censor myself. Anything goes. Editing comes later.

By the time I get closer to Thursday – the day I publish my blog – some kind of theme usually emerges. Why that happens, I don't know. My mind works in weird ways I have yet to understand. When it's time to write, I take a good look at my notes to see what jumps out at me. That's the thing I tend to go with because it triggers something in me.

Other times I know I need to do more research before I can turn an idea into an article. It took me a few weeks before I could write my series on getting paid. Even though blogging is often about subjective experience, I do want to make sure that I get all the facts right.

I'm very busy trying to make a living. How do I find the time to write a blog? Is there a best time to write?

Finding the right time is not as important as making time to write. It's just like learning to play an instrument or learning a new sport.

You've got to build it into your days and weeks. If you don't make it a priority, it won't happen. The more you practice, the easier the ink will flow.

My perfect time is in the morning. I'm still fresh and my mind is most creative. In this crazy world filled with distractions, I find it essential to have uninterrupted time to get into my groove and do my thing. I'm not much of a multitasker. I'm much more productive if I can focus on one thing and one thing only.

Because I am pretty busy, professionally speaking (pun intended), I cherish my moments at the writing desk. It's a time of reflection. It's a time of connection.

It's so easy to get caught up in all the things you need to do to run a freelance business. The buck always stops where you are sitting. That's why I need some space to take a few steps back and think about what I am doing. Are there better ways to work? Am I getting closer to my goals? What's missing that would make me even more effective?

Those types of questions may lead to a new blog post. That's why I often joke that my articles are basically "notes to self."

How many blogs should I publish per week or per month and how long should a story be?

I could start off with a platitude by saying that quality always trumps quantity, which is true. However, some bloggers blog every day and they're phenomenal. Others blog once a month and have very little of interest to say.

Whatever you do, I recommend getting into a routine and to publish on the same day at the same time.

Once you build up a readership, people will know when to expect a new post and they'll start looking for it. Nothing motivates me as much as the knowledge that people are expecting something from me on a specific day.

I know my readers have a lot on their plates and I don't want to take up too much of their time. It still amazes me that they're willing to spend two to three minutes in my company. That happens to be the average time visitors spend on my blog. If I feel I have more to say on a particular topic, I'll turn it into a mini-series.

How long will it take before my blog catches on and how many readers do I need to make it worthwhile?

There's some strength in numbers, but that's only part of the story. I don't write with the intention of attracting a mass audience. I write because I wish to share things that are meaningful to me and helpful to others. One response from one reader can make it worthwhile.

Of course I do my very best to promote my blog. What's the point of publishing something if no one reads it? That would be the epitome of narcissism.

"Success" as a blogger (however you define it) won't happen overnight. To be honest with you, it took me a while to find my voice. I think that's one of the most important things readers are looking for. You've got to have an authentic angle of looking at the world that people respond to. Your readers need you to be relevant and want you to come up with content they can relate to.

In a way, readers aren't much different from the clients we have as voice-overs. Most clients are not listening for a generic sound. They want to hear what you bring to the table. Your voice. They want to be able to relate to how you read their copy.

Never approach a script as a monologue.

It's always a dialogue. Just like a blog.

[27]

Creating a Wave

You and I, we walk a fine line when it comes to drumming up business.

Here's the situation.

Clients won't hire us unless they know we exist.

Colleagues will not recommend us if they have no idea what we are capable of.

Agents might think we're yesterday's news if we don't prove ourselves every once in a while.

Those are all valid points.

The remedy to anonymity is self-promotion. However, we all know people who are constantly promoting themselves. They hijack threads on Facebook to toot their own horn. They pop up in LinkedIn groups to talk about themselves. They spam your inbox with "newsletters" that glorify their latest accomplishments.

They must believe they're very interesting.

If you're one of those people, I have this to say to you:

I'm happy that you seem to be successful, but do you have to rub it in ad infinitum? The louder you talk, the less I hear. The more you post, the sooner I'll ignore you. Is that what you had in mind?

A LOSING STRATEGY

Plastering your achievements all over the web is counterproductive. Think about it.

Why would I send you a job lead when it looks like you're doing pretty well on your own? Why would I encourage you, if you show no signs of modesty and humility? I'm not going to pump up an already over-inflated ego. Think of the mess when that bubble eventually bursts!

But seriously, when we expose ourselves on various social media sites, we deliberately open up a window into our lives and we invite the world to watch us. But not all windows are created equal. Here's a critical distinction.

Those unstoppable self-promotors have covered that window with a silver layer, effectively turning it into a mirror. When they look out, they merely see their own reflections.

When you and I are looking through our windows, we see a world of connections.

This means that if you are one of my friends or fans, I do want to hear from you. I want to applaud you when you've done something special. I want to help you if you need my advice. I am interested in your opinion. I might even take a moment and look at a picture of one of your children or pets.

But when you reach out, do me a favor.

Don't just take.

Give!

Don't just talk.

Listen!

Dialogues excite me. Monologues bore me to tears.

THE FLIP SIDE

Let me ask you this: Should we be suspicious of all forms of self-promotion? Is it better to stay under the radar than to annoy our circles with propaganda?

Not exactly.

At times, modesty is not going to propel your career. As a voice-over, you embody your product and you are the head of your sales department. If you want to sell, you need to advertise, but you need to do it wisely.

Overexposure kills. Underexposure doesn't create any traction.

So, when would be a good moment to stop hiding your light under a bushel?

Whenever you've done something extraordinary, that is the time to create a wave.

Pick something surprising, artistically stunning or deeply personal and moving. A milestone. Something you're really proud of. Make sure it shines and let the world know about it.

Take a look at this video.***

It was created by Studio Smack in the Netherlands for the online magazine of Greenpeace. It's an organization I've supported for years, and when I booked this job, I knew it was going to be something special. That's why I have no problem posting this video on outlets like Facebook and Google+. Doing so promotes two things.

The message and the messenger.

I also did something else.

I made sure this video went out to each and every one of my agents. Normally, I leave them alone because they're too busy balancing many plates in the air. But I know that I'm not the only talent in their roster, and I didn't think it would hurt to send them a reminder of what I have to offer.

Some agents contact me more frequently than others. By sending this video, I'm telling those I haven't heard from in a while that I'm (still) booking jobs. Ultimately, that's the only reason why they should represent me. I can make them money. This video proves the point.

REPUTATION MANAGEMENT

Until recently, I still believed that there are no guarantees in this business. I have to modify that statement slightly because it's only partially true.

If I've learned anything in the years I've been a full-time freelancer, it is this:

Doing good work leads to more work.

Guaranteed.

As long as people know about it.

Just as a writer needs to get in front of potential publishers and a painter has to exhibit his art, we need to show good work to those who can make things happen.

Before we can ride the wave of success, we have to create one.

In all modesty, of course.

[28]

Marketing Demystified

Marketing.

It makes many freelancers uncomfortable.

They look at it as a necessary and expensive evil.

If possible, they'd rather delegate it to someone else.

I disagree.

If you want to run your own business, marketing is something you must master.

A while ago, Chris Kendall of Voice Artists United*** interviewed me about it.

Here's his first question:

Many people rely on just having a website and an Internet presence on Twitter, Facebook or on a Pay-to-Play site to do their marketing for them. Does this work, and if not, why not?

Let's take a step back and start with my definition of marketing:

Any activity that helps you find clients and helps clients find you.

Marketing is all about understanding your clients' needs and connecting your product or service with customers who want what you have to offer.

Effective marketing is a compelling, engaging conversation. It's about building profitable relationships and creating an amazing experience around your brand, product, or service.

If you succeed in these three areas, your marketing works. It's as simple and as complicated as that.

Having an Internet presence in and of itself is as useless as hanging up an expensive billboard in the middle of nowhere. In order to be effective, you have to make sure people find your needle in the online haystack.

Getting people to visit your profile on a Pay-to-Play site or on Facebook is like driving clients to someone else's store. That primarily benefits the Pay-to-Play and Mark Zuckerberg's emporium. You need to drive traffic to a site that you own and control. That way you can maximize your exposure and your sales.

What is the most effective tool to market yourself? Blogging, Facebook, Tweeting?

My blog has certainly proven to be my most effective instrument in my marketing toolbox. I'll tell you why. You can offer the best product nobody has ever heard of and never make a penny. If you want people to buy from you or hire you, they have to find you, get to know you, and learn to trust you. That's exactly what my blog has done for me.

Today's search engines have become much smarter. The number of visitors to your site is no longer the determining factor in its success. It's about what people find on your site and what they do with it. The magic word is engagement. Relevance and social interaction are now built into the algorithm that determines how your pages are found and ranked.

Most experts agree that one of the best ways to boost your SEO is to offer fresh and quality content. A lot of websites are pretty static. Once it's up, not much changes. That's why blogs are so effective. Every day or every week you get a chance to connect with your followers and attract new readers by sharing something of value.

To be effective, how much time do you estimate it is necessary to spend on marketing?

It's a running joke among freelancers that we spend 80% of our time finding the work and 20% doing the work. Marketing never stops.

Look at the big brands. We know their logos and slogans by heart. Yet, they continue to bombard us with messages and they spend millions on Super Bowl ads.

Award-winning colleagues whom we think of as "established," never stop marketing. How do they do it? The key is that marketing is not one special activity reserved to one particular time of the day.

Done right, marketing is never an either/or. It's doing this, that, and a whole bunch of other things in order to influence and reinforce perception. If marketing is not integrated in everything you do, you're not doing it right and you're not doing enough.

To me, one thing stands out, though.

The best form of marketing is delivering a stellar product or service.

Clients are your best credentials. If you exceed their expectations, they will do most of the marketing for you. Remember: tooting your own horn is necessary but suspicious. What others have to say about you is far more credible than all the things you will ever say about yourself.

How do you ensure that you are constantly reaching new people and not just preaching to the choir?

That's a good point. I see too many colleagues spending a lot of time interacting with fellow voice-overs. That's not necessarily a bad thing, but sharing silly animal videos does not get you clients. If you want to find new clients, you have to look elsewhere by asking yourself this question:

What greater community am I a part of?

Most voice-over professionals are:

– Actors & artists
– Self-employed
– Underemployed
– Freelancers
– Solopreneurs
– Small business owners

As a narrator and voice actor, I'm also in touch with:

– Linguists & translators
– Sound engineers & producers
– Bloggers
– Writers
– e-Learning specialists
– Advertisers & Social Media specialists
– People in the entertainment industry

Blogging is a form of content marketing. If I only were to write my blog for a small group of voice-over colleagues, I would be preaching to the choir. That's why I make sure to write stories that (hopefully) appeal to all the groups mentioned above. That way, I widen my reach, instead of making the same rounds in the same circles.

Is marketing yourself the same as bragging?

No, it's not, although it may come across like that if you're not careful. My advice may sound a bit like a contradiction in terms:

If you want to highlight what you have to offer, don't make it all about you.

A blog or brochure is not a public diary about your personal trials, tribulations, and triumphs.

Here's the challenge. You have to show people what you're made of, but avoid the ME, ME, ME-stories. That book is usually very thin and gets very old very quickly.

Focus on your market. Find out what their frustrations are and offer practical tips. Educate without lecturing. Come across as an expert, but not as a know-it-all.

As soon as you have an online presence, you are vulnerable. How do you protect yourself from spam and junk?

Never put your email address on your website. It's an open invitation to spam bots. Use a spam-protected contact form instead. Use an email program with a solid spam filter. Make sure your anti-virus software is up to date. Install anti-tracking software such as Do Not Track Plus.

I check every new subscriber to my blog against a list of know spammers using stopforumspam.com.

Compare the impact of automated tweets, updates, responses, and postings etc. against individually composed postings.

Small businesses have a competitive advantage over big corporations. Small businesses can deal with (potential) clients in a very direct and personal way. Because voice actors embody their product, that's their unique selling point.

Mass emails, tweets, and newsletters can be deleted in seconds.

Personal messages, letters, and faxes are harder to ignore.

Direct your marketing at key individuals as long as you don't give them a sales pitch. People like to buy but hate to be sold.

Address the needs of your potential client and the benefits of your service. Use language and imagery they can relate to. People seek validation and want to be understood.

In an overcrowded marketplace, how do you ensure that you stand out from the crowd?

I am going to brag now, but only because it's based on feedback from my readers.

The number one reason people come back to my blog is because they say they find content that is relevant, entertaining, and helpful, told from my perspective.

If you want to appeal to a wide audience, you must have a unique point of view.

I'm not telling my readers how great I am. I'm simply showing them how they can be more successful if they follow some of my suggestions. In other words: I am not asking them to buy something from me. I'm giving them something that could be useful.

I also try to stay true to myself. If you attempt to be everything to everyone, you end up being nothing to no one. I highly recommend finding a niche and emphasizing your specialty in your marketing messages.

In my case, I market myself as *The Ultimate European Voice*. I realize that this may sound rather pretentious, but for someone living and working in the United States, my European-ness is one quick and dirty way to distinguish myself. More and more clients don't want a British or North-American English speaker for a global campaign.

My neutral English accent seems to meet a real need.

For people who may not be technically minded, do you think it is worthwhile employing someone to do your internet marketing for you?

Before I answer that question, let me say this: Technology is a tool that sometimes stands in the way of true communication. There has never been a generation in the history of this planet that has been more connected, yet millions and millions of people are missing a real connection.

Technology enables us to send a mass email or newsletter to everyone in our database. It's as sad and ineffective as cold calling. You are playing a numbers game, thinking: The more people I send stuff to, the more likely it is that someone will respond.

I always get the best responses from personal contact. There is no marketing guru running my "campaign." The reason is simple.

No one is as motivated and dedicated to my business as I am. No one is willing to work as hard for my business as I am. That doesn't mean I don't ask for help.

We all have our strengths and I do feel that when I look at certain websites, some people should have used a web designer, a copywriter, or a professional photographer. First impressions are vital!

However, it does pay off to learn how to maintain your own website. Otherwise you end up paying your webmaster for every small change or update.

Talk a little about keeping the balance right ... e.g. marketing versus actually doing the job. Is it possible to do too much marketing?

As I said earlier, doing your job to the very best of your ability is one of the best forms of marketing. If you approach it that way, there is no real separation between doing the job and promoting it.

There is a risk of "overmarketing," though. I'm not going to name names, but one voice-over coach regularly plasters the internet with promos for seminars, classes, and the whole shebang. This person uses other people's threads to pimp upcoming webinars and personal appearances. It's overkill, it's counterproductive, and it's rude.

If you yell too loudly and too frequently (especially if it's more of the same), it becomes annoying and people will tune you out.

How do you think marketing will develop over the next five years?

I'll have to take out my crystal ball for that one. On one hand I see that marketing is becoming more and more driven by mobile technology. The results of your efforts can be analyzed instantaneously. On the other hand it's becoming more social. For the first time in the history of the Internet, people spend more time on social media than on porn sites. Social proof is rapidly replacing expert advice.

If you wish to make a dent in the marketing universe, you need to learn to play the technological game, create visual content, and attract, grow and serve a considerable online following.

It is critically important to always remember that you're talking to real people with real problems that need to be solved. It's impossible to meet their specific needs with a mass email. Marketing can be the beginning of a connection, but it's only a first step.

Let me put it this way. Creating an appealing window display is one thing, but no level of technology can force people to come inside, let alone become a (return) customer.

Connecting the dots and creating a seamless approach to marketing – creating your own look, logos, fonts etc. Are they important?

Now we're entering the realm of branding. What's branding?

It's creating a name, symbol or design that identifies and differentiates a product from other products.

With thousands of voice-over talent entering the market each year, differentiation is essential. Having a picture of you with a microphone on your website is anything but unique. Clients are looking and listening for personality and authenticity.

Things like a recognizable logo, a catch phrase, and a consistent color scheme have to reflect who you are and your niche.

Have you seen my website Nethervoice.com?

I do not have a logo per se, but I consistently use a picture of me, holding a bunch of orange tulips. You can see it on the back of this book.

On a subconscious level, people still associate tulips with Holland, and as a native Dutch speaker that's a good thing. Orange also happens to be the Dutch national color.

Then there's the pun "tulips" and "two lips," which for a voice-over professional is a nice association.

What's the most important thing you have learned about marketing?

Does it have to be one or can I mention two things?

1. Marketing is like sowing seeds.

You can't force those seeds to come up overnight, grow into trees, and produce fruit. Marketing is an organic process that requires psychology, persistence, and patience.

2. It is a waste of time to market a bad product, but if what you have to offer is any good, you owe it to yourself to let the world know!

PART FIVE: COLLEAGUES

[29]

Never Bite the Hand

"If a picture's worth a thousand words, why didn't I become a photographer instead of a voice-over?"

That was typical Bill.

No "Hello" or "How are you?" Bill always comes in with some kind of wisecrack.

"Why do you look so happy?" I asked. "Just watching you makes me miserable."

"I think I nailed that last audition, man. I totally rocked the house," Bill said, beaming from ear to ear. "I even added some special effects." He made the sound of an airplane on the runway. I was utterly confused. What audition was he talking about?

Bill is no Shallow Hal. Bill is deep. A while ago, I nicknamed him "Bill the Boomer" because of his powerful pipes.

Most mics aren't made to handle Bill's almighty basso profundo.

Most of his clients aren't either.

Bill and I go way back. This is what you should know about him: he has a heart the size of Texas and New Mexico combined.

Bill has ambition.

Bill has talent.

And... Bill has no social filter for his thoughts. He doesn't listen. He just spits out words. Unminced.

He is always heading for some kind of impulsive disaster.

I have told him many times: "Bite your tongue Bill, or otherwise you'll get in trouble."

He always gives me the same answer:

"I can't bite my tongue. I'm a voice-over. I'd be out of commission for weeks. Besides, you know me: I'm spontaneous."

"There is a subtle difference between being spontaneous and being obnoxious, Bill," I explained. "And you can be both. You know that, don't you?"

One day, I overheard him as he was talking to his agent. I could tell he was not amused:

"If they want me to use my money voice, they should pay me a decent rate! Give me a break. And if they don't like it, tell 'em that they're free to shop at voices one-two-three or whatever. There they'll find plenty of people who'd do this job for a piece of paper with Franklin's face on it."

A week later Bill asked me over for some energy drinks.

"What's the deal with that audition you were so proud of? Did you get the gig?" I wanted to know.

"Funny you should ask," said Bill. "I need to talk to you about that. I want an honest opinion. You see, I thought I nailed it, and this morning the producer called me for something else. He also told me that everybody in the office had had a good laugh when they listened to my demo. They ended up offering the part to that guy who used to do these car insurance commercials. He suddenly became available. Can you believe that?"

"No," I said. "I can't believe that. Nobody likes being rejected, my friend. Were you at least graceful in defeat?"

"Well," said Bill. "I think I might have hit a bit of a snag in that department. You know me and my blabbermouth. I just couldn't help myself."

"Bill, tell me, what did you say to that producer when he told you that you didn't get the part? You know you can be very rude, dude."

Bill took a deep breath.

"I didn't really mean it," he said.

"Didn't mean what, Bill?"

"I told this fellow that he wasn't making any sense and... that I thought he was so gay that he couldn't even think straight."

"Come on, man," I said. "You should have known better than that. That was way off base. Some of my best friends are producers and they would have wrung you out and hung you up to dry. If you ever want to have a long career in this industry, begin by thinking before you open that money-making mouth of yours. And I'll tell you something else: you better start embracing your inner rainbow! You're in show business."

"What's that supposed to mean? Do you want me to start liking Cher and Liza Minnelli?" asked Bill, as he took a sip from his energy drink. "That's not going to happen."

"Can you be serious for a moment?" I asked. "You and I know that some of the best jobs don't necessarily go to the best people. Why do you think that is?"

Before he could answer, I continued:

"Some people know how to schmooze, my friend. They know not to bite the hand that feeds them. They know that if that powerful producer says something that is even remotely funny, they are expected to laugh like Pavlov's dog."

"I didn't know dogs could laugh," said Bill.

"For Pete's sake, Bill," I tried. "How can I ever get through to you? This isn't funny. Show some respect. Call that producer now. Apologize because you were rude. These guys can make or break your career, so you better be on your best behavior. If you don't do that, you'll end up burning all those bridges that you haven't even built yet. Capisce?"

"Point taken. I apperciate the advice," said Bill, pretending to sound like George W. Bush. "But I still think they should have given me that job. I'm telling you: my audition was funny and flawless, but this big-shot producer said that I'd completely missed the mark."

"Alright, mister president," I responded. "Let's play that demo before you call the producer back and eat some humble pie."

Bill's audition was weird. He'd been right about these special effects. It sounded like it had been recorded in the cockpit of an airplane. He also sounded happy but in a forced way, when he said:

"Ladies and gentlemen, this is your captain speaking. We are now flying at an altitude of five thousand feet and the skies are clear.

Why don't you sit back, relax, and enjoy our complimentary peanuts. Organic peanuts from Greener Pastures. Green never tasted better."

"And…?" asked Bill expectantly. "You're a straight shooter. Give it to me."

"Bill, I have to be totally honest with you. What on earth were you thinking?

This demo doesn't make any sense whatsoever," I said. "You're nuts."

"That's exactly what the producer told me," said Bill. He even asked me:

"Why did you spoof Leslie Nielsen in the movie *Airplane!* Why didn't you come up with some kind of silly character voice?"

"And what did you tell him?" I asked.

"I told him that I just followed the instructions that came with the script," said Bill.

"What instructions are you talking about, Bill?"

"It read:

This is for an animated pilot.

How was I supposed to know they meant a cartoon?"

[30]

Ten Ways to Spot a Voice-Over Amateur

"Dad," said my almost eight-year-old daughter, "What does baklava taste like?"

"It's like a slice of heaven," I answered.

"In that case... I don't want it," she replied.

"Why not?" I asked. "It's sooo good!"

My daughter answered:

"I don't want to taste dead people in my mouth."

Moments like that are priceless. This slice of life also reminded me of the fact that things that are apparent to you and me, might not be so obvious to others. Take language for instance.

THE NATIONAL PASTIME

Here in America, we're used to all these baseball-related expressions. Ten years ago, I had no idea what would happen if life would "throw me a curve ball." How could I?

I was born and raised in the Netherlands and the Dutch are crazy about ice-skating. This was a whole new ball game!

A while ago, a videographer touched base with me because he was looking for a narrator. He had used an online service to find a voice, and now he had to sort through 200+ auditions. Before he could give me a play-by-play, I jumped in and asked: "Do you really know what you're listening for?"

"Well," he said, "I don't want a rookie. I want someone who can hit it out of the park. I mean, this script is a can of corn, and I wouldn't want a wannabe to drop the ball on me."

When I heard those words, I knew it was my time to step up to the plate.

TEN RED FLAGS

I've been in the business for over 25 years, and it usually takes me 2.5 seconds to identify someone from the bush league. I don't even need to hear them read a script. Just tell me how much, or rather, how little they charge. Cheap rates are the first red flag.

The second red flag is the quality of the recording. These days, most talent will record in their home studio. It's cheaper that way, but the quality can suffer. Here are a few common problems.

The volume might be too low, or certain words might be too loud and distorted. That's called "clipping." You might also hear cars passing by or a dog barking in the background. This tells you that the recording was not made in a dedicated, soundproofed space. Building a sound booth can cost thousands of dollars. Most beginners don't have that much to invest.

If you happen to hear hissing, it's usually the result of cheap gear and/or the talent turning up volume settings too high. A hum on the recording is typically caused by a ground loop. It occurs when there is more than one ground connection path between two pieces of equipment. Pros know that. Amateurs have no idea and don't know how to fix it.

A third indicator is bad microphone technique. How can you tell? You'll hear popping plosives like Ps, Bs, and Ts. You might also hear harsh and shrill S-sounds (so-called 'sibilance') that tickle your ear drum in an unpleasant way.

Tip-off number four is lack of vocal technique. An amateur might take very noticeable breaths. Breathing is such a natural thing. Most of us aren't even aware that we're doing it. Being close to a mic enhances every single sound. Pros have practiced and mastered the silent breath.

Amateur recordings can also be filled with annoying lip smacks, mouth noises, clicks, and crackles. Some of them can be edited out, but bad edits are a fifth sign of amateurism. Professional edits go by unnoticed.

Sloppy articulation and incorrect pronunciation come in on number six. Some amateurs are lazy speakers. Their delivery will lack clarity, especially when they pick up the tempo. I've also heard beginners over articulate certain words, making them sound unnatural and contrived. A professional narrator will do his or her homework and will correctly pronounce words such as inaniloquent, rastaquouère or nudiustertian.

Poor or inappropriate delivery is clue number seven. You don't want your serious documentary narrated by an overselling wannabe actor who has watched too many infomercials. Local radio show hosts give themselves away because they have cultivated an "announcer voice." You should be listening for a natural delivery. Not for a newsreader.

Number eight: The inability to interpret a script. Any text can be read in a million ways. A voice-over professional will always sound like he knows what he's talking about (even if he doesn't). An amateur will sound insecure, lost, and untrustworthy.

A professional is flexible and appreciates and incorporates feedback fast without fussing. A pro can be coached. An amateur is afraid of criticism; is inflexible and needs a lot of handholding and training. What you might save in terms of money, you will inevitably lose in valuable time (not to mention the aggravation).

Number ten is my personal favorite. You can always spot an amateur by the way certain questions are answered. A few examples:

You: *"What kind of monitors do you have?"*
Amateur: "I have one 18 inch flat screen Dell monitor." (Monitor is another name for loudspeaker)

You: *"How did you stage your gain? Outside or inside the box?"*
Amateur: "I don't really perform on stage. Is there something to gain by doing that?" (Gain staging means setting the volume levels)

You: *"Newman recently came out with a ribbon shotgun microphone. It's only $199! Should I buy it?"*
Amateur: "Really? I thought Newman was a character on Seinfeld." (The correct spelling is Neumann and it is pronounced "Noy-mahn." There is no such thing as a ribbon shotgun microphone. Neumanns never come that cheap).

HOME RUN

"You're an Ace," my videographer friend said. "Thanks for all these tips. You deserve a place in my Hall of Fame. How did you come up with all that stuff?"

"Oh, you know... I've been around the block a few times," I replied. "It's not exactly rocket science. By the way, I think it's time to stop putting all these baseball references into my story. It gets old after a while. People get it."

"I don't know," said my friend. "Can you give me a rain check on that one?"

"Alright, that's it! I'm not playing your game anymore," I said.

"I am going to make myself a nice strong cup of coffee. And guess what I'm having with it?

Some delicious pastry made of layers of phyllo dough filled with chopped nuts and honey."

Ah... the sweet pleasures of life:

Baseball and Baklava!

[31]

The Amateur Infestation

They're everywhere. Haven't you noticed?

Take one good look.

Let's start with your online shopping.

Who's responsible for most reviews on online shopping sites?

Experts? Consumer advocates?

Independent test laboratories?

No. Amateurs!

Who just gave your favorite movie two stars on Netflix? The movie critic of the New York Times?

No. Amateurs!

What kind of people put the "reality" in reality TV?

Amateurs!

Where would talent shows like *American Idol*, *The X Factor*, and *The Voice* be without...

Amateurs!

Credentials are so yesterday. Experience is optional. If it breathes and has half a brain, any Nobody can be Somebody.

On the world wide web, pretenders pose as pros, and social proof trumps scientific evidence. Now, that's what I call progress, ladies and gentlemen!

CULTURE SHOCK

A few years ago, British-American entrepreneur Andrew Keen wrote *The Cult of the Amateur: How Today's Internet is Killing Our Culture****. In it, Keen describes how he holds the participatory Web 2.0 responsible for at least two things:

1. Making it almost impossible to find high-quality material amidst mediocre user-generated web content;

2. Destroying profitable professionalism.

Take Wikipedia, which relies heavily on volunteer editors and contributors. Wikipedia gets more traffic than the online edition of the venerable Encyclopedia Britannica, written by experts and scholars. Keen writes:

> "Every visit to Wikipedia's free information hive means one less customer for a professionally researched and edited encyclopedia such as Britannica."

But why would that necessarily be a bad thing (apart from putting encyclopedians out of business)?

The ever-evolving world wide web is all about user participation. Since the dawn of the egalitarian Internet, experts have had to leave their ivory towers. Information has become democratic.

It's for the masses, by the masses.

We're now living in the age of the Citizen Reporter, the self-styled critic, and open source software.

Anyone can share anything, no matter how profound or pathetic. How liberating is that?

Think about it.

- In this 24/7 global, unfiltered data dump, there are very few well-informed gatekeepers to separate fact from fiction. Any amateur can claim to be an expert, and no one is going to stop them until they are found out. Case in point:

THE ESSJAY CONTROVERSY

In 2007, a Wikipedia contributor using the name Essjay, had edited thousands of articles. He once was one of the few people given the authority to arbitrate disputes between writers.

According to his user profile, Mr. Essjay was a tenured professor of religion at a private university with expertise in canon law. But in reality, Essjay turned out to be a twenty four-year-old impostor named Ryan Jordan, who attended a number of colleges in Kentucky and lived outside Louisville.

"People have gone through his edits and found places where he was basically cashing in on his fake credentials to bolster his arguments," said Michael Snow, a Wikipedia administrator, after Jordan admitted that he had fooled everyone.

Boston Globe columnist Alex Beam called the Essjay affair an illustration of the problems of crowdsourcing and the "wisdom of crowds," saying that the crowd accepts authority unquestioningly. Beam:

> "Who would you rather have write your encyclopedia entries? Bertrand Russell, T.H. Huxley, and Benedetto Croce, who wrote for the Britannica? Or... Essjay?"

Andrew Keen was even stronger in his criticism. He said the whole affair was just one example of people ignoring expert guidance in favor of what he called the "dictatorship of idiots." In this brave new "idiocracy," amateurs rule and professionals are no longer cool.

Thank goodness that's not the case in my profession: the wonderful world of voice acting!

Or is it?

Before I go on, let's just define the territory, shall we?

To me, an amateur is a hobbyist, knowledgeable or otherwise; someone who does not make a living from his or her field of interest, a layperson, lacking credentials.

According to the same dictionary, a professional is a person engaging in a given activity as a source of livelihood or as a career; a skilled practitioner, an expert.

It's no secret that each year, hundreds – if not thousands – of hopeful amateurs attempt to break into the business by presenting themselves as voice-over professionals. It's never been easier, and I'm not going to belittle anyone for trying.

However, if you wish to present yourself as a pro, you must leave your amateur attitude behind. In order to compete with the best, you have to hold yourself to the highest standards of professionalism. If you're not ready, don't enter the market. Otherwise, you're wasting your time.

Now, some of you might say: "I'd rather hire an enthusiastic, talented amateur than a burned-out, uninspired pro. There's an abundance of fresh talent at the online voice casting sites and they deserve a chance. Everybody's got to start somewhere, right?"

Well, let's see how that works out.

HORROR STORY

A colleague with years and years of experience, told me the following story:

> "I'm trying to establish a new voice-over service targeting a specific niche. I listened to hundreds of demos on Pay-to-Plays, and I was appalled at the reads (Radio DJ Syndrome) and by what I call "Audio Quality Disorder" (AQD).
>
> While clicking through the demos, it was like... "no, no, no,no,no,no,no,no, maybe, no,no,no,no, yes. no,no,no,no,no..." Maybe .005% of the people were worthy.
>
> I'm absolutely dumbfounded that the poor quality of the audio that these 'pros' gave me is the same poor quality audio that goes out to clients. I'm dismayed by the unprofessionalism displayed by some of the people.
>
> Bad audio and amateurism are two big reasons the business is going to hell in a hand basket."

ATYPICAL OR TREND

It's very easy to discard this story as anecdotal evidence. If that were the case, why are more and more voice seekers leaving comments like:

> "I cannot emphasize enough that I need high-quality audio. I expect all reads to be performed in some kind of professional or home recording studio with high-quality gear.
>
> Second-rate audio quality is not acceptable for this project."

> "Narrators must be able to record in high quality (either at a recording studio or at home with the appropriate equipment that can produce high quality). "

> "Please do not send me audio that sounds like you recorded with a cassette player!"

"We would need the person hired to record the voice-over in his own home studio with professional voice equipment. We had someone do it on their computer and it sounded awful and unprofessional."

Well, one response would be:

"If you expect professional quality, start paying professional rates! You get what you pay for." My voice-seeking colleague continues:

"When clients have to 'beg' for quality audio, it indicates there is a problem of poor quality in the industry! Why do clients have to specifically demand high-quality audio? We are supposed to be professionals!

The amateur invasion has opened many doors to deserving, talented individuals. But as always, if you don't apply a fine filter, the floodgates will bring a lot of crap too, stinking up the business.

ARE YOU ALARMED?

In a strange way, my colleague's story put my mind at ease. I'm not as worried anymore by the influx of upcoming voice talent as I used to be.

Wikipedia learned from the Essjay affair, and in an article addressing the reliability of the site, writes:

"The Wikipedia model allows anyone to edit, and relies on a large number of well-intentioned editors to overcome issues raised by a smaller number of problematic editors.

It is inherent in Wikipedia's editing model that misleading information can be added, but over time quality is anticipated to improve in a form of group learning as editors reach consensus, so that substandard edits will very rapidly be removed."

I predict that a similar kind of self-regulation will take place in the voice-over industry, or in any type of market that is overcrowded by freewheeling wannabes. Otherwise, something like a Pay-to-Play model will be as unsustainable as the career of an aspiring voice actor.

Erik Sheppard of Voice Talent Productions*** puts it this way:

> "The average lifespan of a voice-over 'career' seems to be about a year. Every year, old names drop off the radar and new ones appear, just to be replaced again the next year. It seems to take about that long for The "Blue Snowball Coalition" of new talent to realize that they jumped into this without knowing what they heck they were doing, and then they are on to the next get-rich-quick scheme. Sad really. I imagine there are a lot of old USB mics collecting dust out there..."

So, what's the final verdict?

Do amateurs cheapen our community, or do they enrich us?

Are they to blame for the steady decline of rates and standards?

Are they stealing jobs that should have gone to seasoned pros, or do they pick up the crumbs no one wants to eat?

Should Pay-to-Plays put up a barrier of entry and be more rigid in their quality control, or will the weakest links just put themselves out of the game?

Here's what I think.

Everybody is entitled to enjoy a few hobbies, but in professional orchestras there is no place for amateur fiddlers.

I wish I could say the same for my line of work!

[32]

Seven Things I Hate About You

It's one of those mornings. I just put on my grumpy pants and I'm not in the mood to write a brilliant new chapter.

I just need to vent about the doubtful delights of social media.

The non-event that triggered the outburst you're about to enjoy, is at the top of my list:

1. Robotic requests to connect, befriend, recommend, or refer.

You know what I am talking about. Automated messages such as:

> "I'd like to add you to my professional network on LinkedIn."
> "You are a person I trust..."

Give me a break! Do I know you? Have we met? Did we do business together? If the answer to these questions is NO, then why are you bothering me? Are you a hacker, a stalker, a spammer, or a child?

Are you truly interested in me, or do you just want to milk my carefully built-up professional network for personal gain?

Should I send you to social media etiquette school and ask one of the teachers to put you in the corner?

Your profile tells me you list yourself as a "PR-specialist."

If your approach is an example of how you conduct business, you will be the first person I will never hire.

How's that for a recommendation?

2. Mixing business with personal info.

Just because we've worked together, doesn't mean I need to know that you came back from your doctor and had a wart removed. Spare me the details!

I don't care what you've had for breakfast, lunch, or dinner. Your kids don't interest me. Your spouse leaves me cold and your high school pictures are just as boring as all the other high school pictures on the Web.

Facebook Profiles are for people. Facebook Pages are for non-profits and businesses.

3. Making it all about you, all the time.

Yes, I know the world revolves around you, but do you have to rub it in 24/7? Thin books become pretty old pretty fast. It's so easy to saturate social media with self-centered fluff. It quickly becomes counterproductive.

I'm happy for you that you landed a new client and I'm sure your latest product looked and sounded great, but do you have an interest in what's going on in the rest of the world?

It's obvious that you like talking about yourself, but can you actually shut up and listen for a change?

And when you do, do you really hear what I am saying, or are you waiting for an opportunity to bring the conversation back to... YOU?

If you're the busy professional you claim to be, how on earth do you find the time to constantly tweet, text, chat, and comment?

4. Using money as your motivator.

What am I to you?

Am I a friend or a business lead? Did you mislead me by befriending me? True friends want to give and share without expecting anything in return. What is it that you really want? Are you trying to warm me up to soften your sale?

I don't want to be reduced to something that's bringing you one step closer to meeting your monthly quota. If you want to lose your friends forever, try involving them in your multi-level marketing scheme. There's a clear reason why it's very lonely at the top of the pyramid.

Stop selling yourself. Do not prescribe a cure before you know the illness. Find out how you can be of service. And if you don't have anything to offer at the moment, leave me alone. Please. I've got work to do.

5. Asking me to do your homework.

You wanted to know how you can become a voice-over artist. You told our Facebook group that you don't have any gear, you have no demos, and you have zero experience. You have no budget and apparently no brain. That's why you asked the community to do the homework for you.

How about doing a quick Google search, or is that too much to ask? Are you perhaps used to things being handed to you on a silver platter? If that's the case, forget about a career as solopreneur.

The self-employed get their hands dirty. If they want something, they go after it. And when they've exhausted their research, then they might turn to a colleague for advice.

I consider myself to be reasonably responsive, knowledgeable, and quite supportive, but there's one thing I will not support:

Laziness!

So: Get off you butt and stop wasting our time!

6. Having no manners.

Picture this: I just took an hour out of my schedule to give you some valuable tips and connect you to a few colleagues. My friends tell me that you followed up with them, so I know you received my three-page email. Did I ever hear back from you?

No Sir! Not even a thank you.

The words "please" and "thank you" are rapidly disappearing from our language. Kids don't use them anymore because their parents stopped using them. After all, what's the point?

Why thank someone for something we take for granted?

Mind you, I'm not looking for an ego-boost and I don't need validation in order to feel valued. But I still believe that it is more than a common courtesy to show some appreciation for something someone has done for you without any ulterior motives.

Secondly, the fact that it's easy to be anonymous online, doesn't give you permission to be rude, insulting, childish, or ill-mannered.

We can't hear your tone of voice and we don't see your facial expressions. That's why it's so easy to take your words literally, so please be careful of what you say and how you say it (notice how diplomatic I am in this rant?).

7. Luring me with the Lord. OMG!

You might have heard the story of the man who got into a serious car accident.

He was rammed by a Hummer with a "G-d is my co-pilot" license plate.

He not only lost a leg. He also lost his faith.

Let me put it bluntly:

I go online for information and communication; not for salvation.

For me, conversion rate is about turning visitors into customers.

Let's not trivialize the sacred scriptures and turn the internet into a stairway to heaven.

Believe it or not, my soul is safe and my religious convictions and affiliations are none of your business.

[33]

The Most Obnoxious Man in Voice-Overs

Characters.

The voice-over world is filled with them.

On-screen and off-screen.

Most of these characters are very likable, but every now and then you'll encounter a rotten apple, an arrogant bully, or a troll.

A week ago, I ran into one of them at a New York audition. I'd seen him before at some other place. He was an older guy, dressed in a classic three-piece suit. His tan was as fake as the color of his hair. When he spotted me filling out the sign-up sheet, he bellowed:

"Hey, Danish guy, I'm surprised to see you here. Did you finally decide to join the big leagues?"

I tried to ignore him, but he went on:

"Tell me, are you union yet?"

"No, I'm still happily non-union," I answered.

"Now, if you'll excuse me. I'd like to take a look at the copy."

"Well, we all have to start somewhere, I guess," he continued. "I was non-union for a while, but then the serious work started coming in. This was back in the day when nobody was working out of a walk-in closet. Of course you wouldn't know this, but I got my big break when guys like Beau and Joe were first making the rounds."

"Could you please keep it down? I'm trying to focus," said a pale, nervous young man standing in the corner.

"I will ignore that," my colleague continued. "Real pros can prepare their script anywhere, regardless of the circumstances. Am I right, or am I right?"

The way he said those last lines... there was something about it. It sounded like a commercial from the fifties or sixties.

Then he turned back to me.

"Let me ask you something, my European friend. What did you think of that Pepsi audition?"

"What Pepsi audition?" I asked.

"You know, the one that every agent in North America sent to his entire Rolodex yesterday," he answered. "Are you telling me you didn't get the memo?"

"I don't think I did," I said.

"No worries," he responded. "You'll get there. Give it some time. It only paid $4,000 for a thirty-second spot anyway. It's ridiculous."

He paused a moment to take a breath mint.

"Here. Have one!" he offered. "These things are small but very strong."

"No thank you," I said. "I'm okay."

"Take it from me, you need one," he said. "I know today's director. He can be hard on people, and if there's one thing he can't stand, it is bad breath. I did my first gig with him when he was still in Kindergarten, so to speak. I remember teaching him a thing or two."

I took a mint, hoping that this would shut the man up. Of course it didn't. I really had to go to the men's room, but he cut me off.

"Speaking of money," he said, "the other day a client called me in a panic. The guy they had hired to do the VO had laryngitis and they needed someone to record a tag line ASAP. 'We can only pay you what we promised him,' they said. 'How does six grand sound?'"

He looked directly at me and continued:

"Guess how many words were in that tag line?"

"I have no idea," I said. "Three hundred and fourteen?"

"Five," said my friend. "They gave me six grand for five words. Now, that's what I'm talking about! Not that it's all about the money for me. Oh no. At a certain stage in one's career, one stops looking at money the way most people look at money: as a way to pay the bills. Do you want to know what money means to me?" he asked.

"Not really," I said, as I was getting more and more annoyed.

"To me, money is a sign of respect," he answered. "And do you know what's wrong with the voice-over industry today?"

And before I could say something he carried on:

"There's no respect. No respect at all. In fact, I didn't even want to be here because the pay is lousy, but I'm doing this as a favor to my agent. Today I'm taking one for the team!"

Now, Peter, what agency are you with, these days?"

I told him.

"Never heard of them," he said. "They must be new. I'll be honest with you. It took me a while before I found a reputable agent. When you need 'em, they don't want you, and when they want you, you don't need 'em anymore. Isn't that ironic?"

I yawned.

"What's the problem? Am I boring you?" he asked.

"No," I lied. "I'm just stretching the muscles in my face. I do that to warm up."

"I see," he said. "I used to do that too, but when you've been around the block a couple of times, you'll discover that it doesn't make a difference. If they like you, they like you. If they don't, you'll never hear from them again.

As long as you don't take things personally, you'll be fine, my friend. By the way, you're auditioning for the Frank-character, right? Don't take this the wrong way, but aren't you a bit young for this role?"

"I don't think so," I replied. "I've played older people before."

The guy was really getting on my nerves. I almost wanted to walk out but he stopped me. Before I had a chance to put the script back on the table, he said:

"Do me a favor. Let's hear it. Give me couple of lines. Just for fun."

Anything to shut you up, I thought, and I began reading the script.

He stopped me after the first two sentences and scratched his ear.

"Are you sure your voice is okay?" he asked.

"You sound a bit hoarse. Did you recently recover from a cold or something?"

"No, I just had the bubonic plague and I'm still contagious," I said.

"Ha, ha. Not very funny, Mister," he said. "Do you mind if I give you a few pointers? You sound like you could benefit from some coaching. Don't worry. It's on the house."

"Don't bother," I replied. "I think it's my turn to audition. Goodbye!"

As I was walking toward the booth, an unconvincing "break a leg" echoed through the hallway. Boy, was I glad that this conversation was over!

The air in the studio was stale, but the director couldn't be more pleasant. "Did you meet Dick?" he wanted to know.

"You mean the older guy with the fake tan in the three-piece suit?"

"The one and only," said the director. "He's a royal pain in the ass, isn't he?"

"You're right about that," I said. "He told me the two of you go way back."

"I suppose that's true," said the director. "Before the internet, Dick was one of the top guys in the industry. Give him a script and he could sell you anything. Not anymore. These days, my clients want a natural voice. Not one of those old school announcer types. As far as I know, Dick hasn't booked a decent job in years."

"Then why is he here?" I asked.

"He's an old and dear friend," said the director.

"Every once in a while I ask him to come in and read for me. He loves it. And then we get to talk about the good old days. You should hear some of the stories he has to tell. He knows everybody in the business. Unfortunately, most of his buddies are no longer with us."

All of a sudden, the studio swung open and one of the assistants stormed in. "Jerry, you better come outside. It's Dick."

We ran to the waiting area and saw a small circle of people looking down. In the middle was Dick, lying on the floor in a strange, twisted way. He looked in pain.

"I'm so sorry, Jerry," he said. "I must have slipped on something and I fell. It hurts like hell. I might be out of commission for a while. Don't cast that audition yet."

"Don't you worry, Dick. We're calling an ambulance," said Jerry. "It will be here in a few minutes." And to the group: "If you came here for the commercial, the audition is over. Go home."

As I was collecting my things, the ambulance crew rushed in. Dick was lifted onto the stretcher and we left the building together. Lying on his back, he looked fragile. Then he pointed his finger at me.

"I want to tell you something," he whispered. "Come closer."

"You know, Peter, you sounded darn good in there. When I'm back on my feet, I'll put in a good word for you with my agent. You'll be joining the union in no time."

"Well, you better get better first," I smiled.

"I promise," said Dick. "I owe Jerry an audition!"

"That's right," I said. "Break a leg."

"Don't worry," said Dick.

"I think I already did!"

[34]

What Some Clients Won't Tell You

*If you don't know what your clients want and need, you'll never be able to give it to them. **Paul Strikwerda***

Throughout my career I have really tried to educate potential clients. Yet, almost every day I get the same old question:

"How much do you charge for a 2-minute voice-over?"

As if we're talking about a pound of sugar or a gallon of milk.

I really can't answer that question, but if you think you can I'd like to know:

What are you basing your answer on?

In the absence of specifics most people start making things up.

Take it from me: Do not assume you know what your clients want.

Ever.

Amateurs make assumptions. Professionals ask questions.

Leave the mind reading to the psychics. Conjectures have destroyed many promising relationships.

In the wonderful world of voice-overs there are many variables to consider before you can come up with a quote.

WHAT YOU NEED TO KNOW BEFORE ACCEPTING A JOB

1. Based on the initial description, are you the right person to do this? Is this a project you can handle, technically and artistically?

Don't just audition to gain experience. It's not a lottery. You do not increase your chances of getting hired by playing the numbers game. Mediocre demos decrease your chances and give you a bad rep.

Advice: Only run a race you believe you can win. Less is more. Choose quality over quantity.

2. Based on personal ethics, can you stand behind this project?

Your voice will be associated with a product, a service, or an organization. You'll never do your best work on something that goes against your deepest convictions and you will resent yourself for doing it.

Advice: Don't sell your soul to the devil. Choose integrity over money.

3. Who is the end-client? Where is this company located?

This relates to number two. Voice-over job posters don't always reveal whom they're working for. Wouldn't you want to know that you're about to be hired by the Church of Scientology or a company that's responsible for one of the biggest environmental disasters in history?

Secondly: Don't quote an American rate to a European company.

Advice: Do your homework before you say yes to a moral mess. Knowing the size and location of a company will help you determine your bid. Do not sell yourself short.

If you're based in the U.S. and you are bidding on a European project, the least you can do is change the dollar sign to Euros when you name your price. Then factor in the cost of money transfer.

4. How did they hear about you?

You can't change what you cannot measure. If you don't know how the client found you, you have no clue which part of your marketing strategy is working and which part needs more work.

Advice: If you don't know already, always ask the client how they found you. If a colleague referred you, send a thank you note. If very few leads come from your website, it's time to rethink, rewrite, and redesign.

Perhaps you need to fire an agent or lose that membership to a voice casting site that doesn't bring you any work. If one of your pipelines proves particularly successful, how can you make it even better?

5. For which medium and market will the audio be used and for how long?

Some clients will happily negotiate a local radio rate for a global multi-media campaign and tell you they're paying for a full buyout (a one-time payment that lets them use the audio for however long and for whatever purposes they would like). I'm not going to blame them.

If you want to look like an amateur, go for it and leave a lot of money on the table. But don't complain to me afterwards when you find out that you've been had.

Advice: A different medium, market, and length of use all come with different price tags. Unless and until you get those specifics, any quote is nothing more than blind bidding.

6. Does the client expect you to deliver unedited or fully edited, ready-to-use audio? Do you need to separate the audio and send each file individually?

Depending on your experience, you can easily spend a number of hours editing sixty minutes of audio. Are you getting paid for that time? Some commentators think voice-overs have lost this battle by automatically including audio editing in their rate.

I still believe we deserve to be compensated for this special skill and time-consuming process. Unless you're using a DAW (Digital Audio Workstation) with batch processing or a program such as Word2Wav, file separation and naming only adds to the aggravation.

Advice: Iron out the details before you name your price and get to work.

If you plan to outsource prooflistening, editing, and mastering, factor in how much that's going to cost you and build that into your rate. If it's included, make sure the client is aware that they're paying for those services. I list them on every invoice I send out. That's how I reinforce the added value I provide.

7. What does the client need you to sound like?

Without a clear map it's almost impossible to get to your destination. You know that and I know that, but so many clients appear to be clueless. It's about time they recognize that very basic descriptions like "English, male or female" are unhelpful to say the least.

Advice: Ask what the client wants to hear and be sure to get specifics.

A few examples:

– Language and Accent: Australian, South-African, or British English? What kind of UK accent? RP, Cockney? Liverpool? Glasgow? Do they want American English? Mid-Western? Southern? New York?

– Style: Announcer, drill sergeant, movie trailer man, best friend, businesslike, girl next door, drama queen, etcetera

– Tone: Serious, sarcastic, soft-spoken, comedic, insecure, confident, sophisticated, old and wise

– Tempo: Are you expected to read to time code, does the client want a relaxed or an energetic read?

– Character: Does the client already have a certain sound in mind e.g. George Clooney, Jeff Bridges, Morgan Freeman, Julia Roberts, Betty White.

– Syncing: Do you need to match the sound and tempo of the original narrator (if you're creating a new language version of an existing video)? If so, ask for a link to the original.

8. What's the deadline for the project and how long will it take you to complete it?

Take a close look at the entire script and your schedule (not just the audition script) and ask yourself: Is this time frame realistic? How much time do I minimally need to get the job done?

How many hours will you spend recording and editing that 350-page audio book and is $500 really worth it?

Some clients tend to want the audio yesterday and pay you many months later.

Remember: Fast delivery, High Quality, and a Cheap Rate do not go hand-in-hand. Getting two out of three often means having to compromise on the third element of this equation.

Advice: Please do not get pressured into rushing a job at the expense of quality.

One of the privileges of being an independent contractor is that you set your own standards and hours. In case the client asks for an ETA, build in an extra day or two. That way you look good when you deliver the goods ahead of schedule.

9. How much, in what way, and when do you get paid?

Don't you love it when a client says: "Budget to be defined?"

They're probably testing the waters to see how low people will go in a desperate attempt to break into voice-overs.

Amateurs plug in numbers. Professionals know what they're worth.

In business I have learned that trust must be earned. Don't negotiate the terms of payment after the client has received the audio. In the worst-case scenario you might not even get paid (and don't think it won't happen to you)! More on this in the "Money Matters" part of this book.

Realize that services like PayPal or international bank wires come with a fee. It's up to you whether you want to absorb that fee yourself or build it into your rate.

Advice: Determine upfront how you want to get paid: per word, per hour, per finished hour, or per project. Make it as easy as possible for clients to pay you by offering several payment options.

Ask first-time clients to pay upfront. Consider offering discounts for fast payment and to returning customers.

Use the power of PR: Positive Reinforcement!

Think about a fee for late payments. Business is a game of carrots and sticks!

WHAT YOU NEED TO KNOW ONCE YOU'VE ACCEPTED THE JOB

In the following, I will assume that you're recording in your home studio without SourceConnect, ipDTL or an ISDN connection.

1. Is the script you received the final and officially approved copy?

Just like people, some scripts are a work in progress. Certain clients believe it's perfectly okay to present you with a new and improved version after you've recorded the original. What's more, they will ask you to record it at no charge.

Advice: Let the client know that if that's the case, they will be billed for a new session. Otherwise you'll end up recording versions 1.1, 1.2, and 1.3 for free, thereby creating an expectation for the next time this client wants to work with you.

Sometimes a re-recording is necessary because of something you did (or failed to do). In that case, the client shouldn't have to pay for your mistakes.

2. Pronunciation: Ask the client to provide a pronunciation guide.

If you're reading a script in e.g. Spanish or Danish with an American brand name, does the client want you to pronounce it the Spanish or the Danish way, or the American way? Don't guess. Always ask!

3. In which audio format does the client want you to record (e.g. MP3, WAV, AIFF) and what's the preferred bit depth & sample rate (e.g. 16 bits, 41,000 Hz).

Advice: High-quality recordings can be converted into recordings of lesser quality. It does not work the other way around.

4. Does the client want processed or unprocessed audio?

If the client is okay with a bit of added compression or equalization, make sure you save a copy of the original, unprocessed audio. If they don't like what they hear, you can always send them the unsweetened version.

Advice: Most voice-over clients prefer unprocessed audio. Always add effects afterwards on a separate track.

5. Does the client want to listen in and/or direct the session?

It's often very helpful to get some feedback during the recording because you'll be able to get a clear sense of what the client wants to hear. There are different ways to set up a simple phone patch.

6. Do you need to sign any forms before you start working?

Think of a Non Disclosure Agreement, Policies & Procedures, tax forms and all that boring small print you really don't feel like reading. Do it anyway!

7. Do you want the client to sign any forms?

If you have a working agreement or a formal contract, this is the time to send it over. As long as your terms and conditions are reasonable (and legally sound), your client should have no problem signing it. If you detect resistance, something might be going on and you need to address it.

8. How does the client wish to receive the audio file(s)?

These days there are many options. To name a few: You can use a digital online file delivery service such as hightail.com or the Dutch company wetransfer.com. You can share your files using drop-box.com, or you can use an FTP host to upload your files.

Advice: Most services will send you an automated confirmation, letting you know that your file has been downloaded. If that's not the case, always ask your client to confirm receipt. That way you have proof that your goods were delivered and received.

9. Ask your client: Is there anything else you need me to know about this project that we haven't covered yet?

Before I end this chapter, I'd like you to promise me one thing:

No more blind bidding, okay?

Be a pro and come up with an informed quote!

Do we have a deal?

[35]

The Four Keys to Winning Clients Over

Do you sometimes wonder why certain clients hire you and others don't? I think about that a lot.

Rather than making assumptions, I often ask them why they picked me over a colleague. That's useful information to have, because it helps me fine-tune the way I run my freelance business and how I position myself in the marketplace.

So, what are clients really looking for?

Even though you and I are likely to have very different clients with very different needs, there are three factors that always play a role in every purchase decision. You might be selling a service or a product. It doesn't matter. All buyers are influenced by the same three things:

Price, **Benefits**, and **Perceptions**

The price is what the customer pays in exchange for benefits received. It's something your client has to give up in order to get something from you. Ideally, those benefits should outweigh or at least equal the cost.

Benefits are the positive effects derived from using your solution or service. It's the pleasure people experience after getting rid of their inner emptiness, frustration, or pain.

Smart sales people sell benefits. Stupid sales people slash prices. Any idiot can close a sale by cutting the price (and go broke as a result). It takes brains to sell benefits.

Perceptions are the result of how people evaluate the benefits and price, the (initial) impression they get from your business, as well as the total experience of using your product or service.

In the end, perceptions matter most. Allow me to demonstrate.

EVALUATING VALUE

Let's assume you've studied the market and you decide to charge $250 per hour for your services. Is that too much or not enough? Does it even matter what you think?

Client A will never hire you because she thinks you're too cheap and cheap equals crap. Client B will hire someone else because she thinks you're overpriced. Client C will happily hire you because she believes your price is just right.

Your fee is just a number in a certain context. It is always evaluated in relation to something else. That "something else" is a matter of interpretation or perception.

People do things for their reasons. Not for yours. Get this:

An anonymous donor paid $3.5 million at a charity auction to have lunch with Warren Buffet, one of the richest men in the world. Is that too much for a few hours of conversation and a meal?

Hedge fund manager Ted Weschler spent about $5.3 million to win both the 2010 and 2011 auctions. To him, it was money well spent.

Buffet ended up hiring him to manage an investment portfolio.

Perceptions are personal value judgments and therefore they are highly subjective. This begs the question:

Can perceptions be influenced? Can we manipulate a client into buying from us?

Even though I believe that lasting change comes from within and cannot be forced upon someone, it is a fact that most people are quite impressionable. Otherwise, they wouldn't be as open to social proof, and all advertising would be totally irrelevant.

Years of being a solopreneur have taught me that there are things you can do to get an interested client in your corner, as long as you play your cards right. Here's what I have learned.

1. First impressions are crucial

We all know that it is unfair to judge a book by its cover. However, psychologists will tell you that it takes us only a few seconds to form an opinion of someone or something. That's why companies spend billions on fancy packaging and people spend millions on make-up, clothing, and cosmetic surgery.

If you can't pique a consumer's interest or instill a level of trust right from the start, he or she will move on to whatever catches the eye next. So, ask yourself:

What is the very first thing new customers see or experience when they stumble upon my product or service? Is it the landing page of my website? Is it a cover of a book or a brochure? Is it... me?

This first impression is the all-important hook. It sets the tone and tells prospective clients enough about your level of professionalism and style, or lack thereof. If anything, this is where you should spend most of your marketing money. To do it right...

2. Your message needs to be clear, convincing, congruent, and consistent

If you want to play the part, you have to dress the part and embody the part. That might seem obvious, yet, so many business owners undermine their own credibility by sending out conflicting signals. A few examples:

– A translation and proofreading service emailed me: *"Your welcome to visit our website."* When I pointed this out to them, they blamed this slip of the pen on the intern.

If you don't even proofread your own material, why would my legal translation be safe in your hands?

– The sign in the front yard said: *"Quality lawn care at a price anyone can afford."* Meanwhile, weeds were growing everywhere and most trees needed pruning.

– The owner of the health food store looked like she was terminally ill. She must be friends with that overweight director of the local fitness center.

See what I mean?

Actions speak louder than words. Remember the four Cs when you craft you core message. You have to be Clear, Convincing, Congruent, and Consistent.

Some things are more subtle:

– You profess to be a pro with years of experience. Then why on earth did you use a free service such as Weebly or Wix to build your website? You don't even have your own domain or a dedicated email address. Is business that bad? Can't you spare a few hundred bucks and hire a professional to take care of your online presence? What image are you projecting here?

3. You have to be responsive

What clients hate more than anything is to be ignored.

It gives them the feeling that their business isn't important to you, and you know what? I think they're right. Time happens to be something we all have the same amount of. How we choose to spend that time, gives us an inside look into someone's priorities and planning skills.

I've walked out of a fancy restaurant because the wait staff couldn't be bothered to serve my table in a timely way. I don't care if you're known for the best food in town. If your service sucks, you're screwed.

I read on your website's Contact page that you'll get back to me within 24 hours. I sent you a message three days ago and I have yet to hear from you. What other promises aren't you going to keep? My project has a strict deadline. If you can't meet your own, how can I be sure you'll meet mine?

Being responsive also means: giving your client concise progress reports. It's a way to reassure them that they're in good hands. If you're right on track, let your client know. If you're experiencing an unexpected delay, you have to let your client know. Don't wait until they send you an email wondering why they haven't heard from you in days.

Communication is key, as long as you're to the point. Anticipate and answer client's questions. Be an open book. Stay in touch. Make it a breeze to do business with you. You want your clients to smile when they think of you. That will happen when you...

4. Go out of your way to be helpful

Not all inquiries lead to a sale. Sometimes what you have to offer is not what a client is looking for.

In my case they might want to hire a female voice actor or someone with an older sound or a different accent.

Does that mean that all my efforts were wasted?

Absolutely not.

If you cut off contact because you can't make an immediate sale, you're thinking about yourself and you're thinking short term.

Everything is marketing.

Any contact with a client, no matter how brief, is a golden opportunity to start building a relationship. A healthy relationship is a two-way street and takes time to evolve. It's about giving and receiving.

So, how do you give to a client who doesn't need your services?

It's simple: Be a resource.

If you're not right for the job, recommend a few colleagues who are. I'm sure they won't mind.

Show your expertise. Build some goodwill. You're sowing seeds, and who knows when they might bloom? There are always new projects in the pipeline that might be a better fit for you.

Here's the thing about giving, though.

Don't just do it for future rewards.

That's not a gift. That's a bribe.

Do it because it's a decent thing to do.

It's all a matter of perception.

[36]

The Customer is Always Right

Do you actually believe that?

I'm not buying it. Not even for a second.

Customers will do anything to get a discount, a freebie, or something extra. At the end of the season they'll return clothes that clearly have been worn, and ask for their money back. They will order a steak medium rare and want a comp because they say it was undercooked. They don't follow instructions, break the appliance, and blame it on the manufacturer. What's more, they'll tell everybody on Facebook and Twitter about it.

Are those customers right? I don't think so.

Customers are calculating, conniving, and self-centered.

Years ago, I worked as a customer service trainer in a call center of a major U.S. bank. I basically had to teach my students how to deal with constant verbal abuse and terroristic threats.

Angry drunks would call to find out why their account had been blocked. Enraged customers wanted to know why they should pay a hefty overdraft fee after spending money they did not have.

These people were beyond rude, and often drove the reps on the other end of the line to tears.

I don't believe these abusive callers were a special breed. They were regular folks like you and me. Perhaps a bit more frustrated. But if you don't think ordinary people are capable of rude behavior, be one of the last people to leave a movie theater and see what a mess they leave behind. After thousands of years of evolution, our civilization has come a long way, hasn't it?

MONEY AND MOUTH

Customers are often wrong because they say one thing and do another. In the late seventies, consumers told market researchers that they didn't need a small cassette player to listen to while walking around. Sony ignored them and the Walkman became a big success. These days, consumers will tell you they're willing to pay extra for environmentally friendly products, but in economic terms it's still a niche market.

Consumers can be wrong because they lack knowledge, imagination, or vision. Steve Jobs told Business Week:

> *"A lot of times, people don't know what they want until you show it to them."*

But there are other reasons why customers aren't always right. It boils down to this: not all of them can be trusted. It's not because they're evil people. Sometimes they cannot foresee what's going to happen.

A while back I negotiated a deal with a corporate e-Learning provider. In exchange for a regular flow of projects, I lowered my rate just a bit.

The client was extremely satisfied with my work, yet, after a while he dropped off the radar. Mind you, my contact at that corporation was a very nice, communicative, and polite man.

Many months and a few emails later, he told me he was no longer responsible for those projects. They guy who had taken his place had his own list of preferred voices, and apparently, I wasn't on it.

From then on, I decided to only offer discounts once a longer-term business relationship had been firmly established. Trust must be earned.

WHO'S IN CHARGE?

Sometimes whom you believe to be the client, turns out not to be the decision maker. A studio once hired me to voice a video to promote a U.S. resort town. If you're familiar with my voice, you know I don't exactly sound like your typical American. The producer told me that my more European accent would give the campaign a "touch of class."

When the Tourism Board of the resort town watched the finished product, they were not happy. They wanted a narrator with a more local sound. Because the producer couldn't use my voice, he proposed to pay me half of what we had agreed on.

Should I have walked away with fifty percent, or do you think the producer owed me the full amount?

UNREASONABLE REQUEST

Customers are also wrong when they're unreasonable. I remember winning an audition to narrate a German script that was taken from an English production. The client wanted me to match the UK narrator precisely, but there was one thing he forgot to mention.

The German translation had about 35% more text. I was stuck with a two-minute script that had to fit into a ninety-second video. I warned the producer about the problem, but he said that as a professional, I should be able to pull it off. After a couple of attempts, I went for it and managed to fit every word in by editing every breath out.

The result sounded unnatural and way too fast. In the producer's mind, the script was not the problem. It was me.

I spent an afternoon recording three more versions of the same text, and I just wasn't able to comfortably fit every word in. In the evening I received an email from the client: "I don't think this is working out. Thank you for your time."

No cure. No pay.

That day I learned another valuable lesson: Never take on a job if you can't meet the needs and expectations of the client.

IS THE CLIENT KING?

If you have been in business for a while, I'm sure you've run into customers with unrealistic expectations. They call you at the last moment and expect the job to be done yesterday at a rock bottom rate which they won't pay until you send them five reminders and threaten them with Small Claims Court.

Some will send a revised script after you've recorded the first and approved version, and expect you to record the new text for free. Of course they want you to take care of the editing and not pay a penny extra. After all, it's great for your portfolio and you're lucky to be selected. In my book, recording a revised script is a new job and I charge my clients accordingly.

No matter how hard you try, it's impossible to make every customer happy. That's not always the customer's fault. Sometimes you have a great day and sometimes you're unable to give 100%.

Feedback will come your way, and it's not all going to be positive. But getting less than stellar feedback doesn't mean you're a failure. It's an opportunity to better yourself.

After dealing with customers for decades, this is what I discovered:

You can never change your clients, but you should do your very best to manage their expectations.

What do I mean by that?

CREATING BOUNDARIES

Only a few years ago, I could go into a studio and be greeted by a producer, someone from the ad agency, the client, the audio engineer, and a director. The recording sessions that followed were often a team effort.

These days, I'm a one-man, home studio band. This saves my clients a ton of money, but I let them know in advance that I don't have all the technical bells and whistles of a million dollar recording facility.

I also let them know that it's up to them to give me clear instructions, because there's no director to guide me. I encourage them to listen in via Skype or a phone line and make sure they get the read they need, but nine out of ten times they leave it up to me.

Some of my clients will get back to me and ask for a faster or slower read. I'm willing to do a retake or two if that's necessary, but that's it. If I give in and keep on fine-tuning indefinitely, I've just trained the client to expect that of me. Yes, I'm willing to go the extra mile, but I'm not running a marathon.

They should also know that I'm not always available. I have other clients. That means I can't just stop whatever I'm doing just because their planning is all messed up and they need me NOW. I take breaks. I need vacation. I have a life.

BE CLEAR TO YOUR CLIENT

I've also learned my lesson when it comes to pronunciation. I refuse to read the client's mind as to how I should pronounce a certain foreign word or the name of a company or a family name.

Last week I had a Dutch script with the name of two global companies that could be pronounced in a Dutch or in an English way.

A client can't expect me to decide how these companies would like to be known publicly. They have to clue me in.

The biggest bone of contention used to be my fee.

In the past, I spent too much time dealing with customers who claimed "they couldn't afford me." By the way, that's a statement that can never be verified.

These days, I manage my clients' expectations by publishing my rates on my website. It's a way to prequalify my customers, and I rarely get an offer to work for a ridiculously low rate anymore.

One last thing.

The customer isn't always right, but you might not always be right for the customer.

You can do your very best to educate your clients, but some people don't read emails, don't know the business, can't follow instructions, or continue to have unreasonable expectations (this goes both ways).

Take my advice:

Let them go before they let you go.

Believe me: Both parties will be much better off in the end.

Am I right?

[37]

Communicating with Domestic and Foreign Clients

Thanks to the internet, any business is now a global business.

Getting through to non-native English speakers can be a serious challenge. Just because your client knows a few English words, doesn't mean he or she understands everything you're saying. Here's an example.

"I have a good one," I said to my friend from France.

"Why do gun-carrying Americans usually wear short-sleeved shirts?"

"No idea," he answered. "You tell me."

"Because they believe in the right to bear arms."

Silence...

"Sorry, but I don't get it," said Philippe. "Explain."

"Well," I said, "I can try, but I don't think it would make the Second Amendment any funnier."

"Oh, was it supposed to be funny?"

"Well, Philippe, some people think that puns are bad by definition."

"What's a pun?" Philippe wanted to know.

Have you ever had a conversation like that? All along you thought that you and your foreign friend were on the same page, but now you're not even sure you're reading the same book. How is that possible? Both of you speak English, don't you?

ENGLISH RULES

I'll be honest with you. Native English speakers are spoiled rotten. Practically the whole planet has adopted your language as the lingua franca of business, and so you expect everyone to be on your page... linguistically and often even culturally.

Not so fast, my Anglophone friends! There is a whole world out there of people who don't get it that you don't get it when they don't get it.

Got it?

Even though your mother tongue blasts out of every radio and television station 24/7, you shouldn't automatically assume that we understand everything you say or write. You really have no idea how complicated Shakespeare's language can be.

Take a simple word like "call." Pick up Webster's dictionary and you'll find fifteen definitions for the noun alone. That's asking for trouble. Here are two actual mistranslations from movie and TV subtitles:

A priest explains: "That's when I got my call from G-d."

The subtitle reads: "That's when G-d telephoned me."

A general has to decide whether or not to bomb an urban target, and he says: "It's a tough call."

The subtitle reads: "It's hard to make a phone call."

As someone who has been breathing in the English language from birth, it is almost impossible for you to imagine what life is like with English as your second or third language. That only changes once the tables are turned and you start learning another language yourself.

Imagine being in a crowded Parisian bakery to get some fresh bread. Suddenly, you are overcome by that embarrassing surge of helplessness, because your French vocabulary is still limited to that of a bed-wetting toddler. All the locals are staring at you as you utter these infamous words, while pointing at a warm baguette:

"Pain pour moi madame. Merci."

Painful, indeed.

Thank goodness the woman behind the counter was merciful.

GETTING DOWN TO BUSINESS

Let's take a closer look at written communication, in particular, when it comes to dealing with non-English speakers.

Even though I live and work on the East Coast of the U.S., at least fifty percent of my clients are on other continents and for many, English is a second or third language. That means that I constantly have to bridge the linguistic and cultural divide as I respond to job offers, negotiate rates or simply share information about my voice-over services. Because English isn't my first language either, I may be more sensitive to translation issues.

This is what I have learned so far:

1. Beware of the power of The Written Word!

Isn't it true that, although we provide less information, printed words always seem to carry more weight? Even though communication experts tell us that we convey most of our meaning through inflection and body language, somehow, the written word seems more authoritative. Especially when coming form a trustworthy source, people are not inclined to doubt what they read.

When I published a completely fabricated story on a fake invention called "the Mic Warmer," most of my blog readers fell for it, in spite of the fact that the news broke on April Fools' Day. The next day I revealed and retracted the hoax, and yet, the serious comments kept coming in. I still get emails from folks who want to know when the Mic Warmer will be on the market and how much it's going to cost.

People believe what they want to believe and they are inclined to seek confirmation of those beliefs without verifying sources. We even have a special term for it. It's called confirmatory bias.

Who has time to fact-check those Tweets coming from ordinary people turned reporters? The need for speedy news flashes has taken precedence over the need for accurate information. It turns out, we can't even trust news professionals anymore.

Mike Wise,*** a sports columnist at The Washington Post, was suspended after purposely spreading false information on Twitter to prove that people would believe pretty much any tweet. Guess what? He was right. Other news outlets picked up his fabricated scoop and ran with it, no questions asked.

Here's one more reason why you should weigh the written word more carefully, not only as a reader.

The private is becoming increasingly more public.

While spoken words disintegrate as soon as they are uttered, your online messages can be kept for years. That hasty, silly comment you left after you drank two glasses of wine, still pops up when people Google your name, even after three years.

Reputation management is booming because...

2. Readers are inclined to take the written word more literally.

People can't see that twinkle in your eyes or hear the subtle sarcasm in your voice when they're reading your email or text message. That's why emoticons were invented. But is it professional to use a smiley face when you're writing to that senior German project manager? Personally, I feel that emoticons should be sent back to where they came from: to the teenage chat rooms. LOL.

The fact that the written word is taken literally, is also a reason why humor doesn't work well. First of all, what seems hysterical to one person could be offensive to another. Secondly, as my conversation with Philippe illustrates, not everyone will be equally thrilled when you throw in a pun or two. Understanding the subtleties of wordplay requires a greater command of a language, as well as a more in-depth knowledge of a culture.

My advice: Be personable but keep things businesslike. And please consider this...

3. Manners Matter.

I can't get over the fact that some folks can be downright rude in their writing. Call me old-fashioned, but I'm inclined to start a movement to bring the words "please" and "thank you" back into everyday language.

How much does it cost to be polite? How hard is it to treat people with a little respect? And what about all the name-calling?

Just because you are used to dealing with people on a first-name basis, doesn't mean that the rest of the world has followed suit. In fact, you'll find that – compared to the United States – most countries are far more formal, and even more so in a business context.

If you're not sure about the correct etiquette, err on the side of caution. As a rule of thumb, I always let the other party take the lead.

If they wish to be addressed by their first name, they will let you know.

I also think it is a common courtesy to proof your messages before you send them. Cheq your grammer and speling. I know its nice to here from me, but your not looking very proffesional right now. Their you have it!

Now, remember...

4. Keep your focus on the client.

Do yourself a favor and look at one of your most recent business emails. How many times did you count the word "I" in that message? What does that tell you? What could you have done differently to make that message less about you and more about your customer?

I once started a "Less Self Campaign" on Twitter in response to the ME, ME, ME mentality that has gone viral. I can understand that people are trying to market themselves using social ME-dia. But could you please stop quoting from that book called 'my career' all the time?

This is what I'd like to ask those Me, Me, Me-people:

Why do you feel the need to make yourself the center of the universe? Did your parents not love you enough when you were young? Does your partner take you for granted? Are your friends unappreciative? Do you think that this is what branding is all about?

Don't you realize that what others say about you is taken far more seriously than what you'll ever have to say about yourself? Your customers are your best credentials.

In business it's never about you. The needs of your client take center stage, whether they live next door or abroad. I also hope you'll embrace the following principle:

5. KISS your clients.

So much to do. So little time.

I just received an email slash novel from a colleague that's listing all her accomplishments, followed by an endless list of clients, projects, and other claims to fame.

Give me a break!

I think that there's much to be said for keeping things short and simple. Perhaps I should leave it at that. But you know me...

Especially when writing to a non-native English speaker, it's important to use plain English without dumbing things down to Kindergarten level.

Simple doesn't mean simplistic. Avoid long sentences, colloquialisms, slang, jargon, and expressions that aren't exactly universal.

The first time someone said he would give me a rain check, I had no idea what he was talking about and it really rubbed me the wrong way. I thought that person was off his rocker.

Also avoid references to politics, songs, TV shows, advertising campaigns, or other phenomena that might be part of your culture, but unknown abroad.

Even though a show like Seinfeld is in syndication all over the world, the impact it has in the context of another country is very different. Not that there's anything wrong with that.

Just realize that things like "double-dipping," the "soup Nazi," or other famous phrases and characters might not have the same effect they have on average Americans. Think about it. How much do you know about Italian sitcoms?

And finally...

6. Relax a little.

One of the biggest adjustments a European needs to make when coming to the States is the fact that work never seems to stop.

Even G-d rested on the Seventh Day, but the American people keep on going. I even receive business emails on national holidays and my U.S. contacts expect me to answer them promptly.

In the Netherlands (my birthplace) we have things called weekends where people actually relax and spend downtime with friends and family.

Don't be surprised if you're not getting an immediate response to that urgent email you sent to a European client on Friday night. You're not being ignored. These crazy Europeans are just unwinding and practicing preventive health care. They will get back to you on Monday. I promise.

If they happen to be on vacation, they might get back to you in three weeks. Did you honestly think that they'd be checking their work email every day? Are you nuts?! Work is work. Time off is time off.

To Americans, vacation is a luxury. To Europeans, it is a necessity.

MINDFULNESS

What I'm really saying is this: Please become a mindful (international) communicator. This doesn't start with acquiring knowledge. If all we needed to change our lives was information, no one would still be smoking or send text messages while driving. Information does not transform people. We have to become mindful first.

Mindfulness is an attitude. It's about being perceptive and sensitive. It's about the willingness and ability to see the world through someone else's eyes. The easiest way to do that is through immersion.

Go away on a shoestring budget! Visit foreign lands. Taste bizarre foods. Become dependent on the kindness of strangers because you don't speak the language.

Don't bribe the locals with dollars to treat you decently. Let's see how long that lasts when pickpockets steal your cash, credit cards, and passports.

Most importantly:

Participate. Don't just observe.

Believe me, on your return, your homeland will never seem the same.

BULLET PROOF

The other day I got an email from my French friend Philippe.

He wrote:

"Paul, I have a good one for you!

I looked up the right to bear arms.

This is what I found.

Your Constitution says it is okay to carry guns.

But it doesn't say that these guns have to be loaded.

Now, that's funny, no?"

"Oh, Philippe," I said, "You just gave me more ammunition to write a whole new chapter.

I guess I better roll up my sleeves!"

[38]

FU or the Power of PR

Dutch soccer star Johan Cruyff once said:

> *"Playing football is very simple, but playing simple football is the hardest thing there is."*

The same applies to running a successful freelance business. On the surface it seems simple, but in reality it can be very challenging. I've been a freelancer for most of my working life, and if there's anything I have learned, it is this:

If you want to do well, you have to master the basics of what it means to be an entrepreneur. One of those basics is that people have to be able to take you at your word. Unfortunately, some freelancers have become masters of hollow phrases and empty expressions.

How many times have you heard the phrase: "I'll get back to you," and said to yourself: "Yeah, right. That'll be the day!"

How many times have you ended a conversation with "We'll talk soon," and sooner became later, and later became:

"You seem familiar. Have we met before?"

One of the basics in business is to always get back to someone.

Be a man or woman of your word and make that follow-up call or write that email. Don't put it off till tomorrow because tomorrow never comes.

Here's what you do after you've spoken with a promising contact:

You use a powerful FU!

As soon as you put that phone down, type up a quick email. Begin by writing something nice followed by something specific.

Let's say you promised to email a prospect an estimate. Always put your promise in writing, and tell him or her when to expect your proposal.

Make it a habit to consistently beat that deadline. Don't allow a hot prospect to cool off or explore other options. Get that proposal in fast.

Be sure to provide your client with all your contact information. You'd be surprised how many business-related emails I receive that are simply signed by some "Jeff" or "Ginny."

My email signature has my full name, my website, how to connect with me on Facebook and Twitter, and three brand names of recent clients.

My goal is threefold:

- to show the client that I am responsive
- to make it easy for them to get back to me
- to reinforce my brand, Nethervoice

In all my years as a freelancer I've heard many clients complain about colleagues. Guess what's number one on their list of grievances? It's lack of responsiveness. Clients tell me:

"It takes ages for John to get back to me. What's going on? I get the feeling that he could care less about my business. Do you have someone else you could recommend?"

Think about it.

If I were to advertise myself as someone who can offer a quick turnaround on a project, and for whatever reason I take three days to respond to a simple question, what is the real message I am sending?

Here's a second blunder many freelancers make:

They only get back to someone when something's wrong.

Unpaid invoices. Unanswered emails. That's when most people feel the sudden urge to follow up. It's a bad habit because it will primarily associate you with problems and negativity.

POSITIVE INTERACTIONS

The secret to building a solid relationship is to make sure that your client, your agent, (and even your life partner) has as many positive interactions with you as possible. That's not rocket science, is it?

Learn from what the Mad Men of Madison Avenue have practiced for decades. The secret to any successful ad campaign rests on the extent to which the agency manages to manipulate you into associating negative feelings with a problem and positive feelings with a product.

Let me be clear about one thing: I am not suggesting that you trick those on whom you depend into liking you. I just want you to be mindful and treat others the way you'd like to be treated yourself.

Sometimes you need to follow up and address things that are no so pleasant. For instance, how do you handle a client who owes you money?

Here's how:

You don't!

Do yourself a huge favor and have your bookkeeper or office assistant handle that outstanding balance. Let your lawyer deal with that contract. Leave it to your agent to negotiate your rate (or to the Union, for that matter).

Stay out of the line of fire and focus on delivering the goods to the best of your ability. That's your job. You don't want to be seen as the bad guy or that nasty girl!

Do follow up to put the power of PR into practice. And by PR I mean:

Positive Reinforcement.

It works with kids. It also works with your partner. It certainly works in business.

Follow up...

- after that meeting
- after your call
- after they've received your proposal
- as soon as you're selected for the job
- when the job is done
- after receiving the check
- to thank your colleague for the referral
- after someone answered your question on an online forum
- to congratulate, encourage, admire, and inspire
- after reading a blog post or book that was really helpful

Here's a third blunder many colleagues make:

Becoming a follow-up freak.

Too much of a good thing is a bad thing.

Remember that it's all about purposeful positive reinforcement, but in moderation.

Just because I have shown an interest in your services at one point in time, doesn't mean that I want to be on your mailing list or that I want to befriend you on Facebook or follow your silly tweets on Twitter.

If I'm interested, I'll make the first move. You don't have permission to cyber-stalk me.

This relationship is not about you.

It is about me – someone you might do business with or have done business with.

Stop leaving those self-serving comments on my blog. I don't need to know what you had for breakfast or that you're a fan of Fox News. That's not a follow-up. That's being a pain in the tush. Don't you have work to do?

UNDERRATED

Used correctly, the follow-up can be one of the best instruments in your freelance toolkit. But if that's true, why don't more people use it?

I think that it's in part due to laziness and sometimes even carelessness. I also believe that it has to do with a culture that seems more intent on punishing unwanted behavior, rather than reinforcing positive behavior.

We tend to take action when things go wrong and we're not grateful for the things we take for granted. We want things for free. We get things for free.

Why follow up and say "Thank You" for something that didn't cost you anything?

If this is a trend we wish to turn around, you and I should lead the way.

Take a minute or two to follow up with that colleague who passed your name on to his client.

Let that company know how much you appreciate the fact that they paid you in full within ten days after you sent them an invoice.

Thank that audio engineer for making you sound better than ever.

Show someone some gratitude, instead of an attitude.

Follow up! Use the power of PR!

Does it always work in every situation?

I'm not sure.

Let me get back to you on that one!

[39]

What Voice Casting Sites Don't Want You to Know

Imagine an international marketplace where buyers meet suppliers. This business environment offers the broadest and most colorful selection of products from all over the globe.

A fast and furious bidding process determines which supplier will sell to which buyer at what price.

Can you guess the name of this marketplace? Could it be eBay? Voices.com? Freelancer.com, perhaps?

Let me tell you what's unique about this particular auction environment. It's actually a cooperative, owned by about 5,000 members who have united to organize their sales. Their aim is to achieve the best possible market position for its members at the lowest possible cost.

The auction I'm writing about offers a transparent market. A fair minimum price is set for each product, based on normalized averages. If that price isn't met, there's no sale.

Here are a few other clues. The items that are auctioned off are of some twenty thousand different varieties.

All of this takes place on the largest trading floor in the world – a conjoined complex of cavernous warehouses as large as 200 soccer fields. That's roughly the size of Monaco!

Inside, 22 million separate items are sold and distributed to buyers every weekday, mostly in Europe and North America.

The "Dutch auction method" is used to determine the sales price. This process uses an electronic clock. The hand of this clock starts at a high price and drops until a buyer stops the clock to bid and accept what he's bidding on. This clock was invented in the 1870's by a cauliflower grower from Holland.

As a voice-over pro who's fighting his own daily bidding wars, I'll tell you what I like about this type of auction:

– The element of collaboration. Although the members of the cooperative are competing against each other, they are working together. What a concept!

– Vigorous quality control based on the highest professional standards, is part and parcel of this business.

– Set minimum prices (based on weighted averages of goods or services in a particular region during a given time period).

– Products or services are sold to the highest bidder. Imagine that in the voice-over industry!

– Transparency. Everyone involved knows immediately what the winning bid was and who won. Only if the quality is not as told, the buyer has the right to complain. The products have to be paid directly.

Of course you know what I am leading up to, don't you? I am going to ask you about the marketplace you do business in: those online voice casting services, known to some as Pay-to-Plays.

Let's say you're paying a nice chunk of money for the privilege of auctioning off your vocal versatility on sites like Voices.com or voice123.com. You spot a project that seems to be a good fit. You record a free custom demo and you put in a bid. Then you wait and wait... and nothing happens. To quote Dr. Phil:

"How's that working for you?"

Could there possibly be a better system to put your voice-over services on the market? Let's go down my list again, and contrast and compare.

OWNERSHIP

1. As a member of the cooperative I described at the beginning of this chapter, you would be one of the co-owners of the business. You would elect representatives and a board that manages the daily affairs on your behalf. In other words: You directly influence how your business is run. The board answers to its members, and every year it must give those members a detailed account of the state of the cooperative.

Compare that to the marketplace where you auction off your services. You are a member of that marketplace, are you not? Let me ask you this: Do you have any say in how this business is run and by whom? And by "say" I don't mean filling out a survey or posting your praises on their website. There is a distinct difference between giving feedback, having influence, and having actual power.

Do you get to see the balance sheet, at least once a year? And if an executive is underperforming, can you vote him or her off?

Do you work together with your colleagues to maximize results, or is it every man and women for him- or herself?

2. Can just about anyone offer their services on this voice-over marketplace you belong to, or is there a screening process based on

professional standards? And once accepted, is there any type of quality control in place to ensure that clients won't be bombarded with third-tier talent?

3. What does your marketplace do to promote fair trade, if anything?

Are buyers and sellers educated about what rates are reasonable for different types of projects? Does your site set minimum prices that allow you to earn a living wage, or is everything left to a market that has no bottom, no ethics, and people who have no clue?

4. Here's a thought. What if our online voice-over marketplace would operate like a Sotheby's, where goods (or in this case services) would actually go to the highest bidder?

5. I saved the big one for last:

Does your online auction site ever notify you of the winning bid?

Let's say a client posts a project with a budget range of $100-$250. Wouldn't it be interesting to know how much or how little he ended up paying?

Don't you want to know if the job ultimately went to an undercutting underbidder or a habitual lowballer? Aren't you curious to find out how successful this site really is in securing fair and reasonable deals for its members? Or is that too much to ask?

Someone who regularly uses Pay-to-Plays to hire talent had this to say:

> "When a job is posted with a $100 – $250 range, over half the people who audition will offer to do it for $100. Another quarter will offer to do it for less."

Mmm, any idea why you're not having much luck, lately?

Of course the voice-over dot-coms could hit back and say:

"That's nonsense. Some people get paid even more than what the job was posted for."

My response would be: Prove it! And don't give me anecdotal evidence. I want numbers that can be independently verified.

Am I wrong, or do you have a right to learn how many posted projects materialized into something concrete, and how many disappeared into thin air? And wouldn't that information help you determine whether or not it would be worthwhile for you to join such a site?

Why aren't these facts available to the members who are paying for these services? What is it that these sites don't want you to know? What are they hiding and why?

GOING DUTCH

My favorite auction is an open book.

The FloraHolland flower auction I was talking about earlier, is the international market leader in floricultural sales. Their auction building in Aalsmeer is the second largest building in the world.

With six locations situated close to the most important production areas in the Netherlands, 9 thousand growers sell just over one-third of all flowers sold in the world, which adds up to about 2 billion Euros each year.

There are 125 thousand auction transactions every day. In other words, 12 billion cut flowers and over half a million plants a year. Business is blooming for this cooperative.

I wonder... is there anything we could possibly learn from this model?

Isn't it about time we add a touch of Dutch to the auctions we take part in?

The idea is definitely growing on me!

[40]

Why Pay-to-Plays Will Implode

It all started with a short article on his company blog entitled:

"A Quick Guide To Selecting The Right Voice Talent"***

The author, Chris Johnson, is co-Founder of Simplifilm, a company specializing in "Hollywood-style Explanation videos." They'll have to make a video to explain what that means, but Simplifilm says it uses animation and storytelling to demo software applications.

Before he became a filmmaker, Chris was Finance Director at Robert Owens for Ohio Attorney General 2008, and he worked as a loan specialist at First Ohio Home Finance. Thanks to his financial background, Chris seems to know the value of a voice-over, and he's not basing it on anecdotal evidence.

This is how he starts his blog:

> "Did you know that the right voice can make a 35% difference in conversion rate? We replaced a voice track in a video – and made no other changes, and the conversion rate went from 2.5% to 3.8% on cold traffic. (Cold traffic is people that are mostly strangers that are coming in via search engines and social media)."

I'm not sure how "2.5% to 3.8% on cold traffic" leads to a "35% percent difference," but Johnson is definitely on to something.

This is not the first time a video company noticed a correlation between the choice of voice and website conversion.

Conversion rate is often defined as the percentage of website visitors taking a desired action. It refers to the number of shoppers turning into buyers. Depending on the size of a company, even a small increase in conversion could mean a significant rise in profits.

San Diego-based Fireclick monitors conversion rates. If you want to get a better idea of industry averages, their Fireclick index*** will provide some insight.

For software, it averages about 2% per year, with a cart abandonment rate of 75%. That means that an overwhelming majority of people shopping for software online, never become buyers!

Could selecting the right voice really change that?

In 2009, Ginger software asked video optimization firm EyeView to develop an introductory video for their homepage to increase the number of visitors that would actually download their software.

EyeView ran a test: 50% of the global audience saw the video with a British voice-over, and 50% saw it with an American voice. Globally, the British voice-over was 4% more effective. For U.S. audiences, the conversion rate for the British accent was 5.5% higher than the American one.

EyeView:

> "The Brits didn't have it all their own way. In India, the American accent was 12% more effective at converting visitors. But the most surprising statistic of all came when we looked at the comparative performance of the two accents in the UK.

For audiences watching the video in the UK, the voice-over with the American accent was 8% more effective at making visitors download Ginger's software than the British accent, representing a significant swing away from the global trend."

Simplifilm's Chris Johnson confirms:

"The right voice is key to converting video watchers into new customers. When you get the right voice, it breathes life into your video productions, and you should take the time it takes to select and respect your voice talent."

Please remember that, next time you're tempted to lowball yet another voice-over project!

With voice talent having such a tremendous impact on conversion, how much does Simplifilm pay their voice of choice per production? Johnson:

"Generally, productions are around a couple hundred dollars. We're not going to lord over them or dangle money like some jerk, we want to do business, be respectful and move on."

FINDING THE PERFECT PIPES

Now, wouldn't it be interesting to know where Chris finds the right voices? According to his blog, two talents work for him on a regular basis and he tells his readers:

"If – for some reason – you need to find someone outside of your network (...) you can start with Voice123.com."

Voice Coach and talent Mark Avery*** read the blog and responded as follows:

"Unfortunately, many producers and end users of voice talent have gone to the "discount superstore" mentality of hiring voices for their projects, and the results often show themselves in rather low conversion rates."

Of course I had to put my two cents in. I wrote:

> "Chris, most online voice casting services will accept anyone with a credit card, talent not required. It's not unusual for voice seekers to receive over 100 auditions for a simple project. Imagine how long it would take you to listen to all these mediocre submissions..."

These turned out to be prophetic words.

That same week, Chris joined the Voice Over Professionals group on LinkedIn, and this is how he introduced himself:

> "Howdy, guys, I'm new to the group. I'm a production company doing software stories. We're looking for a stable of 4-6 males and 4-6 females for future work."

You can imagine what happened next. I'll let Chris tell the story:

> "So, when I asked for submissions here – and other places – they started trickling in. Then the floodgates opened.
>
> Last count was 400+ and I have seen no slowdown... both here, from another couple of sources. I'm surprised because I (hopefully) didn't represent myself as being too "giant." I caused 400+ auditions for what will amount to $5,000 or so in fees annually – at most.
>
> Now, how do I read through 'em all? I put everyone in a spreadsheet, but what's next? How do I sort people out? I need say 8 voices. If I take 5 minutes x 500 voices, that's 2500 minutes or 42 hours JUST listening to voices. I'm not doing that."

At this point I started to jump for joy, thanking Simplifilm's founder for the perfect example. This is exactly why most Pay-to-Plays will eventually implode. Do you get my drift?

Some of my clients have worked with voice casting sites for a while, and they're starting to realize how expensive "going cheap" can be. Think about it for a moment or two.

How long does it take to find a quality needle in a huge haystack made of scrap metal?

Let's look at the numbers.

Of course it's unusual to get 500 auditions for one job, so why not assume that Chris Johnson has to weed through (only!) 100 demos. If he spends 5 minutes on each talent (as he just wrote), this will still take him eight and a half hours!

Imagine being in Chris's shoes. Should he hire someone to do the dirty work for him and weed through hours and hours of audio? That person needs to be paid too.

If Chris is lucky, his hired help might find the perfect voice among the first twenty contenders. However, my clients tell me that the overall level of entries is usually way below the mark. They're forced to listen to a deluge of demos before they finally spot the right voice at the right price.

What an expensive way to find cheap talent!

Critics might say that I am exaggerating the situation just to make a point. Voice seekers don't listen to that many demos. Or do they?

In their Client Experience Report Winter 2011,*** the online voice casting service Voices.com states:

> "(...) it often surprises talent that the majority of clients review all their auditions. I say majority as that includes those who reviewed 'all of the auditions' (45%) plus those who reviewed '50-100 auditions' (8%)."

Fortunately, there is an easy solution.

Some of my clients find it much more cost-effective and less time-consuming to hand their project to an agent and let him or her select four or five voices that can all deliver the goods. Clients might end up paying union rates and agent fees, but in the end they're saving time, trouble, and money.

Bye-bye Pay-to-Play, and thanks for the memories!

THE BABBLE BUBBLE

Online casting services have grown exponentially in the past five years. Fast growing companies often fall victim to their own success. Quality and customer service are compromised and sacrificed in favor of rapid expansion as they're chasing after the big bucks.

It is no secret that more and more (pseudo) voice actors are joining Pay-to-Plays. That means that more dogs are fighting over the same bare bones. With that, the chances of landing a decent job at a decent rate decline rapidly.

Here's my prediction.

At some point in the near future, there is no point in joining such a service anymore. It's not worth it.

Saturation leads to annihilation. Bubbles burst.

Cheaply made balloons will pop first.

What's left is just hot air.

Try fitting that into a 3-minute video demo!

Chris Johnson, here's a word to the wise:

If you need new talent, call a casting agent.

Don't ask for any names of agencies, though.

You might get a list of... about 500!

[41]

Leaving Voices.com

Breaking up is never easy. That's what the song says.

In my case, it was a long time in the making and I didn't shed a single tear.

Yes, she tried to win me back, but I was determined. Our relationship had run its course. It was time for me to move on.

Let me explain.

HIGH HOPES

2009 was the year I joined Voices.com. I was naive. I was excited. I was determined to make it as a voice-over. "Voices" seemed to be the perfect place to hang out my shingle and conquer the world.

Today (in 2014), I have a five-star rating, well over 5400 listens (more than any other Dutch talent), and I have landed a total of... (are you ready?) TEN jobs, earning me a whopping $2,740.89. G-d only knows how many auditions I have had to submit before being selected.

This can only mean one of two things. Either, I stink at playing the Pay-to-Play game, or I'm a talentless, misguided soul who should be doing something useful with his life.

To take up the last point, clients like Harley-Davidson Sharp, Coca-Cola, Siemens and Philips must think I bring something to the table. Otherwise they wouldn't have hired me through my own website.

I just came back from New York where I recorded a radio and TV promo for a new Broadway musical. Later on, I'll be recording two more game characters for a Spanish company and a voice-over for an international documentary produced in California.

LIMITATIONS AND ASPIRATIONS

I know I'll never be the next Don LaFontaine, and frankly, I don't want to be another "Voice of G-d."

I have resigned myself to the fact that I probably won't announce the Oscars next year, and that someone else will do the promos for NBC.

Oh, well... I'm quite happy being me, and I believe that this "me" is still marketable.

That brings me to my first point: playing the online cattle call game.

I've seen the Michael J. Collins' *Book More Work Through Voices.com* video.*** Michael is the #1 All Time Favorite male voice on the site. He's a great guy and he must be doing something right.

I followed most of his suggestions. I've tweaked my profile to perfection. My demos are fresh, my studio is pretty much soundproof and my recording equipment is first-rate. I'm behind the mic all day, and I make sure to be one of the first to submit a custom audition.

What could possibly go wrong?

I'll tell you.

Though not as bad as sites like Freelancer.com, oDesk, or Elance, Voices.com has become a clearing house for those who want more and more for less and less. Voice-over jobs that used to go for $750 to $1500, are now auctioned off for $100 – $250.

Some say it's one of the joys of the free market. Hallelujah! Adam Smith be praised! I'm not playing that game.

For ordinary citizens, life is getting more expensive every year. On sites like Voices.com, talk gets cheaper and cheaper.

Do you want a movie trailer? If you can cough up $150, it's yours. How about a 300-page audio book, fully edited? Give me $250 and I'll find you an ignorant fool who's desperate to build her portfolio.

Mind you, these folks voluntarily pay $349 a year (Premium Plan) for the privilege to be one of 25,000+ members receiving job postings via email. And how are these subscribers treated?

When they audition for jobs, they are not allowed to communicate directly with the client. No other online voice casting service I know of has this overprotective, fear-based policy.

When a job is completed and payment is deposited, Voices.com charges a 10% escrow fee, just to hold on to your cash. "It's for your own protection," says "Voices," yet no one else in the business is that paternalistic or greedy.

And what about accountability?

Does Voices.com ever notify their members of the winning bid? Let's say a voice-seeker posts a project with a budget range of $250-$500. Wouldn't it be interesting to know how much or how little he eventually ended up paying?

LOYALTIES

Over the years I've heard colleagues say that Voices.com seems to care for voice talent, but that it really favors voice seekers.

After all, the client wins when he can hire a voice at a bargain basement rate.

I'm not sure clients always end up on top, though.

In "Why Pay-to-Plays" will implode," I've called sites like Voices.com an "expensive way to find cheap talent."

Who has time to sift through over 100 mostly mediocre auditions for a $200 job? And why are a lot of auditions mediocre? Because of the disregard for professionalism and a lack of quality control.

I often get the impression that quality control doesn't go beyond checking the expiration date on a credit card of a new subscriber. Not talent, but a MasterCard will get you listed as a new member of the Voices.com family.

Once the money is in the bank, you can upload almost anything to the site and call yourself a voice-over artist. Isn't that a boost for the reputation of our profession? Amateur or pro, all are welcome to the table!

And if you think it can't possibly be that bad, do what I did and listen to some of the gifted people listed on the site.

What you're about to hear are actual demos posted by Voices.com members in the hopes of attracting clients and building a lucrative career. Are you ready?

You can find the link to the audio samples in the link library on the website MakingMoneyInYourPJs.com.*** That's where you can find all the other hyperlinks as well.

BEING TOO TOUGH?

Now, some fans of Voices.com will no doubt tell me not to be so hard on the site.

The founders David and Stephanie Ciccarelli are risk-taking, hard-working, church-going, sweet, and successful people. They have created thousands of opportunities and they provide a wealth of free resources to anyone interested in a VO-career.

Voices.com is not the only Pay-to-Play out there, and it's not fair to make one company suffer for the sins of many.

Nobody is forced to join their service and people are free to bid as low as they seem fit. If they want to make a fool of themselves by posting amateur audio and working for peanuts, so be it.

I don't know David and Stephanie personally. We've communicated on Facebook and we're connected on LinkedIn. But my observations have nothing to do with who they are as individuals.

They are a clear example of good people doing a great job working in a flawed system of their own making.

It's a system that does not benefit my career or my community.

THE END OF THE AFFAIR

The rose-colored glasses have come off. The romance is over.

As my career progressed, I was able to compare the Canadians to similar services in North America and Europe. Some are better. Some are worse. I'm riding all of my Pay-to-Play memberships out and will not renew most of them.

Today, I'd rather work for agents who have an incentive to send me quality leads with decent rates. There are no upfront fees.

When I get paid, they get paid. When they negotiate a better deal, they make more money too. That's only fair.

I only pay when I actually get to play.

Most of the jobs I land these days, I get because of my reputation and my website. I like that.

Voices.com and I have grown apart.

We're no longer meant for each other.

It's time to go our separate ways.

What remains is my love.

My love for this crazy business.

It's a love that will never die.

PS Keep in mind that this book is only a reflection of my opinion based on personal experiences. I encourage you to draw your own conclusions and invest in what you think is right for you.

[42]

Rotten Carrots and Cool Clients

In a black and white world, there are two types of clients:

Type A: Pain in the neck

Type B: Pleasure to work with

After many years of freelancing, I think I have developed a sixth sense, warning me ahead of time which type of client I'm dealing with. Usually, this gut feeling is spot-on, but not so long ago, I was unpleasantly surprised.

It all started when I was asked to narrate a Dutch script.

From the first paragraph I could tell that it was poorly translated, probably with the help of software. Some of the language was archaic and the translation was very literal. In the third line I noticed a big slip-up. A noun that should have been singular, was translated with the plural form. Mistakes happen, but this one made no sense whatsoever.

Unfortunately, this wasn't the first time I had to deal with this situation. In this economy, clients are cutting corners and don't bother to hire a professional translator. For some, quality control seems to be a dirty word. Eh... two words, actually.

COMMUNICATING WITH CLIENTS

Whenever I spot really big blunders, I just can't keep my big mouth shut. I have to tell the client, or in this case, the production company that hired me on behalf of the client. It's in my best interest, because I don't like to be associated with a poor product that's going to be all over the web for generations to come.

I always proofread a script before I record it. I don't want to be a brainless nobody who reads whatever they put in front of him. That's what text-to-speech programs do. When clients hire me, I feel I can add value by going over their script, line by line.

I never criticize content, but I'm a stickler for proper grammar. Typos and poor grammar undermine credibility. Take this headline from a web page of an online voice casting service:

"Hundreds of the world's best voice talent. NO AMATUERS to sort through."

This company is trying to position itself as a discerning, professional business, and yet they couldn't be bothered to proofread their own copy! How professional is that?

But let's get back to my story.

When I told my contact at the production company about the poor translation, she promised to pass my feedback on to the client, and she'd let me know what to do next. Two hours later I received an apologetic email:

> "Paul, my hands are tied. The client said the script had been approved by the company, and their legal department signed off on it. You won't believe on how many desks this script has been before

you got to see it. Just read what is written and don't change a word."

Reluctantly, I did because a little voice was telling me that this wasn't the last time I would hear from this client.

A week later the phone rang. It was the production company.

"The client isn't happy," my contact said. "Apparently, their office in the Netherlands had noticed a big error in the third line and they want you to correct it. They also think that the Dutch text doesn't really flow. Could you take a look at it and tweak the translation? You're a native speaker. It should be fairly easy for you and I'm sure it wouldn't take a lot of time."

I told her I'd be happy to do that, but I would have to charge for the translation and the re-recording.

"Well," my contact said, "I'm not so sure the client is willing to pay for that. They sounded pretty peeved that you didn't spot this mistake in the first place. And can't you just throw in the translation? The client told me that they'd be willing to consider you for more work in the future."

I took a deep breath and reminded her that some seven days ago I was told to read the script verbatim.

"Are you sure?" she asked.

"I can send you the email," I said. "I hate to be super formal, but my policy states that I'm happy to record free retakes, as long as they are – and I quote – not necessitated by changes in the script after the initial audio was recorded. The recording of a script that was revised after the first text was officially approved and recorded, is regarded and billed as a new project. Otherwise I would end up recording version 1.1, 1.2 and 1.3 for free... you know how that goes. Just like you, I'm trying to run a professional business."

Having dealt with a gazillion customers, this is what I have learned:

1. You must put things in writing because

2. Most clients have a short memory and a lot on their plate

and...

3. Never fall for the promise of future work. 99% of the time it's not going to happen.

Future work does not pay current bills, (unless you get paid in advance). If that's a no-brainer, why are certain clients trying to dangle that rotten carrot in front of your face?

Who do they think you are? A Voice Bunny?

Clients have two reasons.

One: Because they often get away with it.

Colleagues without a backbone or beginners without business acumen are so desperate to finally get hired, they want to believe the carrot is real.

Two: Because these clients are Type A clients.

As I said in the beginning, over the years I've learned to spot a Type A client from miles away. Here are a few tip-offs:

- They're low-budget and high-maintenance
- They don't ask; they demand
- They have limited knowledge of the business you're in
- You give them a finger; they want the whole hand
- They tend not to read emails and make a lot of assumptions
- Your input is not appreciated because the client knows best
- You're not an equal partner in the project

- They usually pay late and act annoyed when you send them a reminder
- Even though you're an independent contractor, type A clients believe you work FOR them

Type B clients are very different.

- They know what you're worth and what rate is reasonable
- They never demand. They always ask
- They leave you with clear instructions and trust you will do a good job
- They appreciate feedback and are open to your input
- They get back to you promptly
- You are treated as an equal partner
- They pay on time
- You work WITH them, not for them

RESOLUTION

So, how did I resolve the situation with my Type A client?

I didn't.

The production company I was working with was taken off the job, and it took six months before I finally got paid for something that was never used.

Out of curiosity I looked on YouTube to see if I could find the video I had been working on.

It's there and it is horrible.

The script is pretty much the same. Two things were changed. One was the obvious mistake in the third line. That was corrected. Number two was the narrator. They must have found him on Craigslist.

Looking back, should I have given them what they wanted? Why not change that one word and read the darn script verbatim? It would have taken me ten minutes at the most. And why not throw in that translation? What a way to create some goodwill!

I'm all for reaching a reasonable compromise, but I refuse to lower my professional standards just to please a Type A client. Changing that one word would be like adding a fine cherry to a lousy Sundae.

I have a reputation to uphold and I will never compromise quality just to make a quick buck. If a client wants to play games with his reputation, so be it. I'm not going to go there.

Secondly, I deserve to be paid for the work I do.

As soon as I give in and start translating for free, I'm telling the client I believe my time and my work is worthless. I am also taking a good job away from professional translators.

Here's the last thing I learned.

From the day I began publishing my fees, Type A clients started avoiding me.

I have no problem with that.

In fact, it saves me tons of time.

Here's my wish for you:

> *May you be granted the serenity to accept that type A clients cannot be changed,*
>
> *And the courage to attract as many Type B clients as you can,*
>
> *And the wisdom to know the difference.*

[43]

Ten Things Clients Don't Care About

Let me preface this chapter by saying that I feel very lucky. In the past 30 years I was able to develop a strong relationship with a number of clients. The longer we go back, the fewer words we have to waste on what each side is expecting from the other.

It's almost like a marriage. And very much like a marriage, a lasting business relationship needs commitment from each partner. It can be love at first sight and it can also end in a divorce, due to unspoken expectations and unfulfilled desires.

When I just started out as a freelancer, one of my more cynical mentors warned me against romanticizing the relationship with my clients. His mantra:

> *"Business is business and the rest is bullish*t."*

Today, these words resonate even stronger. In these fast and furious times, online matchmaking is getting more popular. And nobody seems to take it slow anymore. Making small talk is so yesterday.

"I need your demo now. Are you available this afternoon?"

Before you know it, you're off into some dark room talking to yourself, and when you're done recording, you dump the files into a dropbox.

As one of my friends put it:

"I almost feel used."

Well, isn't that the whole idea? We offer our services. We deliver our services. We move on. End of story.

Let's be honest. Most times, both parties aren't even interested in getting to know each other before the deal is sealed.

How well do you really know your clients? How well do they know you?

Does it even matter?

In most cases it doesn't, as long as the job gets done. That's why it is time to take off those rose-colored glasses and get rid of your great expectations.

Here's my top ten of things most clients don't seem to care about anymore:

1. YOU

All you are is a solution to a problem; a means to an end. It's your job to ensure that the benefits of hiring you outweigh how much you charge. Your client doesn't have to care about you. It's your work that matters.

2. YOUR PERSPECTIVE

What you perceive to be the benefits of your service is not important. The question is: Do you understand and can you meet the needs of your clients?

Your take on a script (or any other freelance assignment for that matter) may be interesting, but it's often irrelevant.

You're the stylist. The client determines how she wants her hair cut, unless you have permission to be creative.

3. YEARS OF EXPERIENCE

The fact that you've been at it for a certain number of years doesn't automatically mean you're the right person for the part.

Over the years, some people have become very good at being very bad. They're stuck in a rut.

Years of experience entitle you to nothing. In fact, it can make you look like you're old school.

The quality of your experience qualifies you. Not the length.

4. ACCOLADES & OTHER ACCOMPLISHMENTS

An impressive resume tells a client what you have done for others, usually years ago. All he really wants to know is: What can you do for ME, today?

If you can't make that clear, why should he hire you?

Experience can also backfire.

One of my friends specializes in medical narrations. In order to impress a possible new client, he quoted a fine endorsement from a pharmaceutical company he'd been working for, for years.

It was his way of saying: "See... I have a proven track record. I can easily handle your project."

The other party was not impressed. The email he got back effectively said:

"Since you've established yourself as the voice of brand X, it would be unwise for us to hire you. People would automatically associate your sound with our main competitor."

5. YOUR COST OF DOING BUSINESS

Never justify your fee by bringing up how much you have invested in your dream. That's the normal price you pay for being and staying in business.

Be honest. You don't really care about your client's business expenses either, do you?

6. YOUR HIGH-END EQUIPMENT

Clients won't hire you because you happen to own a Steinway. They hire you because they like the way you play, or because you offer the best value for money.

You might impress your colleagues with a brand new Neumann U87 studio microphone. My last client hadn't even heard of the brand.

7. TECHNICAL CHALLENGES

It's lame to blame technology for your lack of preparation.

In voice-overs, home studios are steadily becoming the norm. Even if you record in a stuffy bedroom closet (and call it a 'professional studio'), you're the head of IT, audio engineering and data transmission.

If you can't handle that, don't expect any sympathy from the client. He'll find someone who can.

8. PERSONAL PROBLEMS

Leave them at the door. Clients are clients; not friends or family. You're hired to do a job, no matter how horrible you might feel about your dead cat or a recent break-up.

Put your life on the back burner and focus on the project.

Cry when the job is done.

9. YOUR FRAGILE EGO

You are hired to make your client look good and not to boost your magnificent ego.

If you're in need of praise, visit an evangelical church.

And what's the last thing clients don't care about?

10. YOUR SUBLIME UNIQUENESS

Sure, nobody talks like you or walks like you. That doesn't make you irreplaceable. Even if you've worked with a client for years, don't be surprised if they ask you to re-audition.

One of the joys of being an independent contractor is that there's no long-term contract with severance pay, should things come to a premature end.

You're on your own.

Never take anything for granted.

Complacency will be your downfall.

Be ready to prove yourself, over and over and over again.

If you don't take care of your career, nobody else will.

Business is business.

And the rest is...

[44]

The Secret to Landing Any Freelance Job

Is your freelance business going down the drain?

Are you sick and tired of rejection?

Have you had enough of wasting your time on auditions, bids, and proposals that never lead to anything?

Perhaps it is time to make frustration your friend.

Be sure to add a strong dose of disgust to the mix. According to success strategist Jim Rohn, disgust is one of the four emotions that can lead to life change.

He said:

"The person who feels disgusted has reached a point of no return. He or she is ready to throw down the gauntlet at life and say, "I've had it!"

Once your frustration has reached a boiling point, it is time to make up your mind. Are you throwing in the towel, or are you going to take massive action and turn your business around?

If you pick the last option, the next question is: HOW?

The secret to landing any type of freelance job is contained in these three words:

PRACTICE PREDATORY PRICING

In other words: start offering your service or product at a price which is either below the going rate or below production cost.

So, why don't you crush the competition by underbidding? You gotta pay the bills, right? It is better to have a low-paying job than no job at all. Après nous, le déluge (after us, the deluge).

Most of us live in a capitalist society based on a free market. There are no fixed prices in the unregulated world of freelancing.

Today's economy is based on one principle only: Survival of the cheapest. Is that morally wrong? Please don't be a hypocrite. We're all accomplices.

Let's make a deal.

Stop complaining about business being slow. End the endless self-pity because nobody wants to hire you. Your product is not the problem. The problem is your pricing. So get off your high horse and start lowering your rates right now. If you won't do it, others will. Ever wondered why almost anything is made in China?

Okay. Time-Out.

TV psychologist Dr. Phil McGraw coined the phrase:

"If you choose the behavior, you choose the consequences."

Before you start slashing your fees, please consider the following ten consequences of predatory pricing.

1. Bargain prices attract bargain shoppers.

Low-paying customers are usually high-maintenance customers. As one freelancer put it:

"People that are only willing to spend pennies will argue over every cent, while people willing to spend whatever it takes, care more about the result than the bill."

2. Bargain prices create unrealistic expectations.

You will attract clients that expect a gourmet meal at a fast food price (and at drive-through speed).

Beware: as in mountain biking, it is easier to go down than to go up. Once your price level is set, it is tough to justify a higher price.

3. Bargain rates devalue your work.

Don't be fooled. Predatory prices attract clients that pick you based on your rate, not on your abilities. For them, the value of your work depends on your fee, not on your skills or experience.

People tend not to value things that don't cost them much. Market researchers have also found out that customers are much more likely to be dissatisfied with cheap products or services, regardless of the quality of the product.

Are those the people you really wish to work for?

4. Bargain rates show little self-respect.

A freelance web designer put it this way:

> "I wouldn't think of cutting my prices, because higher prices show that you are confident with your work, and confidence sells a lot more effectively to QUALITY clients – more so than price."

5. Bargain prices foster resentment and jealousy.

What signal are you sending to yourself when you're working for rock bottom rates?

"Is that all I'm worth? Don't they appreciate my work? Why am I only making one-third of what my colleague makes in two minutes and it takes me two hours?"

6. Bargain rates bring your quality down.

Freelance writer Steven Snell:

> "If you are not making very much from a project, you may rush through it so that you can finish and move on to something else. I know. It's easy to say 'I'm only making $X for this work, I don't need to do any better than this.' As a result, your work will be less than your best. If you're making a reasonable amount, you should be able and willing to do your best work."

7. Bargain pricing leaves less time to do well-paid work.

Imagine the frustration of having to say "no" to a golden opportunity because you're swamped with a project paying peanuts.

8. Predatory pricing is unfair competition.

Dumping your product or service is going to isolate you from your colleagues and it will negatively impact prevalent prices.

Don't blame the anonymous forces of demand and supply for a steady decline in rates. You are as much part of the problem as you are part of the solution.

9. Predatory prices leave you working more and earning less.

That's a no-brainer, so let me ask you a question:

Didn't you become a freelancer to have more free time and make more money?

10. Bargain rates lead to bankruptcy.

What do JetGreen, DutchBird, and LowFareJet have in common?

They were all low-cost airlines that practiced predatory pricing.

They went under because they overpromised, underdelivered, and couldn't break even.

Price dumping might win you some clients in the short run, but you will lose your business in the long run.

Is that what you had in mind?

[45]

Paying the Price

Is there a hidden link between price and perception?

Do we get what we are paying for?

Are we more satisfied when we've paid top dollar?

On January 14, 2008, a team of scientists from the California Institute of Technology and Stanford University, published a paper called:

> "Marketing actions can modulate neural representations of experienced pleasantness."

This paper was the result of research*** I would have loved to be part of.

The hypothesis was that the price of a bottle of wine affects the way a person experiences it in their pleasure circuits in the brain. It aims to answer the age-old question:

Does an expensive Bordeaux taste better because of the price tag?

The theory was put to the test using functional MRI scans of people while they tasted wine samples they thought were from different wines at different prices, when in reality they were the same.

Lead author Antonio Rangel, associate professor of economics at the Division of the Humanities and Social Sciences at Caltech, said he was "shocked" when he saw the results.

SHAKESPEARE

Since this is a book about voice-overs and freelancing and not about wine making, here's my question:

"Shall I compare thee to a Chardonnay?"

Well, that's a risky idea, and I'm happy to tell you why. A nice bottle of Chardonnay is probably richer and more expensive!

If you don't believe me, let me give you a taste from the bottom of the barrel (please note: I left the original spelling of the ads intact).

> *Craigslist:* "You have an awesome British accent that Americans go crazy for. I want to have an awesome British accent as the voice of the message on my voice mail. It's really simple and shouldn't take more than ten minutes (at most!). Compensation: $20."

> *Virtual Vocations:* "Voice talent – 60 second recording. You need to be British or sound British. You need to be able to record this at your home with your computer. P.S. I'll happily pay you for this. I was thinking $5 to $15 by PayPal, since it's pretty simple."

> *Odesk:* "Voice-over is for a 20 page presentation naration. If your bilingual that will be the best if you able to do only on just mark it in your letter and make you price in concideration. $50 fixed."

LOW AND BEHOLD

Is it just me, or is there a serious disconnect between what you and I need to earn to make a decent living and what clients are prepared to pay? Of course you can argue that the above examples are extreme. But are they, really?

Here's my challenge.

Sign up for Odesk, go on Craigslist, VirtualVocations, and similar sites, and report back to me in a few weeks. Ask your friends in IT, copywriting, translation, and graphic design to join you in your quest for fair compensation. You might be as surprised as Antonio Rangel.

We're not talking about incidents. We are dealing with a serious downward trend. Ask yourself:

Did the rules of the game change, and did nobody bother to tell us?

Go back a few years.

How did we put a price on our services in the past?

Remember the days we actually had direct contact with a client? A personal connection has always been a pivotal part of any business relationship. It's the grease that makes things go smoothly. Doesn't it all begin with building trust? How do you do that, if your client is purposely hiding his virtual identity?

It's impossible to do your own background check to find out if a company you're hoping to work with is legit. These days, you can't even be sure the demo or design you just sent to a prospect is nothing but a time-wasting test balloon for a campaign you'll never be part of.

But let's continue our flashback. How did we deal with clients in the past? Well, with the rapport going, we could start talking to the project manager about the requirements of the job. Voice-overs could ask simple questions such as:

"What sort of a read do you need? Who's the audience? What kind of person is the narrator?"

It was an opportunity to go beyond the vague descriptions we've become accustomed to. Descriptions such as:

"Male voice. North American. Middle-aged. Non-Union."

How much help are those, do you think?

In the old scenario, we wouldn't have to second-guess the word count, what market a commercial would play in, and details about a possible buyout. Those are things that anyone needs to know before putting in a realistic bid.

And finally, with all the blanks filled in, we could talk money. We could educate the prospect about going rates and why we're worth every penny.

We could discuss a reasonable time frame for the project and counter objections about our fee. It's the back-and-forth that's part and parcel of the sales process.

It was give and take. Negotiate. Communicate.

And now?

Now, you and I just type a few numbers into the "Your Fee" box of an online casting site or other crowdsourcing platform. Then we send our hopes and dreams into cyberspace. It's definitely a change, but I wouldn't call it progress. It has cheapened our industry in many ways.

What does science tell us about cheap?

IN VINO VERITAS

Antonio Rangel and his team discovered that people who were given two identical red wines to drink, said they got much more pleasure from the one they were told had cost more.

Brain scans confirmed that their pleasure centers were activated far more by the higher-priced wine.

With that in mind, wouldn't it make sense to charge a decent price for our services?

One of my favorite TV shows is *Dragon's Den*, where "cash-hungry entrepreneurs pitch for an investment from some of Britain's top business brains." In the U.S. the show is called *Shark Tank*.

In one of the episodes, a young, bright businesswoman made an excellent presentation. The multimillionaire investors were visibly impressed with her product and her poise.

In spite of that, she walked away empty-handed because nobody wanted to invest in her startup.

Here's the mistake she made:

She had lowballed the amount of money she wanted the dragons to invest.

One of them, Peter Jones, summed it up like this:

"What a shame!

Had you asked for more, I would have taken you seriously."

[46]

Finding Your Value as a Free-Lancer

Etymology is the study of the origin of words.

If you love language the way I do, you probably love looking into its history. Delving into the deeper meaning of the things that come out of our mouths is as revealing as it is rewarding.

Take the word *competition*.

To most people it is synonymous with rivalry or a fight to outdo another; a race that can only have one winner and lots of losers. It's Darwin's theory in a nutshell. It wasn't always understood like that.

The word competition comes from the Latin verb competere.

Com meaning 'together' and petere 'to strive or seek.' Hundreds of years ago, competition actually meant 'to strive or come together' or even 'to agree.'

Whenever people tell me that the world of freelancing is getting more and more competitive, I prefer to think of it in terms of the original meaning of the word.

Ideally, it should be about amicable cooperation and not about bitter confrontation. We shouldn't be at each other's throats. Instead, we have to strive together, but for what exactly?

To me the answer is simple: to further our field and to make our profession a profession we're proud to be part of. The way to do that is to set and live by the highest standards.

In a world where the lowest (and cheapest) common denominator often seems to win the day, this is not a popular message. Our culture promotes and rewards passive consumption, and it excels in upholding minimum standards. Take a look around you. Everywhere, highly skilled craftsmen have been replaced by robots and cheesy prefab.

Quality calls for experience, dedication, patience, and passion. It's so much easier to be average. Mediocrity can be phoned in. It doesn't require effort, enthusiasm, or attention to detail. It doesn't ask for sacrifice, continued education, or for high-end equipment.

Perhaps I'm prejudiced, but I see no pride in delivering a perfunctory performance or an ordinary product. There's no value in that.

Some will say that today's culture of coasting is a result of people playing it safe. If you ask me, it's based on laziness, carelessness, and fear.

If you never stick your neck out, you won't get hurt, but you won't rise above the rest either.

Do you know anyone who has ever reached the top of his or her game by playing it safe? It's only good for preventing two things: accidents and unwanted pregnancies.

ADDING VALUE

At this point you might expect a top ten of the best tips on how to increase your worth as a freelancer. But without the right frame of mind, these tips could easily turn into tricks. Tricks are for circus animals and con artists. When discussing value, we need to talk about your motivation first. So, let me ask you this:

What drives you to be in this business?

Fame? Fun? Fortune? Fulfillment? I'm sure you can come up with some other f-words.

Please don't just read on, but take a few moments to really answer the question. But think of it not so much in terms of what you hope to get out of it, but in terms of what you're willing to put into it.

You don't need me to tell you that the more you're prepared to give, the more you're likely to get. Eventually.

Back to the question. What drives you to be in this business?

Write down five to seven things that immediately come to mind. Don't censor or analyze them. Just jot them down.

Now, let's go one level deeper and ask ourselves:

What determines what people are willing to give (and give up), in order to get something that's valuable to them?

That – of course – depends on what's important to them, how important it is to them, and why. Ultimately, this is determined by their values.

Values are the intangible things we really care about; they are the fundamental principles we live by, and they're often compressed into abstract words such as honesty, integrity, health, love, or liberty.

Most of us take these notions for granted and we never really think about what drives us deep down inside.

We're motivated by things that matter to us most.

If I were to use some psycho-babble I'd say:

Values provide an upfront motivation and an after the fact evaluation of the things we do and the choices we make in any context of our life.

Take the value of being truthful.

As with all values, it means different things to different people. To my voice acting friend Fred it primarily means being truthful to himself. He's a lifelong Democrat and he'd never do a voice-over for a campaign ad for a Republican candidate, no matter how much it would pay. Principles are more important than money.

To my friend Julie, being truthful means being truthful to her art, which she translates to being as convincing as possible when reading a voice-over script, whether it's written by a Democrat, a Republican, or a Libertarian.

Julie loves taking on challenging projects, and she has no problem putting her own political persuasions aside. As long as she can sound as if she totally means what she says, she'll happily take the money. After all, she's just playing a role. She doesn't feel she has to vote Republican in order to give them her voice.

NO RESPECT

Fred and Julie have noticed something else. Every time they felt uncomfortable or uncertain about a job or their performance, it usually had to do with their values.

Julie wasn't at all happy with the condescending way a director had treated her in one of her last sessions. She made good money but it came at a hefty price. Afterwards she told me: "I'll never work with that man again, no matter how much he'd pay me."

Not so long ago, Fred was offered a project that seemed to be made for him, and the client agreed.

"Finally, there's someone who recognizes what I'm capable of," Fred said to me, right after his audition. But as soon as he saw what the client was willing to offer for his services, he felt offended.

It turned out that for both Julie and Fred, the value of respect was very important. Julie felt disrespected by the rude director, and Fred felt insulted by the rate they offered him.

When core values are violated, people draw the line.

Now, how does all this digging into our psyche relate to adding value in voice-overs and freelancing? I'll tell you.

Before considering the additional benefits you think you can offer your clients, you have to value what you bring to the table first (and I don't necessarily mean in a monetary way).

It works a bit like self-esteem.

You will never be able to convince others that you believe in yourself, if that timid voice inside of you doesn't believe a word of it. At best, you'd be sending mixed signals. Here's an example.

The worst salespeople are those who don't believe that their product is worth the asking price. They start apologizing right off the bat, and most of them don't even realize they're doing it. They give themselves away by using innocent words like *usually* or *normally*, when discussing their rate or price. Here's what they might say:

"I usually charge...." or "Normally, this would sell for..."

What's the not so hidden message here, and how would you respond?

How about this:

"So, you'd normally charge $350, right? Well, what can you do for me today?"

And so the salesman steps into the hole that he just dug for himself by using one revealing word.

As long as he isn't convinced of the value of what he has to offer, you can forget about teaching this old dog new tricks.

In the past, colleagues have come up to me and said:

"Interesting concept, Paul, but this doesn't really apply to me. I'm a voice-over actor. Not a sales person."

To them I say:

"Believe it or not, you ARE in sales. It is your job as an independent contractor to negotiate the best terms and the best price for your services.

Secondly, as an actor it is your job to sell your character to me as convincingly as you can. If you don't believe you can pull that role off, don't waste your time. I'll be able to tell within a matter of seconds."

Your actions and your results start with what you value. It all begins with what's important to you and why.

People who truly value what they bring to the table state their price with conviction and then shut up. And you know what? These people are more likely to get what they're asking for. They know that quality knows no shortcuts or compromises.

If you are truly committed to furthering the field and make this a profession you're proud to be part of, I hereby challenge you to raise your standards and increase your value.

Let the competition begin!

[47]

Are You Afraid of Raising Your Rates?

Those who can't build value, have nothing left but to compete on price."
Paul Strikwerda

At the end of the 2013 season, slugger Alex Rodriguez had earned $29,000,000 in salary from the New York Yankees. Not bad for a year's work.

Do you think he's worth it?

In 2006, entertainment tycoon David Geffen sold Jackson Pollock's painting *No. 5, 1948**** for 140 million dollars. Assuming you had that kind of spare change, would you spend it on a painting described by some as "stunning drip?"

Can you tell me why actress Abigail Breslin*** reportedly made $65K for five hours of voice-over work for the animated film *Zambezia*? Yes, that's $13,000 per hour! At that time, she was 15 years old.

Let's be honest. What did these people really do?

Mmm... let's see.

Rodriguez is pretty good at hitting a ball with some sort of stick. Pollock simply threw some paint on engineered wood. All Breslin did was talk into a microphone. Why is that worth so much money?

Two words: PERCEIVED VALUE

Before I deal with the notion of perception, let's first talk about the connection between cost, price, and value.

Unless you are selling something that is basic and interchangeable (such as a commodity), there's often no direct correlation between the cost to produce a certain article, the price the article sells for, and the value people attribute to it. Art is an extreme example.

"No. 5, 1948" is one of the most expensive paintings ever sold. Did you ever wonder how much Pollock spent on paints, brushes, and the 8' × 4' sheet of fiberboard he drizzled on? Does it even matter?

What does matter is the subjective value of the painting and not the cost of the materials. In fact, to the new owner, the subjective value of Pollock's masterpiece might be more than 140 million dollars.

Warren Buffet summed it up nicely:

> *"Price is what you pay. Value is what you get."*

That's why people who only compete on price (those darn lowballers), are making a huge mistake. By doing so, they are devaluing what they have to offer, even before the client has had a chance to respond.

As soon as you start competing on price, you treat your valuable service or product as a dime-a-dozen commodity.

Peter Drucker*** was right when he said:

> *"In a commodity market, you can only be as good as your dumbest competitor."*

Perceived value is in the eyes of the beholder. It's intangible. It's a reaction to the assumed benefits you receive from owning and using a certain product or service. It's an emotional response, based on a belief (and I define a belief as "a feeling of certainty").

A belief can be very powerful in overriding logical reasoning. A few examples:

1. As long as we believe that these dirty pieces of paper with the faces of dead people on it represent a certain value, we will continue to use them as money

2. People who were given two identical red wines to drink, said they got much more pleasure from the one they were told had cost more. Brain scans confirmed that their pleasure centers were activated far more by the higher-priced wine (see chapter 56).

3. At least a third of the population consists of what scientists call "placebo reactors."**** This means that if they feel that something is doing them good, it will indeed do them good.

Do you believe that?

Now, I'm not saying that "the market" has nothing to do with the way we put a price on goods and services. But economics is not always about numbers. It's just as much about psychology.

The law of scarcity states that if what you desire is in (seemingly) limited supply, its perceived value increases. This, in turn, increases the urge for people to want it and want it now.

That's why marketers love to create the perception of scarcity by saying things like "for a limited time only," or "while supplies last." Don't miss out, people!

How about the stock market? What causes stock prices to change? Well, the idea is that the price movement of a stock indicates what investors feel a company is worth. For that, they look at things like earnings. Without profit, no listed company can survive.

However, during the dot-com bubble, some internet companies were valued at billions of dollars without ever making a profit. Their value was based on the perception of Wall Street, a strong feeling that these companies would do well in the future.

Feelings overrule facts.

Whoever said "Feelings don't lie," was in for a rude awakening!

For one last blast about the power of perception, let's look at politics.

Why did republican hopeful Herman Cain suspend his bid for the White House in 2011? Did it really matter whether or not he had had extramarital affairs? If anything, his presidential campaign was killed by allegations.

What mattered was that Cain was not able to change the perception of the public. Where there's smoke, there must be fire, right?

Now, let's move away from politics, placebos, wine, and the stock market, and talk about how all of this relates to your pricing strategy.

Let's summarize.

The price people are willing to pay greatly depends on how people evaluate what you have to offer. Value is a matter of perception.

Perception is personal and therefore subjective. Perceptions will influence a client's expectations upfront, and the level of satisfaction after the purchase has been made.

Here's the good news: Because perceptions are subjective, they can be changed. That's what branding, marketing and advertising are for. A successful campaign can turn simple pants made of rugged blue cloth into desirable designer denim.

True Religion's top-selling jeans, the Super T, cost about $50 to make and sell wholesale to retailers for $152 a pair. The average price in stores is $335 (source***). Gucci Low-rise flared jeans sell for as much as $720.

Talk about perceived value...

Most solopreneurs don't have the funds to hire Saatchi & Saatchi and have them create a campaign to convince customers. Luckily, there are other – much cheaper – ways to position yourself in the market and sell your services at a higher price.

This has to start with one question:

Do YOU believe you're worth it?

Alex does. Abigail does, and so do their agents.

And guess what? The New York Yankees and Triggerfish Animation Studios agreed!

They knew that the added value A-rod and Abigail bring to their game, is much, much higher than their salaries.

You and I see price.

They see value.

The pricing of art is an example of the art of pricing.

I can guarantee you that since 2006, the price of Pollock's painting has gone up considerably.

So, let me ask you this:

Are you selling yourself based on price or on value?

[48]

Those Bloody Bottom Feeders

"It's not the crook we fear in modern business; rather, it's the honest guy who doesn't know what he is doing." **Owen Young**

The lines have been drawn.

The time to mince words is over.

Every day, the voice-over community seems to get more polarized around the issue of low rates.

Listen to the buzz. Look at the chatter. Do you think this bubble is about to burst?

Some people are past being polite. They're frustrated and angry. I like that. If you're pissed off at something, it means you give a damn and you want things to change.

Some of my voice-over friends are a bit more diplomatic. Recently, I asked a few Facebook buddies a loaded question:

> "Is charging low rates a sign of fear and lack of confidence, or just a smart strategy to attract more business?"

Here are some of the responses:

"You left out "ignorance" – some don't know what they're worth ..."
*Joe J. Thomas***

"It's not a smart strategy because sooner or later, you will be up to your eyeballs with a multitude of lowball clients and you'll be working 15 hours a days, just to make ends meet. If you have to do this to survive, I respect that but you'll never reach the next level working like this. For every low rate I have to turn down, it's usually made up a few days later when I get a new client who gets it. I would rather work with five good paying clients a week as opposed to fifteen who have $50 for their budget." *Terry Daniel***

"I believe it's mostly the influx of part-timers and hobbyists to VO that drive down rates. They simply don't depend upon the income to pay their bills. Anyone who has to depend on this work to feed, house, and clothe themselves (not to mention a family) could never survive charging such low rates. To them, it's pocket money. And in some parts of the country the cost of living is much lower than in others, so those fewer dollars go further." *Diane Havens***

Not everyone agrees. Of course most colleagues would rather do a well-paid job than a low-budget project, but they say there's no shame in accepting work in the first place. Peter Sandon:

"Many of us are low volume workers, for a variety of reasons, and do not see the need or value in becoming union members. Denigrating comments like "bottom feeders" are not only irrelevant but wrong and rude. For many of us a low paid job is better than no job at all, and there is the chance that someone will hear our voices and offer us a well-paid job. Did the "top feeders" start up there? I doubt it, most worked their way up, leaving low paid jobs for new arrivals, and maybe they don't like the competition coming up behind them, because they may just be better – perish the thought!"

Here's what Phil Sayer*** had to say:

"Do low rates ruin it for the rest of us? No, they don't. They really, really don't. They mop up low-budget work that others don't want.

If they didn't provide that service, the money would simply be spent elsewhere, such as print."

Let me give you my take on some of the arguments that are being used to defend, excuse, or justify low rates.

Even though we're talking about voice-over services, you'll find the same type of reasoning when other freelance rates are discussed.

Lets start with a something I hear almost every day:

1. There will always be a high end and a low end of the market. Accept it and move on.

That's a given and it's not addressing the real issue. We all know that there's a market for KIA and Roll-Royce. The point is: how low is the KIA dealer willing to go to make a sale? Is he prepared to sell his cars at a loss, just to get his business going? How long can he keep that up before he goes bankrupt? It's not a way to get loyal customers either. Next time, they'll just buy from someone who's willing to go even lower.

Bottom line: You need to cover your costs and then factor in a profit. But once you get clients hooked on cheap prices, they will never pay full price again.

2. You may lose money on every sale, but you'll make it up in volume!

That's like buying melons for a dollar each, and then selling 12 for 10 bucks. Does that make any sense? No matter how many KIAs a dealer sells, if he sells them below cost, he's not making any money. A small business owner once said: "Sales numbers feed egos. Profits feed families."

It's not how much you sell, but how much you get to keep that matters. Business is a game of margins, not volume. Bargain airlines tried making money on volume. Guess what? They're gone!

To paraphrase my colleague Terry Daniel: Would you rather do less for more, or more for less?

3. Purchase decisions are primarily based on price.

If that's the case, Mr. client, I will send you your order in two years, okay? I'll also make sure that it will fall apart in two weeks and you won't be getting your money back. Don't bother calling me, because I just closed our customer service department.

Most people do not buy on price alone. They will talk about price, but what they really mean is that you haven't offered enough value to justify paying the price you're asking.

There's this cartoon with a picture of a brother and sister each with their own lemonade stand side by side. The brother's lemonade stand reads "Lemonade 25 cents." The sister's lemonade stand reads:

"Lemonade 50 cents (clean water)."

Do you want your service to be known for being the cheapest on the market, or for high quality? Competing on price is a losing battle.

Lawrence Steinmetz and William Brooks are the authors of *How to sell at margins higher than your competitors. Winning every sale at full price, rate or fee.**** They say:

> "If you want to earn a solid living in sales, you need to remember that you are going to face a consistent challenge to hang on to a higher price, because you will always find yourself competing with a fool who is going broke cutting prices."

The key is adding value. If you don't offer exceptional value, then your product or service becomes just another commodity. People buy commodities on price. If you're just another web designer, voice-over artist, or car dealership, you're in trouble.

Value means offering more for a higher price.

4. Price does not influence the perception of a product.

If that were the case, why are people prepared to pay thousands of dollars for a Rolex, instead of buying a $50 Seiko? Most watchmakers agree that the Seiko is the better timepiece.

Let's talk about brain surgery. Why don't people go to the cheapest surgeon in the area? Because low prices make people think he isn't any good.

Price makes a statement. Cheap = cheap. What does your rate tell the world about what you think you're worth?

5. Some clients just can't afford paying higher rates. I can't change that.

How do you know they can't pay you a better rate? Buyers lie in order to get you to lower your price. It's the oldest trick in the book. If they could get it from someone else at a better price, why are they still talking to you?

Stop making excuses for those who don't respect you enough to pay you a decent fee. Unless you've seen their balance sheet, you don't know what they can or cannot afford.

Know your bottom line. Add value.

Don't compromise so easily. Negotiate. Dare to say NO to a bad deal. Study the art of making the sale. It's part of being a pro.

6. I don't set the rates. The market does.

So, what you're saying is that you don't take responsibility for your prices? They are forced upon you at gunpoint? You're just a helpless leaf in the wind?

Let me put it bluntly: The market doesn't determine your price. Your client doesn't set your fee. YOU do. It's just very convenient to tell the world that you don't have any influence over your rate. If you can't control it, you can't change it. You're a victim of circumstance. End of story. Now go feel sorry for yourself.

Price-cutting is a self-inflicted wound. Should you decide that $10 for an eight-paragraph voice-over script is fair compensation, so be it. Contract law states that parties must agree to enter into a contract freely and must be of sound mind.

I'm not saying that you should ignore the competition or forget about the rate cards that are floating in cyberspace. It's up to you if you want to look at Odesk, freelancer.com, or the $100 voices.com minimum rate, and decide that that's what "the market" is willing to pay. After all, the only thing the client cares about is price, right?

Or you could decide to look at union rates and make those the basis of your pricing structure.

Why not talk to an agent? If you're any good, she might want to represent you. She'll fight for a decent rate because if you do well, she will do well.

7. I'm not a sales person. I'm an artist. I don't know how to negotiate.

No, you're a wimp and you need a firm kick in the pants! Nobody is forcing you to be a full-time freelancer. But if you tell the world you are doing this to make a living, it automatically means that you're the head of the sales department, whether you like it or not. Lawrence Steinmetz has this to add:

> "The first thing you have to understand is that the selling price is a function of your ability to sell and nothing else."

Any idiot can cave in at the first sign of buyer resistance and offer a price cut. That's not selling. That's being lazy and fearful. It's a sign that you don't believe in the value of your product or service. Clients always pick up on that and it will cost you dearly.

Being extraordinarily talented in what you do, does not guarantee instant success. Life might have dealt you a pretty good hand, but if you don't know how to play the game, even the best cards are useless. We all know starving geniuses.

The way I see it, you have two choices. You either learn the rules and become good at playing the game, or you stay out of it. Remember: experience is the slowest teacher.

8. Low-end rates do not affect high-end rates.

If that were the case, why aren't rates going up, instead of down? Why have so many auditions turned into a bidding war? Actor, writer and producer J.S. Gilbert:***

> "While it's not being broadcast, I'm seeing people I know who have made six-figure+ incomes at voice-over for years now, looking at incomes that are fractions of what they were a few years ago."

I understand that we'll never get back to the golden days of Don LaFontaine (a.k.a. "The Voice of G-d") and his limo. Thanks to the internet, the rise in home studios, and online job boards, clients no longer have to book union talent at union rates through an agent. Talk has become a lot cheaper.

As Gilbert pointed out to me, a job that used to cost the client $1000, is now offered at $250. But why pay $250 if some fool is willing to do it for $25?

As I said before, once clients are taught they can get it for less, why should they pay a penny more? Give me one reason why this trend does not impact today's prices, and has never done so in the past.

9. But I'm just getting started. I can't possibly ask full price.

Some beginners admitted to me that they've offered their services for free, just to be able to build a portfolio.

Mind you: they were not talking about doing stuff for charity.

I think a freebie only makes sense if you have something else to sell. That's why a baker hands out samples, and that's why my custom demos are free of charge. But if you're giving 500 dollars worth of services away for free, you're not only creating expectations, you're in fact saying: this is what I think my work is worth. Meanwhile, you're robbing a colleague of the chance to make five hundred bucks.

Jason Fried is the co-founder and President of software solution provider Basecamp. He recommends you practice charging a reasonable rate from day one. But what he said next was a real eye-opener to me:

> "It's very safe to charge low rates, because you don't have to prove anything. But as soon as you charge a customer a good price, it gives them the power to demand something from you, such as good quality and great service. Those are the types of pressures you want on you as a small business owner. You want to be forced to be good. Charging for something forces you to be good."

10. I don't need to make a full-time income. It's only a hobby.

If it's only a hobby, why are you advertising yourself as a voice-over professional?

I play the piano, but I don't market myself as a concert pianist.

If you enjoy reading to other people, why not volunteer at your local children's hospital or elder care facility? You will probably get more appreciation for doing this, than for anything you've ever done before.

Most talents I know are only freelancing part-time, because they're still building what they hope will become a full-time business. A part-time teacher only gets paid less because she puts in fewer hours. Does a part-time cab driver fix the meter so he can drive you around at half-price? So, why should you offer your services at bottom dollar?

Oh... I see. Your partner has a steady job and the money you make doing the occasional voice-over doesn't have to pay the mortgage, right?

Guess what? In this economy there's no such thing as a steady job anymore. What would happen if your partner gets laid off and you become the sole breadwinner? Can your beer money pay the bills? Do you really think you could raise your rates to make ends meet?

Price buyers are the first to look elsewhere. They don't care about your personal situation. They care about cutting costs. But stop thinking about your own situation for a moment.

There are people who depend on doing this for a living right now, and they think your price dumping is nothing but unfair competition. I admit: you're quite talented, and by charging these low rates you are making it harder and harder for them to justify their fees.

I think it's time for you to think about the bigger picture.

This is not about shameless greed or about becoming filthy rich and famous. This is about being able to provide for your family; being able to send your kids to college and save some money for a rainy day.

Your voice could help sell millions of dollars worth of product. It can introduce people to brilliant books that enrich their lives.

Your voice can be the voice of a mentor, teaching valuable skills to e-learners across the globe.

Your voice can inform, entertain, sell, and assist. Surely, that must be worth something?

However...

Those who can't build value, have nothing left but to compete on price.

[49]

The Lowdown on Lowballing

You've probably heard the story of the priest who preached the same sermon every Sunday. After a few weeks, the parishioners got tired of it and demanded an explanation.

"Do you really want to know why I'm repeating myself at every service?" asked the priest. The crowd nodded.

"I will continue to tell you the same thing over and over again, until you take it to heart and do something with it. If you don't change your behavior, I don't see any reason for me to change my sermon."

Well, I may be the son of a minister, but as a writer, I can certainly relate to this priest. When it comes to setting rates, I sometimes feel I'm talking to a sea of people with frighteningly short memories and no backbone.

Watch me as I go to my pulpit and address the crowd:

FELLOW FREELANCERS, do you know how much you're worth?

Do you have a good sense of how much to charge when a client asks you for a quote? Do you have an idea of how much your full-time and unionized colleagues are charging, nationally and internationally?

If you don't, you shouldn't even think of responding to that latest online job offer. Don't you dare come up with an estimate. You have no business being in this business until you've figured out a basic fee structure.

Imagine going to a photographer to get your headshot taken. Of course you want to know how much it is going to cost. "Well, let me get back to you on that," is not the answer you expect to hear from a pro, is it?

How on earth are you going to determine your basic rate?

Let me get one thing out of the way first. It's not the responsibility of your clients to offer you a good rate. It would be the decent thing to do, but it's your job to negotiate a fair fee.

That fee is determined by how much you need to make in order to survive and by how much you want to make in order to thrive (today and thirty years from now).

In my experience, most freelancers aren't capable of giving a clear answer to both questions. Can you? If not, you are running your business based on guesswork and you're setting yourself up to be taken advantage of.

Your rate should be high enough for clients to take you seriously, and reasonable enough to still attract business in your segment of the market.

As a beginner, here's the worst thing you could do: trying to break into the business by working for stupendously low rates. If you don't know what I mean by a low rate, it's time you do your homework. Don't you know that low rates flag you as an amateur?

If you want to be a pro, grow up and act like it! It is self-evident that as a beginner you're not yet in a position to command top dollar, top euro, or whatever currency you prefer. But that doesn't mean that you should sell yourself short and become a predatory pricer.

A quick reminder. Predatory Pricing is the practice of selling a product or service at a very low price, intending to drive competitors out of the market. It is a strategy for losers and I'll tell you why.

Bargain prices attract bargain shoppers. Low-paying customers are usually high-maintenance customers. You can either believe me, or find it out the hard way. Your choice.

Secondly, people tend to not value things that don't cost them much, and they're much more likely to be dissatisfied with cheap stuff, regardless of the quality of the product.

Third: you will attract clients that expect a gourmet meal at a fast food price and at drive-through speed. As in mountain biking, it's easier to go down than to go up. Once your price level is set, it is hard to justify a higher price.

Fourth: predatory pricing is unfair competition. Dumping your product or service will isolate you from your colleagues and it will negatively impact prevalent prices. Don't blame the anonymous forces of supply and demand for a steady decline in rates. You are as much part of the problem as you are a part of the solution.

Last but not least: show some self-respect! If you don't value your own work, why should I? You have a unique talent. You have invested so much time and money in making it this far. Why would you want to put yourself up for sale in the bargain basement? Don't you deserve better than that?

Now here's a question for you:

Would you charge the same fee for the same type of work to a client in Europe and let's say India? If you don't know the answer, that's okay. Just stop reading and think about it for a moment.

The internet has turned every business into a global business. Sooner or later, you'll have to deal with this issue.

Have you ever heard of the Big Mac index,*** the Tall Latte index, or the iPod index? Clever economists came up with these lists after a lot of hands-on research to illustrate the idea that identical goods have different prices in different markets.

Most prices are based on a local standard of living, the price of raw materials, transportation, labor, taxes, and frankly, on what companies feel they can get away with. That's why pharmaceutical companies sell the same drugs at different prices in different countries.

Economically speaking, the product or service you provide is not so different than a burger, a cup of coffee, or an iPod, iPad, or eyeliner. That means that your client in India is likely to have a different budget than your client in Denmark.

Whether or not you want to work for that budget is up to you. You know what you're worth.

If you're okay with an Indian salary as a US-based freelancer, just tell me how you intend to make ends meet in the States. I don't think your local gas station has started accepting rupees yet. But let's make a deal. Once you've chosen to accept a low rate, stop contaminating social media with complaints that it's so hard to earn a living.

By the way, I don't blame a Chinese company for trying to hire talent at the lowest possible price. They're probably working for a US-based firm that has outsourced certain activities because labor is cheap. After all, we all want our Black Friday bargains, so we're driving that demand for cheap products and services.

I do blame North American and European clients that are trying to make us work for rates that would only be acceptable in countries like India. I also blame online job boards that enable those clients to set these bargain basement rates. And lastly, I blame so-called colleagues who willingly devalue our business by accepting jobs at these rates.

So, how do you determine your fee in an international context?

Let's recap.

First you have to know what your bottom line is before you do anything else. That means answering the question: How much would you minimally need to charge to turn a profit? You are running a for-profit business, aren't you?

Once your bottom line is covered, find out how much this particular job would be worth in the country of the client. If you can live with that rate, that's where you want your quote to be... minimally!

Don't quote that German client 250 US dollars if the going rate in Germany is 250 Euro. Why should you leave any money on the table?

If you start working for less, don't be surprised that this same client will post his next project for 180 Euro. We teach people how to treat us, and this is how rates go down. Clients aren't stupid.

And remember: just because a client needs you, doesn't mean they can afford you, or that you can afford to work for them.

If you would charge $1000 for a project and they're willing to pay $800, it's totally worthwhile to see if you can meet in the middle. But don't spend any time trying to sell champagne to someone on a beer budget, no matter where they live.

These would-be customers don't care that you're using the latest equipment or that you recently completed a project for a prestigious brand. They just want to know how low you're willing to go.

Got it?

Thus endeth my sermon.

[50]

Are You Still Hiding Your Rates?

Whether you're a voice-over artist, a photographer, or a freelance copywriter, sooner or later you'll have to answer this question:

Is it wise to put your rates on your website?

I used to be vehemently against it, but I have changed my mind. To give you an idea why, let's explore both sides of the argument.

Business writer and voice-over professional Maxine Dunn[***] describes herself as a savvy solopreneur. Does she think it's a good idea to post rates? Maxine:

> "No! Definitely not! No way! Never! What if you had a rate on your website that said you charge $600 for something, but the client's budget was actually $3000? Talk about shooting yourself in the foot. Or what if your rate appears too high for a prospective client and you've lost the chance to negotiate with them? I think putting rates on your website makes the client focus on price right away and that's not what you want. It's about your value and how you can help them, not appealing to price shoppers. It's always best to negotiate a rate with a client when you have all the information about a project."

In an informal poll on Facebook, 88% percent of voice talent agrees with Maxine. 9% was undecided and only 3% (one person!) thought listing a rate was a good idea.

Voice actor Mara Junot*** is with the 88%:

> "Years ago I read an article about thinking like a pro and not putting a "ceiling" on oneself with listed rates, and it has undoubtedly served me well. When listing rates up front in the past, I found it was much harder for me to make room for any flexible negotiating of fair fees based on specific factors (...). Most top performers and their agencies don't even have rates in their vocabulary as far as their website is concerned, so as not to create that pre-determined sense of value, especially for the higher-end consumer."

One argument that always comes back is that we are selling a complicated service, not a simple product. It's virtually impossible to come up with a standard rate card because we are dealing with many variables that can all influence our voice-over quote. To name a few:

- the medium (radio, television, internet)
- the market (local, national, international)
- the length, the nature, and the use of the audio
- the value of our expertise, experience, and reputation

Furthermore, rates can be determined per project, per length of script, or per word. Good luck fitting all of that on a neat sheet. It will take several pages to cover all the details. Who wants to read that?

There's also this golden rule in sales that says: "Never mention price until value has been established." Once the client is convinced of your quality, it's much easier to negotiate a decent rate.

Then there's the element of competition.

Do we really want to give our colleagues the information that will allow them to put in a lower bid?

Arno Lubbinge*** was one of the first Dutch voice-overs with an online presence. He has always been open about his pricing. He explains:

> "I see no reason to be mysterious about my rates. When I do an online search for a service or product – whether it's a vacation rental, a vacuum cleaner, or a handyman, I have to get a good feeling about it and I want to know what I'm getting myself into. What does it look like? What do others think of it? And lastly: how much does it cost?
>
> I tried to translate that in terms of my situation as a voice-over pro. I book most of my voice-over projects without ever speaking to the client in person. That's why I think it's important to come across as reliable and to put all my cards on the table. My voice is a valuable investment and my prices and my demos reflect that.
>
> I'm not afraid of undercharging a client with a bigger budget. Usually, it's the opposite. People think my rates are quite up there, which is absolutely true."

PRICING AS A FILTER

Voice-over professionals are by no means unique. We all need to figure out ways to spend our time wisely. In the past, I've spent countless hours with potential clients explaining my services and my rates, only to find out that they had a champagne taste and a beer budget. If you're in sales, you learn not to spend too much time on unqualified buyers.

A freelance photographer was asked about posting prices on his website. He was tired of tire-kickers:

> "If you want to deal with the people who want to haggle, then you shouldn't list the prices. It leads to wasted time spent dealing with folks that in the end aren't going to make you any money anyway.

I have found that listing my prices on my site is good for business. I don't have to spend a whole lot of time replying to emails from people wanting to know prices. When they contact me, they know what to expect."

Clients can be clueless. That's why you need to educate them and manage their expectations. If you're dealing with customers who have no idea how much your service costs, why not tell them upfront? What's the big mystery? Have you ever thought of the fact that you might actually lose business because you're not open about your rates?

The owner of a transcription service added:

"When I'm looking for a service I will generally look at lots of different websites to compare prices. If there isn't a price list I usually don't bother with the company because I assume that their prices are high. It is also a lot more effort to contact a person to find out their prices."

But what about the argument that you might be losing money by posting your rates, because a big budget client could be willing to pay way more? Audio book narrator Jeffrey Kafer*** isn't buying it:

"If my rate for something is $300, then that's what I charge. I don't charge more if the client's budget is higher. When I walk into a grocery store to buy bread, the cashiers don't ask me how much is in my wallet and then charge accordingly. I actually have a rate calculator on my website that covers all kinds of different types of projects. Once they fill it out, I follow up with an email."

MORE THAN MONEY

Let's keep one thing in mind. Just because we're talking about rates doesn't mean that price is always the predominant factor in the selection process. Maybe it is for low-budget clients, but that's not the crowd I wish to attract. The clients I usually work with pick me because of the way I sound and for my ability to interpret their script.

Most of them are willing to pay my going rate and if they're not, they'll find someone else.

Should we still be worried that a rate sheet might scare potential clients off?

Piehole is a voice casting site based in Ireland run by Priscilla Groves and James Kennedy. In one of their blog posts, they discuss reasons why some of us land a job and others don't:

> "For most people hiring a voice-over, they've put a lot of effort into this production. It's more important to get the right voice than haggle over fifty quid. When it comes to voice-over gigs, the majority of the time it's someone in the middle price range who wins the gig (you know the way you never order the cheapest wine on the wine list, same thing). The law of averages says that you have the best chance of being "average," so just knock out your quote and don't think too much about it. The only thing you don't want to be is the bottle of plonk. Everything else is ok."

LESSONS FROM THE POOL GUY

You already know where I stand in this discussion. I'm with Marcus Sheridan.***

Marcus used to sell fiberglass pools until he became a successful speaker on sales and social media. In an article for the Social Media Examiner*** he writes:

> "People like to know how much stuff costs. That's just the way we're all wired. Notwithstanding, the majority of businesses around the world have elected to skirt the subject of pricing on their websites for a variety of reasons, the most common being fear of losing a prospect before he or she ever contacts the company.
>
> And although this "hidden approach" may have worked in marketing five or ten years ago, I'm here to say that today's consumers don't like their core questions to be left unanswered.

Furthermore, if we are truly to embrace content marketing and the essence of social media, we must learn to embrace every question consumers ask our company.

In other words, if your customer is thinking it, you should be addressing it. This transparent, common sense approach is the essence of successful modern-day marketing."

Here's my takeaway:

1. Think like a customer.

If you're not posting your rates online because you believe it might cost you business, you're thinking about yourself and you're probably acting out of fear. A winning website is never about you.

2. Being open about rates attracts business.

Because Sheridan didn't beat about the bush and started addressing the cost of his pools, traffic to his website skyrocketed. Transparency is a good thing. Customers appreciated the fact that he was open about pricing.

3. Listing rates is good for SEO.

My voice-over rates page at Nethervoice.com is one of the most visited pages of my website. Clients check it out all the time, but it also attracts many visits from colleagues.

Once people land on that page, they tend to stay a while to read my blog or to listen to my demos.

4. Be proud of your price.

Your rate is a statement about the quality of your product. You offer great value for money, don't you? Why keep that a secret?

5. Fear paralyzes. Confidence gives you wings.

THE PERFECT RATE SHEET

With a fiberglass pool there are hundreds of factors that can determine the ultimate price. When it comes to voice-over rates (and other freelance rates for that matter), there are also a lot of variables that go into the mix. What to do with that?

When shopping for services, most customers like to get a sense of how much things will cost. That doesn't mean you have to give them a definite number.

Should you decide to be more open about what you charge, I highly recommend you build in some flexibility by either giving a price range or by listing starting rates.

That way, potential customers have a ballpark figure and there's still room for negotiation.

In other words, give potential clients an idea what a project could cost and not what it eventually will cost.

Isn't that the best of both worlds?

[51]

When a Client Owes You

Imagine walking into a fancy restaurant. You like what you see on the menu and you order a three-course meal plus a bottle of Bordeaux. After a short wait, the food arrives, meticulously prepared by an expert chef. The meal is delicious. The wine is divine.

When it's time to pay, you tell the waiter:

"I'd be happy to take care of the bill, but I'm afraid I can't do that right now."

"What seems to be the problem?" the server asks. Your response:

"Well, I'm a little low on cash right now. I'm waiting for someone to send me a check. Once that money is in my account, I can pay you. That could take a few weeks or even a month. I'm sure you understand the position I'm in. I promise you'll get your money. Just not today."

It's an absurd scenario, but if you're a freelancer it's not uncommon. According to the Freelancers Union, almost 80% of independent workers will be stiffed by clients in their careers. Right now, two of those clients are telling me that I'll get paid as soon as they get paid. Is that how it works?

These clients wanted me to deliver ASAP, and now they are urging me to be patient. They were hired by another company to deliver a package of e-Learning modules to a third company. If one company delays the pay, everyone has to wait and pray. That's the idea.

What the people I work for are really saying is this: It's not our fault that you're not getting paid. We're just as much of a victim as you are. And then they always add this line:

"These things happen, especially in this economy."

Excuse me?

Sometimes I feel like saying:

"I understand what you are trying to tell me, but how you deal with your clients is none of my business. Literally. Recession or no recession. Your clients didn't hire me. You did. We have an agreement. I have kept my part of the deal. Now it's up to you to do the same. Don't order things you can't pay for."

Unfortunately, freelancers (over 42 million in the U.S. alone) are easy targets. Unlike more traditional employees, freelancers have very little payment protection. Most of them run small operations and don't have the time, the means, or the energy to go after deadbeats.

So, what to do when a client fails to pay you?

Before we get practical, let's talk about something I've noticed time and again when this subject comes up.

Some freelancers feel funny about money.

Even though they know their client owes them, they have a hard time confronting that client. The same people cave in during negotiations soon after the first objection is raised.

After coaching a number of colleagues on money matters, I noticed that these people have a few things in common, personality-wise:

- They have a tough time dealing with conflict in general
- They have issues related to self-worth
- They tend to take things personally
- They haven't learned how to be professional
- They don't know how to deal with fear

Does some of this sound familiar to you?

ARE YOU A DOORMAT

Let's start with number one. As long as you see your client as your boss, you will act and react as a subordinate and the client is in control. After all, a boss is an authority figure, and from an early age you have learned to listen and obey. Heaven forbid you'd challenge their position.

By playing that game as a child, you earned the love of your parents and you received praise from your teachers. You always did what you were supposed to do. You never caused any trouble. It's the tragedy of the "good child."

Those who avoid conflict never learn to stand up for themselves and allow the world to walk all over them. Guess what? The world is more than happy to oblige! If you have a rather weak spine and a client owes you money, there are a few things I need to tell you.

First of all: Your client is not your superior. As an independent contractor, you work *with* someone, not *for* someone. It's a relationship of equals. Didn't you become a freelancer so you could be your own boss?

Secondly, it is important to remember that you did not create this situation. You have honored your part of the contract or verbal agreement, right? If that's the case, then there's no reason to feel wrong or guilty about asking for your money. You've earned it... unless deep down inside you feel you didn't.

I'd be the last one to suggest that someone's sense of self-worth is directly and totally related to what's in his or her bank account. However, I have noticed a correlation between a person's level of self-esteem and their level of confidence when it comes to pricing.

To put it bluntly: those who don't feel they deserve it (consciously or unconsciously), have a hard time asking for it. If that's you, you have also fallen into trap number three: you think this whole money-thing is personal.

I like to be on good terms with my clients. Some of them go way back. It's wonderful to see their businesses grow, knowing that I have played a part in their success. But even though we're on a first-name basis, they are not my friends. They are the people I work with. At the end of the day, I offer a solution to their problem.

My voice helps them sell their service and it praises their products. I educate their employees and welcome their customers. In exchange, I get paid a very, very small percentage of their profits. It's business. It's a professional relationship. Keep that in mind when a client tries to play the "I thought we were friends-card," after you've kindly asked him or her to pay up.

BE A PRO

In my experience, those who are rather reluctant to put their foot down when it comes to payment, find it challenging to act as a professional across the board.

They expect the world to treat them the way they treat other people. They operate on the basis of trust and good intentions. They jump on a new client like a dog in heat, assuming that everything will work out for the best. I'm sorry to burst your bubble, but clients have to be qualified and trust needs to be earned. Otherwise you'll get burned.

Qualifying clients means finding out whom you're dealing with. In other words: You've got to do your homework!

Ask them to sign a contract or working agreement, and if they refuse, it's a red flag. Some colleagues won't get to work unless the client pays up front or puts fifty percent down. If they refuse, that's another red flag. When I make these suggestions, I almost always get the same reaction:

> "But what if the client walks away because he doesn't like my terms and conditions? Then what?"

This brings me to point number five: Fear.

Not all fear is bad.

The population of the Netherlands knows a little bit about that.

After a disastrous flood killed thousands of people in 1953, they were afraid it could happen again. Instead of running away from the problem, the Dutch became damn good at building dikes to protect the lowlands. Nowadays, those who live close to the sea can feel confident that they're safe, even when it storms.

As a solopreneur, it's your job to protect your own interests or you'll go under. No one else will do it for you. This means keeping a paper trail on all your clients. If you don't use a formal contract, you must save that email in which your client hires you to provide a certain service. Make sure they know and agree to your terms of payment. If you'd like to formalize the relationship, check out the free Contract Creator*** from the Freelancers Union.

Having such a contract shouldn't scare a legitimate company away. If anything, it proves you're a pro. Would you really trust a new client who refuses to sign anything that's more than reasonable, especially if that client is located on the other side of the globe? Don't be afraid to lose business you're better off not having in the first place!

The mistake many people make is that they confuse uncertainty with fear. With the freedom of being a freelancer comes the unpredictability of being in business. Even those whom you might think of as "established," have months that are great and months that are not so great. That's why they never stop marketing themselves.

If uncertainty is too hard to handle, get a job as funeral director or tax collector.

I've been a freelancer for most of my life and at times I despise the unpredictability of my career. One company I worked for had contracts with Fortune 100 companies. The man who managed my accounts promised me a constant stream of scripts from the best global brands in the world. For a while I thought I had hit the jackpot.... until he was replaced. His successor never called.

When business is slow, the temptation to compromise is greater. Clients pick up on that in a heartbeat and will start twisting your arm as much as they can. Insecurity does not win contracts and fear will never pay your bills.

When dealing with an unpaid invoice, be confident that you can work something out instead of being afraid that you'll ruin the relationship. Successful people focus on what they want. Fearful people focus on what they don't want.

You're more likely to attract what you focus on most.

RISKY BUSINESS

And finally, an entrepreneur is often defined as:

> "a person who organizes and operates a business or businesses, taking on greater than normal financial risks in order to do so"

Some people say that if you own your business, you should expect that at least one percent of your bills will never get paid. The older the debt, the harder it is to collect. Common sense dictates that you should build that risk into your rate.

A few questions remain.

Should you hunt your debtors down like a hungry bloodhound, or is it better to write things off and focus on those clients you can rely on?

And how did I resolve the situation with the two companies that still owe me money?

More about that, later.

Right now, I think I'll try out that new restaurant in town.

I've worked hard today.

I believe I have earned a nice meal and a good glass of Bordeaux.

Cheers!

[52]

Give Me My Money!

The previous chapter may have disappointed you slightly. Perhaps you thought I was going to give you a few quick tips on how to handle non-paying clients. Instead, I asked you to take a good look at your relationship with money.

"I am not the one to blame," said one colleague. "Why should I feel guilty when a client refuses to pay me when the invoice is due? I delivered my work on time. Don't make me the bad guy!"

I wasn't trying to guilt-trip anyone, but there's a reason why I wanted you to take a look in the mirror when it comes to finances. As a freelancer, you are responsible for how you run your business. If you've done everything right and your client still isn't paying, remember this:

It's not your fault, but it is your problem.

"Doing everything right" means being on top of your finances. To you that might be a given. That's because you are a pro. However, you'd be surprised how many freelancers don't keep track of how much goes out and how much is coming in. They're simply not that interested in money. Yes, they'd like to get paid, but that's not the reason why they do what they do.

346 | *Making Money In Your PJS*

Every year, wonderful, sweet, talented, creative, intelligent, and trusting people go bankrupt because their finances are a mess. Not being on top of your finances can lead to embarrassing situations.

CARELESS MISTAKES

One colleague got mad at a non-paying customer and wrote a rather firm email. In response, the client told him they were still waiting for the invoice that was never sent.

Another colleague got all worked up because he thought he'd be paid within a month. Before he contacted the client, he looked at the contract he had signed. It said he'd be paid within 90 days.

"What's the big deal?" said one of my voice-over friends. "One client owes me $250 and another $300. I'm not losing any sleep over these small amounts. It's just money, anyway."

The last time I heard from him, he was selling some of his equipment on eBay. Small amounts do add up, and apparently, quite a few of his clients had taken advantage of his happy-go-lucky attitude.

So, before you moan and groan about your deadbeat clients, think about what you can do to decrease the chance that you'll be taken advantage of.

MANAGING YOUR MONEY

Now, we all have our strengths and weaknesses. I'm pretty good with words, but numbers do not thrill me. They never have. My wife on the other hand, is a great bookkeeper. She's efficient and organized, and that's why she's my Chief Financial Officer.

When a client needs a gentle reminder, she usually takes care of it. That way, I don't have to be the enforcer and potentially sour a relationship with a late-paying customer. I can be the good guy who delivers the goods with a smile.

You cannot manage what you don't measure. Should you decide to be your own CFO, then you must choose a system suited to your business that clearly shows your income and expenses.

Services such as FreshBooks,*** ZoHoBooks*** or Invoicera*** are meant to make accounting and invoicing less intimidating. Secondly, you have to develop the discipline to keep your records up to date. Reserve one day a week to do the books. That way you'll know exactly where you stand.

TERMS & CONDITIONS

With an accounting system in place, you need to figure out how you'd like to get paid and when. The only way you can be sure you get your money, is to require payment up front. That sounds great in theory, but not every client is going to say yes to that. Unless you have a unique, rock solid position in the market place, or your customer is desperate to hire you, you do not have a lot of leverage to get paid before handing over the goods.

Second best is the 50-50 system. Ask for half of your fee as a deposit, and for the other half when the job is done. Once the invoice is paid in full, you release your work. Not a day earlier. If the client wants proof before paying the remainder of the balance, simply send a sample of the completed project.

If the client insists on paying after the fact, you must decide how quickly you want your money: net 7, net 14, net 30. Some clients will ask you to sign a contract with different terms. Let's say company X reserves the right to pay you after 90 days and your policy is net 30. Try to meet in the middle and get to net 60.

Whatever you agree upon, always put things in writing and have the client sign on the dotted line or confirm via email. A verbal agreement only carries weight if you can prove it in court. That usually means that witnesses need to be present when you shake hands.

Otherwise you might end up in a costly he-said-she-said situation. Even with a written agreement in place, there's no absolute guarantee that you'll be paid on time. That's where incentives come in.

You have two options to motivate your client: the carrot or the stick.

You can either offer a discount for early payment in full, or institute a penalty for those who pay late. If you decide to take 10% off for good behavior, I would raise rates by 10% before instituting that policy.

In general, I'm all for reinforcing desired behavior. If a client has been systematically ignoring your requests to be paid, a late fee might not make a huge impression.

EASY DOES IT

And finally, remove all obstacles and possible excuses clients may come up with to not pay your bill. Make it easy for them to send you money. Sometimes it means educating your clients.

I require international customers to use PayPal.

One of my clients was hesitant because she thought she'd have to sign up for that service. Once I told her membership was optional, the client asked me to send a money request. Thirty minutes later, I got paid.

Quite often, the person who hired you is not in charge of payments. Always ask to whom you should send your invoice and deal with that person directly. You do not want to hear that the department that processes payments never received your invoice.

Whenever you send the finished product, always ask the client to confirm receipt. That way they cannot claim they never got it.

If your rate includes a limited number of retakes or corrections, be explicit about it. You don't want to end up recording more versions every time a copywriter has a new idea, and not get paid until everyone is satisfied.

GETTING PAID

In a perfect world, every client could be trusted and everyone would always pay on time. We all know that reality is not like that. So, what to do when a client keeps you waiting or does not pay you at all?

There is no straight answer because I think it really depends on your relationship with your client. Here's what I do:

1. I am willing to cut returning clients with a solid payment history a lot of slack. They've been there for me. I've been there for them. We'll work it out.

New clients, on the other hand, still need to prove themselves before I give them any credit. I'm not going to trust someone just because he or she sounds nice on the phone.

2. I tend to build in more safeguards with clients outside of my geographical area or jurisdiction. It's much harder to recoup money from clients on the other end of the globe than from those in my back yard. The more money is at stake, the more guarantees I'll need.

3. When a client owes me, I refuse to get emotional. I usually send a few polite and understanding reminders. I'll send the first one a month after the invoice was due, and the other a week after that. Nine out of ten times I get an apology and a check. If that's not the case, I get on the phone to find out what's going on.

4. The more flexible I am, the greater the chance that I will see my money. Flexible doesn't mean letting someone off the hook. It could mean offering a payment plan. By being willing to work with these clients, I can save the professional relationship and create some goodwill. I would hate to lose a good client over something as stupid as money.

When things go downhill, it helps to have some leverage, A few weeks ago, a client who still owed me asked if I could record a second video in a series for a specific client. I told him I'd be happy to do that once the outstanding invoice was paid. That same day the situation was resolved.

5. If nothing seems to work, I will notify the client in a certified letter that I have no other option but to turn them over to collections. Most of the time that will do the trick for domestic clients.

ESCALATION

So far so good, but what to do when things get out of hand and the client isn't open to reason?

At this time it's fair to say that your relationship is pretty much ruined. It's time to put your foot down and apply some pressure.

6. Sometimes it helps to contact the end-client. Let me give you an example.

A few years ago, I voiced a video for a small Scandinavian production house. They were hired by a manufacturer of appliances to produce promos for the European market.

Months went by and I had yet to be paid. My friendly reminders fell on deaf ears. Meanwhile, the videos with my voice were all over cyberspace. Not cool.

I decided to write an email to the CEO of the appliance manufacturer explaining the situation. He apologized profusely, and promised to get in touch with the production company. Two days later I received my payment. Needless to say, the Scandinavian production house never contacted me for other work and that was just fine with me.

7. Of course you can hand your case over to a collection agency. If you're in the U.S., companies like the Media Recovery Group, Inc.***

and Cambridge Receivable Solutions, LLC,*** specialize in debt collection for freelancers and small businesses.

ZenCash*** offers a collection solution that connects to your current invoicing software (such as Quickbooks, FreshBooks and others) to automatically send out notices to your customers when they are late on a payment. This is not a free service, but you only pay for what you use.

GOING TO COURT

8. If the non-paying client is in your jurisdiction, you can take him or her to small claims court.*** Depending on where you file, your claim may not exceed between $3,000 and $10,000.

Attorney, actor, and voice talent Robert Sciglimpaglia Jr. – author of *VoiceOver Legal**** (a book every voice-over should own) – notes that you can put a clause in your contract saying that your client agrees to submit to the jurisdiction of the state court where you are located. Should you have to sue, you can sue them in your own court, without having to travel to them. You could also pursue a lawsuit out-of-state and include filing costs and travel expenses in your claim.

One word of warning. Winning your case in small claims court does not mean that you will see your money. The court rules but does not collect. Follow this link*** to read about how one freelancer won her case. It will give you a good idea of what's involved.

Before you decide to go to court, figure out whether or not the amount owed is worth your time, energy, and money collecting it. One colleague told me that anything under $1,000 isn't worth the trouble and aggravation. This brings me to your last option.

FORGET ABOUT IT

9. You can decide not to collect the money; never work for those deadbeat clients again, and tell the world about how you've been

treated. Shame your non-paying clients publicly and warn your colleagues. Social media can be devastatingly powerful.

The Freelancers Union has a client scorecard*** where businesses are rated by members. Bear in mind that this is a work in progress. Many companies have only been evaluated by one person. When more contributions come in, this could become a very useful tool.

By the way, membership in the Freelancers Union is free.

THE FINAL WORD

In closing I'd like to suggest that it's easy to talk and think about money in abstract terms. But money is more than a bunch of boring numbers in a bank account.

By charging a decent rate, you tell the world that you firmly believe your service is valuable. By paying you, clients show that they value and respect your work.

Those who use your work without paying for it, are thieves and they deserve to face the consequences.

The bottom line is that you are not powerless.

You can protect yourself against crooks and criminals.

In order to do that, you need to organize and guard your business to the best of your abilities.

As a freelancer, you probably put a lot more hours into your business compared to people with a regular job. You also run a bigger risk.

For that, you deserve to be well compensated.

You owe it to yourself.

[53]

Asking for a Raise

The project was perfect.

It had my name written all over it.

Better still, I didn't even have to submit a demo. It was mine!

There was only one problem: the budget. It was a bit low.

I asked myself: "Shall I do it anyway?" It would certainly be nice to add another prestigious brand name to my portfolio. And if they liked me, perhaps they'd hire me at a better rate next time.

Seconds later I knew I wasn't making any sense. Big brands have big budgets. Even for voice-overs. And every sales person on earth knows that the first offer is never the best.

It's a test.

Assume I'd say yes to what they were offering right now. I'd set a precedent. Why would a client feel inclined to pay me more next time?

If I really wanted this job, there was only one solution: I had to ask for a raise.

Now, if you ask the average American worker what they fear most, it is negotiating salary. Most people feel lucky to have a job or a job offer. They'd rather take what's on the table, than risk losing everything.

If we are to believe recent polls, less than a third of respondents say they negotiate salary after receiving a job offer, and that number is going down every year.

One-fifth of U.S. workers never even bring it up. Almost half of the people who were interviewed didn't bother to ask for a raise during an annual performance review. What does that tell us?

When it comes to asking for money, most people are terrified and insecure. Women more so than men. They're also unprepared.

Let's start with that.

The first lesson in "Asking for a raise 101" is to know what you're worth. That means doing your homework. Some colleagues are more diligent than others. Take the folks who don't have a clue how much they should charge. As a result they are practically asking for peanuts.

I don't believe that every lowballer bidding on a specific freelance job is purposely trying to undercut the competition. They're offering to do it for less because they believe their rate is perfectly reasonable. They'll tell you:

"A hundred bucks for a two-minute voice-over is good money. It beats bagging groceries at the supermarket."

What they forget is that they're comparing apples and oranges. Voice-overs don't bill for their time or for how many customers they can serve during an eight-hour shift.

Like so many other creative freelancers, voice-overs get paid for their expertise and their experience.

You cannot compare the salary of a steady job with benefits to the unpredictable position of a freelancer who has to build things like health insurance and a pension plan into his rate.

A freelance fee also has to pay for the many hours spent looking for work; it has to pay for marketing, for materials used, rent of work space, an internet connection, a smart phone, a laptop, continuing education, et cetera. Those are expenses employees with a nine-to-five job don't have.

Uneducated and inexperienced freelancers can leave a lot of money on the table because they're bidding blindly. They plug in a number without bothering to check how much others are asking for similar services. That, by the way, was how I knew that what this client with the perfect project was offering, was not enough.

Here's the thing. If you're going to ask a potential client to increase the budget, you need to know how much you want and why you want it. Don't assume the client will understand. Tell him or her why you believe you deserve it. Make clear how much work is involved.

If he's offering a local rate for a nationwide commercial, explain that a greater reach comes with a different price tag. If the job requires hours of editing, let the client know that you have to build that into your fee.

Communication is crucial.

Providing your client with information is just one part of the negotiation process. How you present that information is even more important. If you're just trying to get a few extra bucks out of the deal but you haven't convinced yourself that you're worth it, you won't get anywhere. Clients aren't stupid. They pick up on all the non-verbals.

If you're not confident that you should be paid a certain amount, you will sound insecure. You'll use words as "perhaps" and "maybe."

356 | Making Money In Your PJS

Your voice will quiver and go up at the end of a sentence as if you're not really sure of yourself. You'll cave after the first objection.

If, on the other hand, you feel strongly about your case, your voice needs to reflect confidence. You're stating facts.

You're not opening the door to a discussion. Your fee is your fee.

I'm not asking you to act like an arrogant jerk. I'm simply asking you to stand up for yourself. Be respectful and keep it businesslike.

What you're actually doing is selling. You're telling the client: Trust me! Buy me!

Would you rather buy from someone who sounds confident or from someone who doesn't sound sure of what he or she is doing?

In my case, I didn't need a confidence boost. The client had contacted me, and of all the voices they could have picked, they wanted me to do the job. That put me in a stronger bargaining position. Still, there's always the possibility that they could go shopping for a cheaper voice. That brings me to lesson number three:

Be prepared to walk away from a bad deal.

You've done your homework. You know what you're worth and you've stated your case with confidence.

Be ready to be rejected.

Should that happen, don't take it personally. It's just money and you'll get better job offers. Besides, if you get a sense that there's a willingness to continue the negotiation, you can always try to meet in the middle. Know your bottom line and give them a new number. Don't quit the game while you're still playing.

If you really feel that there's no wiggle room, don't waste your energy. Thank the client for contacting you and refer them to a colleague who you know charges even more than you do. That will give them something to think about.

Don't be surprised if the client gets back in touch once they realize that your rate wasn't so bad after all...

I didn't have to go that far to secure my perfect project. All I needed was a brief email exchange.

Based on the word count, I told my client how long it would take me to record his script. He was new to voice casting and had no idea it would take that many hours. After checking in with his supervisor, he accepted my quote and that was that.

Looking back, it didn't take much and it didn't take long for me to negotiate an amount I could live with. That doesn't make me special. Anyone can do it, yet, not everyone will. It depends on your mindset.

Realize this.

If you decide to leave money on the table, it means your client isn't paying for it.

You are!

[54]

Breaking Down an Audio Book Rate

"Attention Voice-Mart shoppers, in aisle seven you'll find a fresh selection of promising audio book narrators, ready to read your epic 300-page novel for only $499.99. But hurry! Only today, they'll throw in free editing. That's right, a $299.99 value could be yours, absolutely FREE."

The shrill sound of my phone woke me up out of a bad dream. So much for power naps!

Ever since I had helped my friend Fernanda with her website, she regularly calls me because she wants to pick my brain about the voice-over business. Her enthusiasm is contagious, and sometimes I feel almost guilty to be the one who has to bring her down to earth again.

The thing is, Fernanda is incredibly talented. I could listen to her voice for hours, and as it turns out, I'm not the only one. Not only is she blessed with amazing vocal cords; Fernanda has the uncanny ability to take you on a journey to a place where time and space no longer exist.

Her unique talent is only matched by her youthful naiveté about the less artistic aspects of our work; minor details such as contracts, rates, self-promotion... you know, the boring stuff. In other words: she's the ideal candidate to be taken for a ride. The other day it almost happened again.

A GENEROUS OFFER

"Paul, I found this amazing project online. Can I read it to you?" Fernanda asked.

"By all means," I replied. "Shoot."

"Well, it's for an audio book," she continued, "and they're offering between 500 and 750 dollars."

"Wow," I said positively underwhelmed. "Why so much? How many pages does this book have? Thirty?"

"Oh, I don't know," said Fernanda. "Are you going to be a party pooper again?"

"It depends," I said. "Any other information about this masterpiece? Is there a script for a custom demo? Do you know the word count? Are you sure these are not the sordid memoirs of some perverted, monstrous mind?"

She gave me the web page with the job posting and I glanced over the details... that were not there. The voice-seeker did offer a link to a page on Amazon.com, and lo and behold, we found the book. It was called *Ahead of the Curve: A Commonsense Guide to Forecasting Business and Market Cycles*, by Joseph H. Ellis.* Even the summary looked promising:

"Economic events are not as random and unpredictable as they seem. This book will help readers recognize and react to signs of change that their rivals don't see – and win a sizable competitive advantage."

"Alright. This doesn't sound like the autobiography of a madman to me. That's a definite plus," I said. "Let's find out who this Mr. Ellis really is." Harvard Business Publishing had the answer:

"Joseph H. Ellis was a partner at Goldman Sachs and was ranked for 18 consecutive years by Institutional Investor magazine as Wall Street's No.1 retail industry analyst."

COUNTING PAGES

The Harvard web page also gave us another vital missing piece of information. I learned that we were talking about a 304-page hardback.

"Now, how long do you think it would take you to record this book?" I asked Fernanda. "Two hours, a day, a week?"

She admitted that she didn't really have a clue. That was my signal to go into my Sherlock Holmes mode.

"So far we have established that this guide is over three hundred pages long. We don't know anything about the actual word count, though. That will depend on the font, the font-size, the spaces, and the margins. It's amazing what some academics manage to fit on a page by using a 10-point font.

On the other hand, I've seen four hundred page volumes packed with graphs and other illustrations, printed in a 12-point font, double-spaced, and with wide margins. In other words: the pages were filled with fluff."

Fernanda sounded discouraged. "What do you suggest I do? Go to the bookstore and buy the book? If I don't put in a bid within the next five minutes, four dozen others will have jumped on this project and I might as well forget about it."

"If I were you, this is what I would do," I said. "Why don't you come up with an estimate that's based on the assumption that the average manuscript is printed in 12 point Arial, double-spaced, margin-to-margin. According to the handy-dandy Edge Studio Words-to-Time Converter,*** the typical reading time for such a page is one minute and forty seconds. Based on these parameters, how long would it approximately take you to read this book?

300 pages x 100 seconds = 30,000 seconds = 8.33 hours

The next question is: How much would you charge for a minimum of eight and a half hours of work?

Here's the easy answer. You are an independent contractor, are you not? Theoretically, that means that you can charge whatever you think you're worth. If your name is Julia Roberts, you'll probably get it. If you're not, dream on.

Bear in mind that audio books usually pay per finished hour (the length of the final product) rather than based on the length of time you spend in your studio.

A completed hour includes the time you need to prepare yourself for the recording. I spent hours and hours reading and researching my last audio book. It was filled with foreign names. I had to practice unusual accents and I had to annotate the script.

My scripts are usually packed with symbols and colors. Just as an opera singer would make notes on where to breathe and where to place accents, I do the same thing. Every character is highlighted in a different color, making it easy for me to change my voice and speech patterns. All of this takes time. Lots of time.

Back to this offer. Does the client expect you to do all the editing and mastering? You know very well that editing an hour of audio could easily take you two to three hours.

Now, add all of that up: prep time, recording time, editing, and mastering. When you're negotiating your rate for a finished hour of audio, make sure you're getting paid for all these things. Of course you could always outsource your editing and mastering, but that's going to come out of your fee.

UNION OR NON-UNION?

If we were to take out the table of contents, the footnotes, and any other fluff, you're probably looking at eight completed hours on CD.

New narrators who happen to be SAG-AFTRA members, can charge $150 per hour, which would give you $1,200 (The 2014 SAG-AFTRA rate ranges from $150 to $240 per finished hour).

If you don't belong to SAG-AFTRA, the world you live in looks very different. The Edge Studio explicitly says that their published voice-over rates are "pure suggestions for less experienced, non-union talent. Rates reflect average and realistic rates being fairly charged within the industry, and do NOT include editing."

For audio books their rates are:***

- Inexperienced narrator – $85 to $100 per completed hour
- Moderately Experienced – $90 to $150 per completed hour
- Very Experienced – $150 to $250 per completed hour

In other words: according to Edge Studio, the very, very inexperienced reader could realistically charge $680 for eight completed hours (8 x $85). Her colleague on the other end of the spectrum could charge $2000.

But we're not done yet. There are other sources we can use to determine your bid for this Wall Street saga.

The Voices.com resources rate page*** has an overview per project category. The indicated range for audio books is $250-$500 per finished hour. Voices.com suggests that clients pay vocal artists $300 for the first hour of work and then another $100 for every finished hour thereafter.

Voices.com has a second online rate sheet.***

Based on this overview, the site suggests $150 for a one-hour audio book recording session or $500 per finished hour.

Let's say that you'd minimally need 20 hours to produce an 8-hour audio book. That would mean $300 plus 19 x $100 = $2,200 in the first scenario, or 8 x $500 = $4,000 in the second scenario.

On top of that, the client would pay an extra 10% SurePay escrow fee.

GUESSWORK?

I'd be the first one to agree that these numbers are based on a few assumptions, because the voice-seeker left out vital information when posting the job (either by accident or on purpose). However, the rates I used are in the public domain.

Fernanda, remind me, what book were we talking about again?"

"A 304-page guide, written by former Goldman Sachs partner and Wall Street's No.1 retail industry analyst that 'will help readers recognize and react to signs of change that their rivals don't see – and win a sizable competitive advantage.'"

"And how much is the client offering again?"

"Between 500 and 750 dollars."

"How many responses did the voice-seeker receive so far?"

"Only 105."

"How much do you think the client will end up paying for a narrator?" Fernanda asked. "And is there a minimum rate per project?"

"Unless you happen to run into the person who put in the winning bid, you'll never know," I said. "But I would be very surprised if all 105 hopefuls would bid the $750 maximum. Can you even call it a winning bid, or is it more realistic to speak of a losing bid?

Anyway, Voices.com has a minimum project posting requirement for any job posted publicly, and this amount is $100. Privately it can be even less.

But let's not turn this into another Pay-to-Play issue. Take a good look at a majority of the projects posted on these sites. I don't think we're exactly talking about the high-end of the market.

When it comes to determining reasonable voice-over rates, we've only just begun to scratch the surface.

If you really want to discuss what you should charge, there are two crucial questions you need to ask yourself first:

- How much do I need to make?
- How much do I want to make?

But let's talk about that some other time. I think I need to get back to my power nap now."

I put the phone down.

The comfortable couch was still there waiting for me. I rearranged a few pillows and curled up in a ball.

As soon as I closed my eyes, a soothing voice whispered into my ear:

"Thank you for shopping at Voice-Mart. Please come again soon."

* The author of the book that was used as an example in this chapter, was not the voice-seeker for this project. However, this was a real project posted on a well-known voice casting site.

PART EIGHT: THE INNER GAME

[55]

Why Some Will Never Make It

I remember exactly where I was when it happened.

On my way to Las Vegas, I popped in a Tony Robbins CD from his Personal Power series.

Tony Robbins is a hugely successful motivational speaker, trainer and writer. If you have a million dollars, he'll give you his private number and you may call him 365 days a year for a private coaching session.

People either love him or hate him.

Those who hate him are usually put off by his hyped up, in your face presentation style. Those who love him are pumped up by his towering presence and contagious enthusiasm, whether it's on CD, during a live seminar, or on TV.

Robbins built his career on the study of success. Following in the footsteps of NLP-creators*** Bandler*** and Grinder,*** Robbins developed a toolbox based on what he calls Neuro Associative Conditioning (NAC). It's a mix of positive attitudes, beliefs, and strategies that help people design and live the life they've always dreamed of.

At the basis of NLP and NAC is the process of modeling.*** I'm not talking about the catwalk in Milan, but about the study of exceptional people: business tycoons, sports icons, therapists, artists, et cetera.

The idea is that these people, in order to achieve something extraordinary, have set themselves up for success. They have carefully (and often unconsciously) conditioned themselves to accomplish astonishing things. Modeling is all about uncovering and learning from what goes on behind the scenes: what instructions do these people give their brains and bodies?

Take Steve Jobs, Richard Branson, or Oprah Winfrey. None of them seemed to be destined for greatness. Jobs was given up for adoption by a Syrian Muslim. Branson suffers from dyslexia and was academically challenged. Winfrey was born into poverty to a teenage single mother and raised in an inner-city neighborhood. Look at what they have accomplished!

What is the secret to their success? Is there a recipe? Can it be broken down into bits and pieces and taught to mere mortals such as you and me? Robbins firmly believes it can be done, and one of the key ingredients of this recipe for success can be captured in a single word:

MINDSET

You might not be able to choose the cards life has dealt you, but at least you control how you approach and play the game. Your mindset is the filter through which you look at reality and interpret what it means to you and which actions to take.

A mindset is not something you were born with that operates outside of your awareness. A mindset is a choice. You determine whether the glass is half empty or half full. Not your mother or father or teacher or upbringing or education or race or any set of circumstances.

What separates Winfrey, Branson, and Jobs from the rest, is a foundation of empowering beliefs. An empowering belief is the difference between looking at the world in terms of problems or in terms of opportunities.

An empowering belief is the difference between looking at obstacles as roadblocks or as stepping-stones. An empowering belief is the difference between "I'll never be able to do it" and "Yes I can!"

WHAT DRIVES YOU

As I was cruising through the dry Nevada desert, Robbins talked about another powerful principle he had modeled. Whether in sports, politics, business, or in the entertainment industry, all leaders had this in common:

They knew the difference between being interested and being committed.

The interested person is merely exploring options.
The committed person is going for it.

The interested person says: "I'd like to," "I'm thinking of," "It would be nice..."
The committed person says: "This is my path," "This is my passion," "Nothing can stop me."

The interested person reactively responds to opportunities.
The committed person pro-actively creates opportunities.

The interested person is not invested in the outcome.
The committed person does whatever it takes to achieve the outcome.

The interested person is conditioned to "trying."
The committed person is conditioned to "doing."

The interested person always has reasons.
The committed person has results.

When I look at my own voice-over community, I hear a lot of whining and complaining about how hard it is to break into the business and earn a living. Reading between the lines, I notice an undeserved sense of entitlement and lack of respect for what it takes to make it.

Sorry folks, but there are no silver platters, silver bullets, or golden shortcuts to the top. It comes down to this: what are YOU willing to DO to build a solid career and live a meaningful life?

Are you merely interested or are you truly committed? Of course you're entitled to your hopes, your dreams, and your aspirations. Don't let me take them away from you. But it's up to you to make them a reality.

It's nice to be 'interested' in something and fantasize about your future. I'm all for creative visualization. But without ACTION a dream will always be a dream: something you intend to do... one day. And you know what they say about the road that's paved with good intentions.

According to Robbins, successful role models know how to turn those intentions into a magnificent obsession. They channel their energy and focus it like a laser beam. To the rest of the world, it looks like these people are working their butts off, but to them it doesn't even feel like work. They're having the best time of their life!

Committed people don't let things happen. They make things happen.

Committed people don't complain about something. They do something about it.

Committed people don't quit. They learn from experience and move on.

Commitment is a solemn agreement you make with yourself to do everything it takes to achieve a goal, and then some.

STARTING OVER

If you're sick and tired of all the excuses and rationalizations, the ifs, the buts, and the maybes, perhaps you are ready to commit yourself and decide that your time has come.

If that's the case, I have a question for you. Please don't answer it until you have fully considered it.

What's the one thing you can do today, to show the world (and yourself) that you're truly, madly, and deeply committed?

Use the Power of Now*** and DO IT.

For losers, there's always "tomorrow."

This moment is yours, today.

Embrace it and hold on to it, for the rest of your life!

[56]

That Dreaded Audition

"Do you ever get nervous before an audition?" a colleague wanted to know.

Let's name him Jack.

"Not really," I said. "I find nerves to be extremely unhelpful. Most of the time they're the result of future memories.

"Future memories? What do you mean by that?" my colleague wanted to know.

"Well, in my mind, a memory is a reconstruction of an interpretation of what we think has happened to us in the past.

A future memory is something we've made up that we believe might happen one day. It's equally unreliable, and yet people can get all worked up over them. Especially those who are into worst-case-scenario thinking. Nobody can say with certainty what's going to happen. Take it from me, there's nothing as unpredictable as the outcome of an audition."

"Why is that?" asked Jack.

"Because it's not something we can completely control."

"But what about things like talent and preparation?" said Jack. "Talent is something we can cultivate and it's up to us to prepare for an audition as best as we can. Isn't that control?"

"To a certain extent," I replied.

"Let's assume you're getting ready for a trip to the mountains. You bring the right gear and the right maps. But as soon as you board the train, you notice it's heading for the beach. You're perfectly prepared for the wrong destination.

That's what often happens when you're doing an audition. You think you've done everything right, but the client has a very different direction in mind. Who is to blame?"

"Good point," said Jack. "Most of the time, audition instructions are either lacking or they are incredibly vague. I just got a script asking for a narrator who could exude a humble confidence. What's that supposed to mean? How does that even sound?"

"In order to come up with that," I continued, "you'd have to create something based on your imagination and experience. Who is to say that your version will resonate with what the anonymous client has in mind? I was once asked to do a Dutch-accented voice-over and the director didn't like it at all. Now, I'm from Holland so I should know what a typical Dutch accent sounds like, right?"

"So, what was the problem?" asked Jack.

"The director had seen the movie *Goldmember* in which Mike Meyers plays Johan van der Smut who supposedly has a Dutch accent. Apparently, that's what he wanted to hear from me. I didn't know that. How could I?

People have these unspoken preconceptions and unless you can read minds or they tell you, you'll never find out what goes on between their ears."

"You just described my previous marriage," said Jack with a faint smile.

"Often," I continued, "people get nervous because they are unsure they can live up to expectations they're not even certain of. It's an impossible situation. Yet, they desperately want to please and be accepted. They're so afraid of the word NO.

Especially those who let their sense of self-worth depend on what others think of them, are vulnerable. And when they don't get the job, they blame themselves because they feel they weren't good enough or undeserving. If you don't have a thick skin, this business can get really tough."

"So, how do you approach an audition?" asked Jack. "Do you ever try to second-guess what the client expects to hear from you?"

"Not anymore," I replied. "Unless I have the opportunity to ask the client or director all kinds of questions before the audition, I usually ignore the instructions and do my own thing. It's a crapshoot anyway. At least I get to put my own spin on the script. They might like it. They might hate it. As long as it doesn't leave them cold.

The other day I did the opposite of what the audition specs called for. Guess what? The producer called and told me I got the job. 'We had never considered doing it the way you did it, and we were sold!' he said."

"But isn't that a risky strategy?" Jack asked.

"What's wrong with taking a risk?" I said. "Nobody has ever won an audition by playing it safe. If you don't put some personality into your part, why should they hire you? It's your most powerful weapon against the competition.

You don't want to be a generic brand. Nobody wants Mr. or Mrs. More-Of-The-Same. The way to truly stand out is to be yourself.

376 | *Making Money In Your PJS*

History was never made by people who follow instructions. It's made by the contrarians, the renegades, the ones who went against the grain and followed their heart."

Jack looked slightly peeved. Then he said, "I'm not here to change the world, Paul. I'm simply trying to figure out how to tame my butterflies before an audition. I take this very seriously and I don't want to make a fool of myself. I audition as much as I can and I'm not getting anywhere. What do you suggest I do? I've got bills to pay!"

"Relax, Jack," I said. "Start by accepting that you cannot control people's expectations or how they will respond to you. You can only be responsible for your part.

Speaking of that part, some (voice) actors get stuck because they're overthinking the script and they're overanalyzing their performance. They end up recording take after take until all the spontaneity and life is beaten out of the words.

Take my advice. Stay in the moment. Stop the internal dialogue. Focus on the external dialogue instead. Have fun with your lines. Don't be too serious. Get out of your comfort zone. Embarrass yourself. Nobody's watching.

Do you think you can do that?"

"I'll try," answered Jack.

"Try is the worst word in the dictionary, Jack," I said. "It's as non-committal as should, maybe, or perhaps. When someone tells you they'll "try to be on time," you just know they'll show up late.

Stop trying and start doing.

Record less and you'll win more. It took me years to find that out, so learn from my experience. The wheel has already been invented. And one more thing.

Whether or not you get the part, that's not your call. As long as you know that your audio was clean and you're happy with your read, you've done all you could do.

Treat your audition like a balloon. Let it go! The end result is up in the air anyway."

Jack's eyes lit up. But I wasn't done yet.

"Now, I understand that you're worried about paying your bills," I said. "You've given up a lot to make this career work. You've invested in coaching and first-rate equipment. You've got a nice, quiet home studio. It's all good, but that just enables you to do what you want to do. It entitles you to... nothing.

If you care about your income, stop worrying about the outcome. It's paralyzing.

What you focus on most, tends to grow. So if you're insecure or fearful, it will come out, one way or another. It's a sign that you're too occupied with future memories of your own making. People pick up on desperation.

Clients will never hire you because you need them. They'll hire you because they need you.

In the end, you have a choice. If you're that good at creating disempowering future memories, why not use your imagination to create positive, empowering memories? I'm telling you: it's much more motivating and life becomes a lot lighter!"

"Have you ever tried motivational speaking?" Jack asked.

"What do you think I'm doing right now?" I asked. "Can you tell I'm the son of a minister? All I seem to do is preach!"

Jack laughed out loud.

"But you know what, Jack? Motivational speaking is one thing, but I'm much more into motivational doing.

When I do what I love doing when I'm in my studio getting ready for an audition, I feel funny things happening in my body.

You might call it nerves, but to me it's just excitement that's building.

I'm like a kid on the night before his birthday, filled with dreams of what might happen the next day.

Future memories.

I know I won't always get what I want, but I'm ready to be surprised!"

[57]

The Emotional Dilemma

For most of my life, I have been running away from my emotions.

I grew up believing that showing emotions was a sign of weakness. Strong people keep everything inside. They don't lose their temper. They don't act impulsively. Strong people are always in control.

Strong people stay detached in order to make rational decisions. They look at facts and disregard feelings. In my old-fashioned model of the world, it was okay for women to be emotional. Being strong was masculine, and I wanted to be a "real man," whatever that meant.

Looking back, this attitude of "nothing affects me" might have been a coping mechanism that helped me deal with the breakdown of my parents' marriage. I was in my teens when my dad left and I became the man of the house. I needed to be there for my mother and my younger sister.

Later on, my emotional detachment served me well in my career. As part of the news team of an international radio station, every day was a confrontation with death, disaster, and human tragedy. The newsroom was and is no place for tears.

What I had yet to learn was this:

In one context, certain behavior is necessary in order to function. In another context the same behavior could be highly inappropriate. Being all business and unmoved might work when you're anchoring the news, but not when you're coming home and your significant other needs warmth and affection.

Looking back, my emotional detachment was a protective wall that helped me survive. It also made it hard for me and others to connect with the real, vulnerable me. But it went deeper.

The fact that I wasn't letting the pain in, also subdued the pleasure. Without lows there were no big highs either. Because I felt the need to stay calm and collected, I lost a part of my enthusiasm and spontaneity. Deep inside, I was fearful. What would happen if I would take off the lid that kept my emotions at bay? Would people still like me? Would I like myself?

At this point you might wonder what all of this has to do with voice acting. Stay with me. I'll get to that in a minute or two.

OPENING UP

It took me several decades and lots of soul-searching to discover that daring to be vulnerable can be a sign of strength. The world wasn't going to crash down on me just because I showed some emotion. Keeping my feelings to myself had left me lonely. When I finally started opening up to people, it became easier for people to reach out and open up to me.

It was freeing to be able to tap into my anger and frustration. In the past, bitterness and resentment would fester inside and grow. Inward anger would lead to darkness and depression. Once the wall had been broken down, I felt light and alive.

Looking back, I wasted so much energy on keeping the lid closed. Today, I use that energy to move forward, and I spend much of my life following my gut feeling. I use what Malcolm Gladwell describes in his book *Blink: The Power of Thinking Without Thinking.****

Even though I'm happy to have opened my emotional house to all kinds of guests, there are consequences to wearing my feelings on my sleeve.

I'm more easily moved by the kindness of strangers and the cruelty of friends. When I see someone hurting an animal or hitting a child, I feel it in my body. I tear up when I see the veterans' parade through our town, knowing that they have risked their lives so I could live in liberty. Life has become more intense, and I have become a sentimental wuss! Professionally speaking, being more easily affected by my emotions has made me more effective and less effective. Let me explain.

PAINTER'S PALETTE

As a (voice) actor, I believe it is vital that we can tap into a whole range of emotions. I often compare it to the colors of a painter's palette or the instruments in an orchestra. The more colors or instruments we have at our disposal, the greater our dramatic range.

If we wish to convey genuine enthusiasm to our audience, we must access that state ourselves first, in order to be convincing. The same is true for other emotions such as disbelief, amazement, rage, being heartbroken, in love, feeling rejected, et cetera.

When our words, our tonality, and our body language all say the same thing, we become believable. However, we cannot unleash those raw emotions unfiltered and unpolished. That's where we become ineffective.

I once asked one of my students to read a page of a novel that touched her deeply. It was about someone who had just lost her father. Little did I know that my student had recently lost her dad.

It didn't take her long to feel the emotional impact of the story. After reading a few lines, she was overtaken by emotions and I could barely understand what she was saying. Then she started to cry.

Once she had calmed down, we talked about the experience. She soon realized that there and then, she did not go into character or into what I call "narrator-mode." She was merely being herself, reading the lines as if it was her autobiography.

It's understandable, but unprofessional.

NO EGO

Acting is a most selfless profession. It can never be about ego. We don't serve ourselves. We serve the authors, the screenwriters, and the playwrights. It requires a detached involvement. If we do it well enough, the audience will believe that we are the character we portray.

In order to create that character, we need a frame of reference. It can be completely imaginary, or we can tap into our life experiences.

Our emotions are like a goldmine. We can delve into it, but we must transform the gold ore into something we can melt and mold according to our desire and design.

As a (voice) actor, we must channel and manage these emotions to create the guise of spontaneity and authenticity. We don't act out reality. We're merely the creators of something that looks and sounds like it.

Director Richard Linklater put it this way when he talked about his movie *Before Midnight*.*** He said:

> "There is no reality in film. It's all a huge construct. But what we're trying to construct is something that feels like there's nothing there, like it's just unfolding very simply."

Great actors are like the violinist who's so much in control of his technique that he can forget about it and give an amazingly passionate performance.

Instead of playing notes, he's allowing the music to unfold.

While we personify the characters we play, I believe it's healthy to keep an intimate distance to them, if only to preserve our own sense of self.

Without emotion, there is no character, but if we become too emotionally invested, we may cross the line between reality and fiction.

We all know celebrities who have become their characters. Wherever they go, they've always got it turned on. I know a few voice-overs who can't stop doing funny voices or strange accents no matter where they are. They have forgotten the difference between playing a character and being a character. It is useful to learn to turn it on and turn it off.

At home, Tom Kenny (the voice of SpongeBob SquarePants) is just Tom Kenny, Jim Carrey keeps a straight face, and Steve Martin is not this Wild & Crazy Guy.***

There's another reason why we need to keep an intimate distance to our copy and character. If we allow ourselves to be overtaken by personal grief, joy, or disappointment, it can easily lead to overacting.

Here's my rule of thumb:

The more dramatic the language and the more powerful the images, the more we must restrain ourselves as voice-overs. Otherwise, our delivery could be overemotional and could become a distraction.

Sometimes though, that's easier said than done, especially for those who have embraced their inner emotional selves at a later age.

SAYING GOODBYE

A while ago, I was asked to lead a Celebration of Life for a dear friend of mine. After battling with brain cancer for many years, he passed away at the age of 41.

Leading the memorial would be honoring one of my friend's last wishes, and of course I accepted. In the days before the gathering, I had no idea how I would handle my emotions. I was afraid that I would break down in the middle of a reading, putting the focus on me instead of on my friend. Then I thought of the concept of intimate distance.

In order to fulfill my job as officiant, I made sure to become intimately acquainted with what I wanted to say that day. In voice-over terms: I thoroughly familiarized myself with the script.

Preparation is one of the best ways to deal with nerves and other emotions.

I also realized that in order to be there for friends and family, I had to distance myself from my own feelings. In voice-over terms: I had to focus on my role by separating the personal from the professional. It was the only way I could truly serve the purpose of this Celebration of Life.

MAKING A CHOICE

In my studio I use the same strategy. When I decide how to approach a particular script, I ask myself: For what purpose was this written? What are the intentions of the author or the client? How can I best communicate these intentions without me getting in the way?

I no longer run away from my emotions. They're my friends. Being able to tap into them has strengthened me as a voice actor and it has made my life a lot richer. But like any color on a painter's palette, there is a place and a time to use them.

Sometimes I listen to an audition I just recorded and I know something's missing. It sounds too detached.

When that happens, I tell myself: "Once more, with feeling."

Sometimes I hear myself overdoing it. I sound too sentimental.

When that happens, I hear Arnold Schwarzenegger's voice in a scene from *Kindergarten Cop*, telling me the following:

"It's time now, to turn this mush into muscles!"

[58]

Overcoming Self-Sabotage

There are a million ways to start a successful business and there are at least two millions ways to mess it up.

The worst of those two millions ways is when you become your own opponent.

Most people don't do it on purpose. They really want to succeed. They invest in their business. Financially and emotionally. They work long hours to build their dream. And – miracle of miracles – after a while things start going well.

Clients are happy. Cash is coming in. The future is looking brighter every day. And then this inner voice starts nagging you:

"Perhaps you're on a lucky streak. This will never last. You're not that good anyway. What were you thinking, leaving a secure job with benefits behind? This is never going to work and you know it."

Even after receiving rave reviews, the self-doubt continues:

"Get your head out of the clouds and get real. People are so easily impressed these days. They just want to kiss up to you. You don't think you deserve this, do you? What makes you so special?"

Sometimes these inner voices sound very much like one of our parents or like that nasty teacher who seemed intent on making our life difficult.

One of my colleagues wrote:

> "I went to Catholic school and one nun always picked on me. It happened a long time ago but I can still hear her penetrating voice as she humiliated me in front of the class. That's the inner voice I hear when I tell myself that I'm not good enough.
>
> Tell me, why can't I take a compliment? I know I'm pretty good at what I do. Why don't I trust other people's opinions of me? Why don't I trust myself? It's the one thing holding me back from reaching what I feel I'm truly capable of."

THE REAL ME

When I read emails like that, I wish there was something I could say to magically make someone more self-confident. But by definition, self-confidence comes from within. It has to do with someone's core beliefs, and those beliefs usually have very deep roots. Besides, I'm not a psychologist, therapist, or other kind of specialist.

I can tell you this, though: I am too familiar with the feeling of self-doubt. I was one of those geeky, glee-club kind of kids who always got picked last for team sports. Classmates called me "the professor" and mocked me because I was into classical music. They thought I had a high opinion of myself because I spoke with what they considered to be a posh accent.

I tried to fit in, but I just couldn't. On the outside I pretended that everything was A-Okay, but underneath I wasn't nearly as self-assured as people thought I was. Their comments got to me like a slow-burning fire, eating me up from the inside. Frankly, I hated high school and till this day I have kept my vow to never attend a class reunion.

For years, this internal "who-do-you-think-you-are" voice kept on bugging me, especially at times when things seemed to go well. It was lurking around the corner during exams, in romantic relationships and yes... when I was auditioning for jobs.

Think about it. How was I going to convince clients I could bring their script to life if I couldn't even convince myself? How could a loser ever run a successful business?

PEELING OFF THE LAYERS

As I started digging deeper into my psyche and the literature on self-esteem, I (re)discovered a thing or two.

One: The question "Why am I doing this" is overrated. Those who ask "why," often expect a rational answer to explain irrational behavior. They're trying to make sense of something senseless. In my book that's not very sensible.

Knowing the "why" behind the "what" does not mean one can make the unwanted behavior or self-deprecating thought patterns stop. Knowing why you just cut yourself cannot ease the pain or make the bleeding stop, can it?

Most people know why they overeat and why overeating is bad for them. But knowing why doesn't make it easier to kick the habit.

It gets worse. Trying to answer the WHY often leads to finding plenty of reasons to justify and perpetuate unwanted behavior, especially if we start blaming others and "circumstances" for the unhealthy things we do. As long as we blame others, we can't help ourselves because – in our mind – we're not the problem.

Two: We cannot change the past. We can only reinterpret it with the knowledge we have now. If we keep holding on to the past, we give it power it does not deserve. That nun who used to pick on my colleague died a long time ago. But in my colleague's mind, she's still alive.

Those classmates who made fun of me, have moved on. But in my brain, they're still the same! They did not grow up, just as that part of me had yet to grow up.

As long as your ship is anchored to the past, you can only go as far as the anchor chain allows you to go, and you'll never be able to unleash who you really are and explore new destinations.

Forgiveness is one way to let go of parts of the past that disempower us and hold us hostage. If it is true that we sometimes are our own worst enemy, maybe it's time to forgive that enemy.

Three: To learn how to deal with our negative internal dialogue, it helps to separate behavior from intention. What do I mean by that?

To put it bluntly: we sometimes do something bad in order to feel good. This may sound silly but remember: I'm not talking about the logical mind here.

Any type of behavior (conscious or unconscious) fulfills a certain need. It serves a certain purpose; a purpose that might very well be positive. Take overeating. People don't overeat because they want to get morbidly obese and diabetic. They overeat to feed a deeper need.

For some, eating a lot of food can be comforting. Hence the name "comfort food." It's one way to show self-love. It can literally be a full-filling experience.

Food is often associated with fun. It's instant gratification. Eating doesn't only change our body, it also changes our state of mind thanks to the endorphins that are being produced. So, eating can lead to an overall feeling of well-being. Food is also a great stress buster. Once the plate is finished, relaxation sets in.

It might not be a pleasant or efficient way, but do you get the idea that something bad may have some benefits? It's the basis for any addiction. Learning to separate the negative behavior (overeating) from the positive intention (comfort), is often an Aha-moment. It's also a key to positive change.

OUR INNER VOICE

Let's get back to those negative inner voices telling us we're not good enough. What could be a positive intention behind those negative words?

When I did some soul-searching, I found out that deep down inside, part of me wanted to protect myself from failure. And if I didn't try, I would never fail! Telling myself that I wasn't good enough often stopped me from trying. Ultimately, I wanted to feel safe.

Then there was this part of me I'd call "the perfectionist." That part also told me "it" wasn't good enough or I wasn't good enough. Behind that negative self-talk was a person who always wanted to do better. It's that part of me that wishes to learn and grow and reach new heights. Once I recognized the positive intention, I could ask myself a different question:

What better ways can I come up with to honor that ultimate positive intention, that would not require beating myself up? Mind you, I'm not completely opposed to a firm kick in the pants, but in general, negative motivation is harsh and causes a lot of stress, which is not healthy for mind and body.

Back to the question: How could I possibly better myself and gain more confidence? One way to do it was to become more competent. That meant getting more training and gaining more experience. I also promised myself to be kinder and to treat myself with more respect. It was time to cut myself some slack.

I realized that cultivating one's talent is a crockpot, slow cooker kind of process; not a microwave meal. I did not have to be perfect and nail every audition. That's not humanly possible. Some roles I auditioned for in the past required a level of skill and maturity I didn't have. At that time they were not meant for me, and that was okay.

Even the roles I thought had my name written all over them, I would not always get. That was fine too. As long as I had done my very best during the audition, I had nothing to be ashamed of. On some days, my "very best" would be better than on other days.

Here's another concept I learned to embrace:

Everyone deserves to be successful, including me. The universe is abundant and there is enough work for everyone.

Not everything will go my way, but as long as I learn from the things that don't go as planned, I cannot fail.

Here's one more:

I am not my work. My job is just a small part of who I am. So, if I don't land that job I hope I will get, it's merely a reflection on something I do and not on who I am.

As my beliefs started to change, my internal dialogue started to change as well. I felt better about myself and people said they could hear it in my voice and see it in my posture. Everything's connected.

Does that mean I never doubt a thing I do anymore? Of course not. That would be dangerous.

Every now and then, I hear that nagging little voice question something I am about to do or say.

If only to keep my big fat ego in check!

[59]

Is Your Freelance Career Fueled by Fear?

> *Do not anticipate trouble, or worry about what may never happen. Keep in the sunlight."* **Benjamin Franklin**

WARNING: Do not read the following sentence.

Yes, this one!

Why did you read it when I asked you not to?

Don't even think of reading the next line either.

Are you blind? You just did it again. What's up with you?

Why is it so hard to follow simple instructions?

You're a grown-up, aren't you?

Kids are different. You go to the store and make them swear upon their teddy bear's life not to touch anything. And what do they do? As soon as they get a chance, they start picking up stuff left and right. You tell them not to cross the road and before you know it, they run to the other side of the street. But that's youthful spontaneity, isn't it?

What about you? When you tell yourself not to do something, do you do it? Or rather: not do it?

Then why is it so hard not to hear that stupid but very popular tune that has totally taken over your brain? By the way: this is not a test. There's no need to remember the last time that silly melody got stuck in your head. It wasn't one of those cheesy, catchy songs that kept following you around from store to store, was it?

We've all experienced this phenomenon:

The more we don't want to think about something, the harder it is not to think about it. Why is that?

It turns out that our brains have a tough time processing negatives, as demonstrated by the famous blue elephant experiment. You'll play along, won't you?

Just for a moment, don't think of a blue elephant.

Really, whatever you do, try not to think of a blue elephant...

... with big blue ears, blue eyes, and deep blue tusks.

Thanks for being a good sport. We'll get back to the elephant later. If anything, this little thought experiment demonstrates that...

We can't think about what we don't want to think about without thinking about it first.

Think about that for a moment!

Why would this be extremely relevant to you personally and professionally?

It has to do with the power of focus. Focus is sometimes defined as the concentration of attention or energy on something. Are you having a hard time staying focused?

Are you easily distracted? Is your freelance business all over the place? Well, you're not alone.

We live in an age of information overload and a culture that has embraced distraction. People prefer being entertained to being educated. Never has there been a generation that is so bombarded with a constant stream of nonsensical stimuli. Doesn't your head feel like Times Square times ten, sometimes?

With so much going on all the time, can we even attempt to shut it off and try to separate what's truly important from the trivial? Especially, when the trivial is constantly seducing us with the brightest colors and the loudest sounds?

The trivial is all about the immediate. The latest is automatically the greatest. It doesn't matter whether it is relevant or even important. Who cares about yesterday's paper or this morning's tweet? That's old news.

The trivial also tends to tap into to very basic emotions of pain and pleasure, hoping to elicit a gut response by emphasizing the simplistic, the outrageous, and the grotesque. A few examples:

- Newspaper editors will tell you: If it doesn't bleed, it doesn't lead.
- Madison Avenue knows that boobs and babies boost business.
- The masses prefer Twitter chatter to in-depth intellectual arguments.

We don't read anymore. We scan texts. And if the author doesn't get to the point in the next paragraph, we move on. Are you still with me?

Meanwhile, shouldn't you check your email? I think someone wants to chat with you on Facebook. NOW! It's rude not to respond.

Did you just receive a new text message? I wonder what it says. You'd better look at it pronto. It might be important!

Distractions, distractions, distractions.

ENOUGH ALREADY!

The French philosopher Blaise Pascal hit the nail on the head when he said:

> *"All men's miseries derive from not being able to sit in a quiet room alone."*

I would add to that:

"sit in a quiet room alone, and do absolutely nothing."

Life's like a glass of water.

Someone or something comes along and drops some dirt in it. Then someone else comes along and does the same thing... and they start stirring and stirring until the water's all murky and muddy. When that happens, it's impossible to see clearly and think clearly.

Only when you let it rest and allow the dirt to sink to the bottom, things start to become transparent again. And when the water is clear, what do you choose to focus on? On the fact that your glass is half full or half empty?

I happen to believe that what we focus on consistently is more likely to materialize (emphasis on "more likely"). That's not something I came up with.

Just think of a few people who "have made it." Do they seem distracted or dedicated? Are they bad planners or are they well organized? Do they focus on futilities or do they lead their lives "on purpose?" More importantly: do they zoom in on what they want or on what they don't want?

As of today, start listening carefully to the language people use when they describe what drives them; what they pay attention to and why.

Then look at their results and discover how the words we choose to use are translated into the outcomes we achieve.

Don't take my word for it because I can't convince you of anything. Just open your eyes and ears and dissociate yourself from what is being said. Content is irrelevant. Concentrate on *how* things are said.

FEELING BLUE

I remember running into one of my freelance friends around the holidays. He looked absolutely miserable. Christmas was coming up and he was trying to figure out how to pay the most basic bills. In desperation, he had taken on a couple of low-paying jobs and now he was dealing with overly demanding clients. A few things he said stood out for me:

- I don't want to go broke
- I don't want to go back to my old job
- I don't want to miss that deadline
- I don't want to lose another client
- I don't want to mess up again

No wonder he was down in the dumps. He was clearly thinking of blue elephants. Focusing on what you don't want is a tried recipe for self-sabotage. People who habitually focus on what they don't want, usually do that out of fear. They're willing to do more to avoid something than to accomplish something. Ironically, they may end up with more of what they don't want.

Fear is paralyzing. Fear smothers creativity. Fear is reactive, not pro-active. Fear activates our fight-or-flight response, purposely limiting our behavior to a few options. Fear makes us run away, instead of going for it.

Don't get me wrong. Sometimes, fear can be a good thing. It is perfectly normal to stay away from burning flames or roaring lions.

But quite often, fear is nothing but an irrational, conditioned response, linked to our interpretation of something that we believe happened to us long, long ago.

STUCK TO THE PAST

In places like Thailand and India, people still use working elephants. What always amazes me is that these mighty, intelligent animals don't run away into the jungle. Instead, they stay where they are and help their masters with logging and other heavy lifting. They seem to know their place. Why is that?

Someone once told me that at a very young age, these elephants are tied to a strong tree. Whenever they try to get away, the chain will pull them back. Once they're a little older, the tree is replaced by a heavy ball, restricting their range of movement. These elephants are trained to stay put.

Later in life, there's no need to restrain them anymore. They have learned their lesson and have become conditioned to stay within a limited space, even though they're technically free to go and explore the world.

That's what fear will do to you.

Fear makes you play things safe. Instead of focusing on the future, it ties you to the past – even though those ties are long gone.

Are you still mad at your dad or afraid of your mom, even though they have passed?

I'm not telling you we shouldn't pay attention to the past. Our roots are part of who we are. But we should learn from the past and move on. It is time to grow some wings and leave the nest!

There's another reason why it's counterproductive to focus on our fears. It causes stress. Stress is not just a state of mind. Physical, emotional, or psychological strain is harmful. Stress negatively affects immune responses, and it also affects how well the body heals itself.

But here's the thing: we can't get rid of it by focusing on what we don't want. That's why I have to laugh when I see an ad for the "Less Stress Center" or the "Pain Clinic." Don't think of a blue elephant, folks!

It's just as bad as that disturbingly distracting billboard, urging us not to become a distracted driver. But it goes even deeper and it becomes more personal.

At times, it seems we just love to identify ourselves by what we don't want, or by what we no longer are:

– I'm a scientist against global warming
– I'm an anti-war activist
– I'm a non-smoker
– I'm a cancer survivor
– I have been sober for 15 years. I am an alcoholic.

Comedian Tina Fey once joked about former vice-presidential candidate Sarah Palin on the Tonight Show: "They address her as Governor Palin, which is like calling me Dairy Queen employee. I was once, but I quit."

In order to move forward, you have to think of who you are NOW and imagine what you can be, instead of focusing on what used to be or on what you don't want to happen. You are not an elephant! You are free. You are a freelancer!

HOLDING UP THE MIRROR

Let's wrap this up by talking about YOU for a change. I've asked you to listen to other people talk, and find out what drives them. Now it's time for you to start analyzing your internal dialogue.

Are you a closet masochist and do you beat yourself up on a regular basis, mistaking it for motivation? Do you prefer the stick to the carrot? In that case, stick to the carrot.

Are you moving away from what you don't want? Do you even know what you really want?

Now listen to yourself as you're talking to others.

If you intend to calm a friend down, do you tell her not to worry? If your partner panics before a presentation, do you tell him not to be nervous?

Do you tell your daughter not to get sick when she sneezes? Do you ask your husband not to forget the keys? Do you tell your team that failure is not an option? Do you tell your client: "No problem!"

If that's the case, you have some work to do.

The Indian sage Patanjali is known for a collection of aphorisms on Yoga practice, the Yoga Sutras. Thousands of years ago,

Patanjali suggested:

"Repel disturbing thoughts by pondering the opposite."

Back in 1902, James Allen, author of *As a Man Thinketh*,[***] put it this way:

> "Mind is the Master power that moulds and makes,
> And Man is Mind, and evermore he takes
> The tool of Thought, and, shaping what he wills,
> Brings forth a thousand joys, a thousand ills: —
> He thinks in secret, and it comes to pass:
> Environment is but his looking-glass."

[60]

What To Do When You Are Down

We've all had them.

Days, weeks... months perhaps, during which very little seems to go our way.

Clients stop calling. Agents have gone AWOL. Lots of auditions and hardly any bookings.

You're busy but unproductive. You try to stay positive but it feels fake. Something's not right.

Meanwhile, colleagues are telling the world how well they're doing:

> "Just booked another spot for a national brand!"

> "Signed a long-term narration deal with a successful author!"

> "I'm recording my first big video game!"

Rub it in, folks. Rub it in!

I'm happy you're happy but can you please shut up about it?

One part of you is hopeful, though. You tell yourself: "If these guys are still getting work it means that there's money to be made." But another part of you wonders why those people were picked and why your career is going nowhere. What do they have that you don't? They're certainly not more experienced or more talented. It all boils down to this question:

"What's wrong with you?"

Are you too old? Are you charging too much? Should you have bought better equipment? Does your website need an overhaul? Perhaps it's time to call that famous coach and get a second opinion. But who's going to pay for that? It was hard enough to come up with the money for this month's rent.

The only reason I can describe this state so well is because I've been there. Several times. I felt like I was pushing and pushing to get my career moving and very little happened. Mind you, I wasn't counting on an overnight miracle. I just wanted my business to grow steadily. I wanted to be one of the few that would beat the odds. Instead, the odds were beating me and it showed.

Gradually, I became depressed, distracted, and disenchanted with what I was doing. Worse even, I began to resent the success others were having. One day, I heard the voice of a friend in a commercial I had auditioned for. He had done a good job, but he did not blow me away. The script was kind of dumb too.

Before I knew it, my internal dialogue took me on a dark path. My inner voice became rather sarcastic and whispered:

"Sure, it would have been nice to have booked that commercial, but when you think of it, the pay may be good but the job is trivial. That's the thing with commercials. I mean, do we really need to sing the praises of yet another car or computer? Does mankind evolve when we're all drinking more diabetes in a bottle and sell it as soda?

How beautiful is America really, when a majority of the population is obese; something my voice could help promote?

Why should I encourage shallow consumerism while our planet is dying? Is that the most meaningful thing I could do with my life right now? Does this world need more voice-overs, or do we need more doctors, teachers, scientists, and aid workers? I might as well give up and do something useful with my life."

The point is this: I wasn't feeling good about myself and my work and as a result I didn't feel good about others and their work. But those are two very different things.

In times of crisis, I was looking for something we're all longing for: a way to find meaning in who we are and what we do. If you don't find enough meaning, it's so much harder to bounce back and carry on.

In this process I was reminded of three things that are as simple as they are profound. Here's number one:

It's hard to find positive reasons for pursuing a certain path if you're in an unresourceful state.

Knowingly and unknowingly, I had talked myself into a state of gloom and doom. One way of doing that was by asking myself a loaded question:

"What's wrong with me?"

It's a question that can only lead to a distorted view of reality. First of all, it put the blame of what's happening entirely on me, which is unfair. There's only so much in life we can influence and there's very little we can control. The fact that a casting director prefers another voice doesn't mean that you're a miserable failure, does it?

Secondly, if we ask ourselves "What's wrong with me," our mind starts searching for answers, and I can guarantee you that you'll get a laundry list of shitty reasons, which will make you feel even worse.

You can never find what's right by looking for what's wrong.

To turn things around, you need to do at least two things. One: you have to get out of your "Woe is Me" state. Take a break. Literally. Go to a different place, physically and mentally. Go for a walk. Hit the gym. Listen to some great music. Do something healthy that makes you feel good. Take a time-out to change your state of mind.

Two: once you're in a more resourceful mood, ask yourself a very different, more positive question, such as:

"How can I turn this situation around? What's a small, concrete thing I can do today that will help me and my business?"

Keep it simple and manageable. Massive success is often the result of a series of small steps in the right direction over a long period of time.

Now, the next thing I rediscovered in this process lifted a huge weight off my shoulders. It had to do with how I felt about myself. Here's my realization:

Who we are and what we do are connected but they are not the same.

It's so easy to confuse those two things because when someone asks what we do for a living, we're inclined to say: "I am a voice-over, I am a teacher, a trainer, et cetera." It points to our identity. To me, my work is something I do. I "do" voice-overs. I write a blog…. among many other meaningful things.

If we believe that what we do professionally defines who we are as a person, any blow to our business is personal. The truth is, what we do professionally is only a small aspect of who we are and how we contribute to the world. There are many ways to make life worth living:

first and foremost through our relationships with the ones we love and care about.

If we invest in these relationships and they are strong, we have a support system that can get us to the end of the tunnel, no matter how long or how dark it may be.

Strong relationships make us resilient. How?

Because we don't need to prove anything to those who are close.

No matter how well or how poorly we do professionally, the ones who are near and dear will love us no matter what.

The third and last rediscovery is more of a personal belief. It's a mindset I find tremendously empowering. It goes like this:

"No matter the challenges, I will always find a way out."

Sometimes a dry spell will last for days. Sometimes it takes a few weeks or even months to get back on track. Eventually, the tide will turn.

As long as I don't wallow in my misfortune and I take small steps to improve my situation every day, I will find a way out.

And you know what?

You will too.

You better believe it.

[61]

Woulda, Coulda, Shoulda

What would you do if you knew that your time on earth was about to come to an end?

Would you go back to work and pretend nothing happened? Would you go on a cruise around the world? Would you visit as many friends and family members as possible? Or would you stay inside, close the blinds, and curl up with a pint of your favorite ice cream?

Phil Keoghan,*** the U.S. host of *The Amazing Race*, was 19 when he almost lost his life.

On one of his first TV shoots under water, he got trapped in an up-turned interior cabin of a sunken cruise liner and couldn't find his way out. With very little air left in his tank, he panicked, realizing that his next breath could be his last.

After what seemed an eternity, the support crew on the surface sent a rescue diver to find him. In the nick of time, Phil was pulled to the surface and he survived. The next day, he went back to repeat the dive that nearly killed him.

That was not all.

After his near-death experience, he promised himself to live life to the fullest and he made a bucket list of all the things he wanted to do, from climbing Mount Everest and hand-feeding sharks, to setting a world record for bungee-jumping.

Phil Keoghan:

> "A lot of the things I wrote down on this early list involved thrill-seeking – and I've since come to understand what was going on. I was looking for a way to replicate that "rush" of coming face to face with death. It seems crazy, but when you have an episode like that, you come out feeling more alive than ever before – and for a while, I almost became hooked on trying to recreate that feeling by way of life-threatening stunts: I jumped, I dove, I strapped myself onto speeding objects.

> Eventually, I would come to realize that there were many other ways to lead a fuller, more interesting life, without constantly risking my neck. And I also came to appreciate that a good List for Life should be more mature, emotionally richer, and much more varied than this one. (But hey, I was 19)."

Keoghan turned his lust for life into a List for Life, and into a philosophy that became his mantra: **No Opportunity Wasted***** or NOW.

A few years ago, I had a chance to meet Phil Keoghan at the Great New Jersey Country Bike Ride, benefitting Multiple Sclerosis.

Phil is not one of those celebrities who make an obligatory appearance for a good cause just because it looks good to do good.

If you've followed his career, you may know that in 2009 he travelled over 3500 miles on his bike in just forty days, riding from coast-to-coast to raise awareness and money for the National Multiple Sclerosis Society. His journey was documented in *The Ride*.***

Phil set out to raise $500K for MS. He exceeded that goal by raising $1M (and counting). But there's more to this story.

Later, his NOW organization teamed up with Novartis Pharmaceuticals Corporation for the *Together in MS* Campaign.*** This campaign involves tandem cycling teams that take part in Bike MS rides across the country. Each team is made up of a professional female cyclist from the NOW and Novartis for MS team, and someone living with MS.

For the Jersey ride, my wife Pamela Taylor teamed up with pro-rider Christina Gokey-Smith for the fifty-mile tour. Novartis was kind enough to take me along for the ride as team photographer, not knowing that the MS Society is the official charity of my business, Nethervoice.

To me, this ride was one of the most uplifting and empowering events of the year. Imagine a thousand cyclists, all riding for a reason, connected to a common cause. People helping people.

This is what I learned from them and from Phil:

1. You don't need a near-death experience to decide to live your life to the fullest.

Don't wait for that heart attack to finally change your lifestyle. You don't need to get into a car accident to become a safer driver. Why risk your life doing dangerous stunts to prove to yourself that you're alive?

You can decide right now, that life itself is an opportunity not to be wasted! Every day is a new chance to touch the lives of others and create positive change in your own.

However, it can be very tempting to live life on automatic pilot. For many of us, life has become too comfortable. We'd rather watch other people achieve great things, or complain that our life is boring and meaningless. Before we know it, another year has passed and nothing's happened.

That's why it helps to create a Life List of goals you want to accomplish. Writing things down is the first step to making them visible and concrete. Don't stop there, though...

2. The NOW is all you have. If you wait, it might be too late.

Bronnie Ware*** is an Australian nurse who spent years caring for patients in the last weeks of their lives. Ware has written about the incredible clarity of vision that people gain at the end of their lives. When she asked them about the things they would do differently, she noticed common themes that came back again and again. The number one regret of the dying was this:

I wish I'd had the courage to live a life true to myself, not the life others expected of me.

No one can live your life for you. Others can inspire, encourage and offer support, but it's up to you to lead life on someone else's terms or on your own. At the end of the day and at the end of your life, "Woulda, Coulda, Shoulda" doesn't cut it.

Now, there's a big difference between those who stay true to themselves and turn dreams into reality, and those who end up with regret because they played it safe. The ones that manage to tick things off their Life List know that in order to accomplish meaningful goals they need to...

3. Get rid of excuses.

When my wife told one of her young friends that she was about to embark on a fifty-mile bike ride, the response was:

"Oh, I'd never be able to do that."

"Why not?" challenged my wife. "You're at least half my age and you don't have MS. You might not be in perfect shape, but that's something you can change. A few weeks ago, I climbed the tallest tower in the Netherlands. You're talking about 465 steps. Granted, not everyone with MS is able to do that, and yet, life doesn't have to come to a complete standstill because of it."

To emphasize the point, my wife joined 7,500 cyclists for the Bike MS City-to-Shore event, named one of the best cycling experiences on the East Coast of the United States. This time, she rode on her own bike and she finished ahead of most of her team.

In order to rid yourself of excuses, you have to be completely honest with your friends and family, and with yourself.

You might be able to fool the rest of the world, but you know deep down inside when you're just making stuff up because you're not ready to commit.

Do things for the right reasons and...

4. Never use money or fame as motivators.

Let's say you're a successful reality TV show host. You've won multiple Emmys and you have more money in the bank than you can possibly spend.

If you were solely driven by a nice paycheck and a shallow sense of importance, what would you do when you've "arrived?" Your goal is accomplished. You're rich and famous. Now what?

Where's your motivation?

There is a reason why some "stars" try to fill the emptiness with substance abuse. Others overspend and go bankrupt, still hoping that money can buy happiness and true friendship. Fame and fortune are fickle.

Phil Keoghan has done well for himself – no doubt about it – but that's not how he measures success. It's not what motivates him.

For Keoghan, it's about how well he can do for others.

He saw his celebrity status as an opportunity that could and should not be wasted, and his motivation turned out to be highly contagious.

So, has some of Phil's philosophy rubbed off on you?

Are you thinking of making a Life List?

If the answer is yes, what's going to be on it and why?

What will you do today to get one step closer to one of your goals on that list?

Are you ready to turn it into a reality, or will you forever wonder what could have been?

[62]

Are You a Winner or a Whiner?

We all do it.

With the best of intentions.

We tell ourselves that this is the year we will turn things around.

Finally.

We even tell the world.

And then we move on with our lives and forget about it.

A year passes, and we wonder why nothing has changed.

And we always find something or someone to blame.

Our greatest accomplishments and our greatest disappointments are well planned.

People are good at setting themselves up for failure, and good at setting themselves up for success.

It starts between the ears.

413

Winners understand the power of planning.

Whiners live from day to day.

Winners say: There's no day like today.

Whiners say: There's always tomorrow.

Winners take action.

Whiners sit around and wait.

Winners get their hands dirty and dig in.

Whiners expect others to do the work for them.

Winners produce results.

Whiners have excuses.

Winners are proud of their accomplishments.

Whiners feel sorry for themselves.

I could fill an entire page with these bold statements, but I think you get my drift. It's all about attitude.

Instead, let's delve a bit deeper into the anatomy of a loser. Yes, I know. It's a derogatory term and I'm only using it for dramatic effect. I'm not writing anyone off and I'm not pointing any fingers.

Here are some surefire ways to sabotage your own success.

1. WISHFUL THINKING

Life's not a fairy tale where three wishes are granted to the humble but noble underdog. Yet, most of us keep on wishing things would change for the better, but are we willing to work for it?

You can spot lack of commitment from a mile a way by the language someone uses. You'll hear a lot of:

"I would like to…"

"I may or might…"

"That sounds interesting. Perhaps I should explore that…"

Their favorite word is "but," as in: "I really wanted to do that, but…."

If you want to get something done, get off your butt. Take that first step, no matter how small.

Life is overwhelming. That's why we break complicated processes down into small pieces. It makes them more manageable.

Nobody expects you to finish a full meal in one bite.

2. LACK OF URGENCY & MEANING

A goal is a more than a dream with a deadline.

No one gets excited about the things they want to accomplish… some day.

Be brutally honest.

If you don't want it badly, it probably doesn't mean a lot to you at this point in time. Otherwise, you would feel that inner urge burning inside of you like a fire that makes you unstoppable.

The feeling of being driven comes from doing things that matter more to you than anything else. This feeling will excite you when things go well, and it will give you the energy to climb those mountains that still stand in your way.

So, stop talking about the things you've always wanted to do.

Start doing them. NOW.

3. BEING NON-SPECIFIC

If you don't know your destination, how will you know you have arrived?

Vague ideas are daydreams. Vague ideas never inspire. Vague ideas let you off the hook, and you know it!

The statement: "I just want to be happy" is a great example.

What does happiness mean to you? It's not even a goal. It's a touchy-feely by-product of something else, but of what exactly?

Here's another one: "I want to be better."

Better than what? Compared to what?

What's preventing you? Who's preventing you?

A favorite of motivational trainers is the statement:

"I want to make more money."

Some self-help gurus will walk up to you and give you a dime, saying:

"Look, you've just accomplished your goal. You now have more money! Are you happy now?"

Besides being unspecific, making more money is not what they call an end-goal. It's a means-goal, meaning it is a means to an end.

Concrete goals have a starting point and a finish line. They require careful planning and a clear vision of the end result. Once you have that clear vision, ask yourself:

"What is the last step I take that will get me to accomplish my goal?"

Then you work your way back, figuring out all the steps you have to take to get you to that point, until you arrive at the present.

It's – to quote Steve Jobs – connecting the dots looking backwards, in advance.

Unfortunately, most people find it easier to sum up what they don't want. Take it from me: You'll never get anywhere by focusing on the things you wish to avoid. In fact, you're more likely to attract the very things you're running away from.

Great goals are always stated in the positive.

4. BEING OVERLY DEPENDENT ON OTHERS

Waiting for others to make your dreams come true is not only lazy, it also means you make yourself dependent on others as you're giving away your personal power. How many times have you said to yourself:

"I would feel so much better, if only this person would…." You fill in the blanks.

Forget it. People won't change unless they want to.

A great goal is self-initiated and self-maintained. You OWN it. You're the captain. It's your ship. Why is that essential?

No person in the world is ever willing to work as hard to accomplish something that's meaningful to you, as you are.

Yes, it's nice to surround yourself with the right type of supporters and critics. But you don't need cheerleaders chanting empty slogans or Debbie Downers that rip your plan to pieces before it's even born.

You need friends that can give you an honest assessment and who can help you fine-tune your grand plan. You also need the right people who have the expertise you don't have, and who are willing to put their weight behind your project.

However, it is your vision and your responsibility to make it a reality.

5. BEING SELF-CENTERED

You might reach your goal and feel like a winner, but I see it as a failure if you're the only one benefitting from your success.

There's no doubt that it's an accomplishment to get out of the ghetto and become a successful multi million dollar-recording artist. But all your golden showerheads and bling don't mean a thing if you spit on your roots instead of giving back to where you came from.

Results come with responsibilities. Decisions have consequences. That's why I encourage you to look at the impact pursuing and reaching your goal will have on the world around you.

Pursuing a goal with passion means you're willing to pay a price. Remember that you don't live on an island and that sometimes that price may be too high.

In William Shatner's documentary *The Captains*,*** Kate Mulgrew (Captain Kathryn Janeaway), reveals that her two children resented her always being on the set, working 18 hour days. To this day, they still refuse to watch *Star Trek Voyager*.

Both Shatner and Patrick Stewart (Captain Jean-Luc Picard) link the breakdown of their marriages to the demands of their careers. That is, the choices and sacrifices they willingly made to "make it."

One last example.

Your company might have successfully launched a new product, boosting business like never before, but if your production process is poisoning the wells and killing wildlife, is it worth it?

Think about the bigger picture. It's a matter of ecology.

Before you commit or decide to quit, here are four questions I want you to ask yourself.

1. What will happen if I do X?
2. What won't happen if I do X?
3. What will happen if I don't do X?
4. What won't happen if I don't do X?

The answer to these questions will help you determine whether or not the price is worth paying.

And finally...

The greatest goals are never about personal fame and fortune, and they will never come true the way you imagined them to come true.

At the end of the day, every goal is a picture of what you believe you're capable of, with all the resources you have available right now.

That means that every goal is limited by your imagination and your perception of what is possible.

The most ambitious goals will seem unrealistic and unreasonable, and yet, even those are confined by what you think you can or cannot accomplish.

That's why some of the philosophers of the world will teach you to set clear outcomes, and then ask you to let go of the form.

That way, you allow the universe to exceed your expectations.

Steve Jobs' sister Mona Simpson, was there when her brother died. She told us what his last words were:

"Oh wow. Oh wow. Oh wow."

We will never know what prompted him to say these words, but whatever Steve saw in his final moments, I'm pretty sure it exceeded all his expectations.

[63]

The Freelancers Creed

To my past, present, and future clients:

I AM A FREELANCER and my added value will always be higher than my rate.

I am here to make your life easier, to solve a particular problem, to work on a project and save you money by getting the job done more efficiently and more skillfully.

When you hire me, you can rely on my expertise, my experience, and my enthusiasm.

Unlike so many people who go to work and go through the motions just to collect a paycheck, I became a freelancer to do what I'm good at; to do what I love… and I love what I do.

I need no time tracker, no handholding micro-managing supervisor, or never-ending on-the-job training.

When your 9-to-5 crew leaves the building, I'm still going strong and move things along because I focus on the job and not on a punch clock or office politics.

I'm as flexible as it gets.

I don't waste time on water cooler conversations, endless meetings, or team huddles.

You are my priority and I'm only a phone call or email away.

I AM A FREELANCER and my added value will always be higher than my rate.

I need no company car, designated parking space, business cards, or a security badge.

You don't have to get me a cubicle, office furniture, phone, tablet, or computer.

I took care of that.

My equipment is state of the art, and I keep up with the latest developments in my field.

You're not paying for expensive hard- or software, conferences, Continuing Ed, silly incentives, or motivational seminars. That comes out of my pocket.

All I ask for is a detailed description of your project, a reasonable time frame, and fair compensation, and I'm good to go.

I AM A FREELANCER and my added value will always be higher than my rate.

I need no 401K, no end of the year bonus, or stock options.

I won't ask you for paid holidays, sick days, or vacation time.

You don't have to worry about Workers' Comp or unemployment insurance.

You're not paying for my health care benefits or my retirement plan, either.

I pick up that tab.

Why?

Because ...

I AM A FREELANCER and my added value will always be higher than my rate.

Staying in Touch

If you feel that this book has been helpful to you in any way, there's no need to thank me.

The biggest compliment you could pay me today, is by sharing your experience with friends and colleagues, especially on social media.

I'd be absolutely thrilled if you could take a few minutes, and write a review on Amazon.com.

You can find other fans of *Making Money In Your PJs*, and connect with them on a special Facebook Page:

www.facebook.com/moneyinyourpjs,

and on Twitter:

https://twitter.com/MoneyInYourPJs.

There's also a website that's dedicated to this book:

http://makingmoneyinyourpjs.com.

On this site you can find all the hyperlinks, read the latest reviews, and you can contact me for guest posts, interviews and speaking engagements

I hope to see you there!

About the Author

Born and educated in the Netherlands, writer, coach, and voice-over professional Paul Strikwerda started working the mic for Dutch national radio at the age of 17.

After a career in international broadcast journalism (BBC, Radio Netherlands), he became a sought-after media coach.

In 1999, Strikwerda moved to the United States where he founded Nethervoice, providing voice-over services in native Dutch, neutral English, and sometimes even in German.

In his studio in Pennsylvania's Lehigh Valley, Paul records audio books, videos, virtual tours, commercials, and documentaries for major clients on all continents. His weekly blog deals with issues facing voice-overs and other solopreneurs, and is read by thousands of people every month.

Paul is an expert-contributor to Internet Voice Coach and the New York headquartered Edge Studio, as well as to the International Freelancers Academy and recordinghacks.com.

Previous books include *Building a Vocal Booth on a Budget*, and *Boosting your Business with a Blog*.

For Paul's blog, audio samples, and more, please visit his website www.nethervoice.com

16940172R00263

Made in the USA
Middletown, DE
28 December 2014